Who are the Turks?

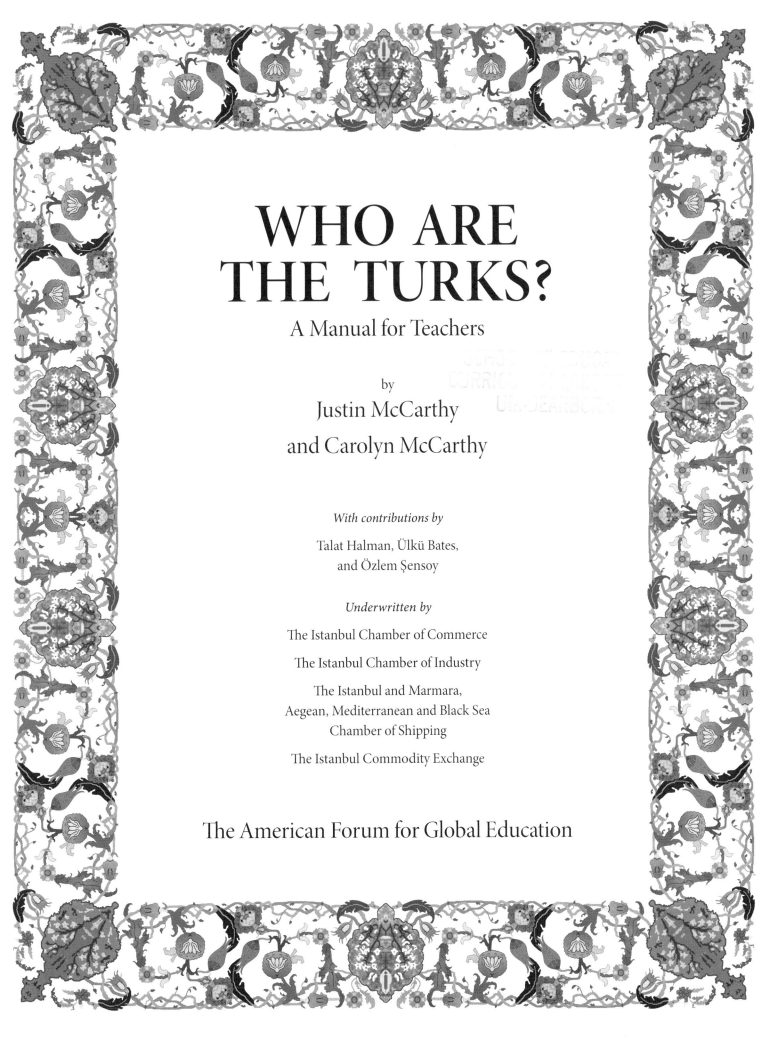

WHO ARE THE TURKS?

A Manual for Teachers

by

Justin McCarthy

and Carolyn McCarthy

With contributions by

Talat Halman, Ülkü Bates,
and Özlem Şensoy

Underwritten by

The Istanbul Chamber of Commerce

The Istanbul Chamber of Industry

The Istanbul and Marmara,
Aegean, Mediterranean and Black Sea
Chamber of Shipping

The Istanbul Commodity Exchange

The American Forum for Global Education

Who Are The Turks? Educational Resource Guide

A Publication of the American Forum for Global Education

Hazel Sara Greenberg, Project Director
Linda Arkin, Project Director

ISBN: 0-944675-71-9

Book Design by Beth Lamka

Cover Image: Detail of a tile from the Selimiye Mosque in Edirne, Turkey, 1569-1575.
Photo courtesy of The Ministry of Foreign Affairs, Turkey.

The American Forum for Global Education
120 Wall Street, Suite 2600
New York, New York 10005
Tel: (212) 624-1300
Fax: (212) 624-1412
email: hsg423@aol.com
Web address: www.globaled.org

To Melih Berk

Acknowledgements

The authors wish first to thank those who provided the financial and editorial support that allowed *Who Are the Turks* to be produced: the American Forum for Global Education, Inc, the Istanbul Chamber of Commerce, the Istanbul Chamber of Industry, the Istanbul and Marmara, Aegean, Mediterranean and Black Sea Chamber of Shipping, and the Istanbul Commodity Exchange.

We are indebted to those who provided illustrations: Boğaç Güldere, *Hürriyet* newspaper, *Image of Türkiye* magazine, the Istanbul Chamber of Commerce, the Istanbul Karaköy Rotary Club, Ersin Karabudak, Pinar Korun of *Time Out* magazine, the Library of Congress, the Los Angeles County Museum of Art, the Metropolitan Museum of Art, Namık Tan, Yücel Tanyeri, and the Turkish Foreign Ministry. We depended on Bürçin Karagemicioğlu and Melih Berk to find illustrations and request them from sources in Istanbul, and we owe them many thanks.

We acknowledge the great contribution of those who created the first teachers manual on Turkey for the American Forum, Spotlight on Turkey: Linda Arkin, Abby Barasch, Ülkü Bates, Karl Benziger, Robert Croonquist, Talat Halman, and Hazel Sarah Greenberg.

Finally, we would like to thank Leslie Friesen, for invaluable advice and criticism.

This manual is dedicated to Melih Berk, whose tireless effort and desire to portray Turkey accurately was responsible for the existence of *Who Are the Turks*.

Contents

This book is divided into two main parts: history and related social disciplines, and art and literature. Each part contains a number of lessons that include: 1) a **LESSON** plan with notes to the instructor, key concepts for the material, vocabulary terms, and suggestions and strategies for teaching and for projects, 2) **HOMEWORK** readings and **WORKSHEETS** to photocopy as handouts for students. Some lessons also include maps and full-page graphics for copying and distribution to students. Additional material is available in Appendices at the back of the book.

Sources of Illustrations

Ersin Karabudak: 227, and as credited in color plates.

Fotografla Türkiye (Matbuat Umum Müdürlüğü, Munich, 1930): 24, 28, 30, 71, 188, 189, 192, 194, 199, 200, 206, 234, 236.

Hürriyet: x, 72, 79, 80, 82, 90, 102, 103, 106, 109.

Image of Türkiye: 96, and as credited in color plates.

Istanbul: the City Where the Continents, Seas, Roads, Merchants Meet (Istanbul Chamber of Commerce, 1997): 107, 177-179.

Istanbul-İnançların Buluştuğu Kent; Birlikte ve Yanyana (Istanbul Karaköy Rotary Club, 1996): 42-45, 172, and as credited in color plates.

Justin McCarthy: maps.

Library of Congress: 52, 54, 55, 60.

Los Angeles County Museum of Art: as credited in art section.

Metropolitan Museum of Art: as credited in art section.

Pınar Korun of *Time Out:* as credited in color plates.

Republic of Turkey, Ministry of Culture, *Masterpieces of Turkey* (Ankara, 1997), 172 and as credited in color plates.

Spotlight on Turkey: 203, 205, 211-220.

Turkish Foreign Ministry: 22, 84, 88, 105.

Turkish Seismology Directorate: 110.

Yücel Tanyeri: 56, 59.

Introduction for Teachers:
Who Are the Turks?

In 1992, The American Forum, Inc. developed a curriculum guide primarily designed to assist secondary school teachers and students better understand Turkey. We worked closely with three eminent scholars in the field: Professor Justin McCarthy from University of Louisville, Professor Talat Halman, then at New York University and Professor Ülkü Bates from Hunter College in New York City. The resulting publication was very well received across the nation and much of the material was introduced into American classrooms. The responses from educators, as well as from Americans of Turkish descent, indicated the great need for this material to redress some of the material written about Turkey and the Turks in current textbooks. Moreover, many Turkish-Americans especially commended the guide because of our efforts to present a fairer portrait of the Turks and Turkish history.

In the ten years since the original publication, Turkey commands a much larger role in world affairs. The secular state remains different from its Middle Eastern neighbors, as well as a strong ally of the United States. On a national level, educators have come to realize that the teaching about Turkey in all our curricula has been biased or totally ignored. The development of National Standards in social studies areas now includes a good deal of Turkish history, again proving the importance of the area geographically and historically. We began to comprehend that what was a small project had far greater significance and there was the need to revise and update the original publication.

Teaching about Turkey is currently a major priority in world and global history courses. There has been a re-examination of this region, a re-emphasis on the "contribution" of the peoples of the area to history and a re-evaluation of the role of the Turks not only in Turkish history but also in Central Asia, Western China, Eastern Europe and Russia. The Turks cannot be relegated to the backwash of history, especially in the current political climate. This is a particularly significant moment for Americans to learn about Turkey, as well as her neighbors.

The material in this guide is developed with a humanities perspective. We are interested in classrooms which explore the Turks from the viewpoints of their history, their geography, their myths and stories, their literature, their art and architecture and their cultural heritage. In each of these areas, we have provided lessons and materials for teachers which can easily be included into their existing curriculum. Although we have provided "lessons," we do not feel that teachers cannot be more creative in developing strategies for this material. Our primary objective is to help supplement the material currently available and help enrich the classroom with wonderful readings and visuals. We hope this guide will be useful to American teachers and help inform our young citizens about other regions of the globe.

Hazel Sara Greenberg, Director
Linda Arkin, Director
The American Forum, Inc.

Top: Bridge between Europe and Asia over the Bosphorus.

Middle: Dancer.

Bottom: Hot springs and formations at Pammukkale.

Who Are the Turks?

The purpose of this lesson is an attempt to develop a "frame of reference" when we speak of Turks. History books tend to represent the Turks in a somewhat negative fashion and current newspapers, especially in Europe, refer to Turks in pejorative terms. However, the name Turk is historical in origin and often geographic in location. Students need to look at the issue of Turkish identity and try to determine the factors which help contribute to the name "Turk."

Performance Objectives
1. to develop a definition of the term "Who Are the Turks?"
2. to understand the complexity of working with this definition
3. to assess the validity of trying to define the term Turk.

Springboard
If you were asked to define yourself (e.g. Hispanic, Chinese, African-American, Irish, etc.) what ingredients would you consider when you craft that definition?

Strategy
▷ Students will have been given the **Reading**, *Who Are The Turks,* for homework reading. Each group will be given (a) a map of Turkey and (b) a map of Central Asia from the Pamirs to the Mediterranean. They will now be assembled into groups of four to discuss the following statements and questions:
- The simplest definition for the term "Who are the Turks?" is political.
- Turks have uniformly nomadic origins.
- Using a map, trace the travels of the Turks into what is modern-day Turkey.
- What is the ethnic origin of the citizens of modern-day Turkey?

Students will work in groups for about 15 minutes reviewing the reading and the maps and answering the questions. Teacher will then debrief the class and develop a semantic map:

The Turks are...

Summary
What are some of the problems we faced when we tried to define the term "Turk?" Would this occur if we tried to define other groups? Why? Please explain.

Application
Each of us has some ethnic or national origin. Write a short paragraph similar to the long one on the Turks, attempting to tell who you are.

Who Are the Turks?

THE SIMPLEST QUESTIONS CAN BE THE MOST DIFFICULT TO ANSWER. THE TURKS ARE OBVIOUSLY A PEOPLE SEPARATE FROM OTHER PEOPLES, but a people can be defined in many ways — language, religion, cultural traits, citizenship, loyalty to a ruling house or many other feelings of kinship. The Turks of today are citizens of the Turkish Republic. The name Turk is also used to describe the people in Turkey who share the distinctive Turkish culture, especially the Turkish language, which all Turkish citizens do not share, no more than all Americans speak English. Or a Turk can also mean a member of the great linguistic and cultural family of the Turks, a family that stretches from China to Europe, bound together by language and history. The best way to define the Turks may be to consider which people make up the Turks of Turkey and how they defined themselves politically, first as subjects of the Ottoman Empire, later as citizens of the Turkish Republic.

The original speakers of the Turkish language lived in Central Asia. They roamed as nomads over a vast region that today lies in Siberia, Western China, Kazakhstan, Kyrgyzstan, and nearby regions. They were known at an early time to both the Chinese and the Middle Eastern Persians and Arabs, but they first appeared in the Middle East in large numbers, as nomadic soldiers, in the tenth century. Finding the Middle East more pleasant than the cold steppes of Central Asia, they conquered and remained.

The Turks had converted to Islam while in Central Asia. Although some of the Turks in history had been Christians and Jews, Islam became the religion of the vast majority and remains so today.

The Turkish nomads expanded westward under the leadership of the Seljuk family of sultans.[1] The Seljuks quickly took Iran and Iraq, capturing Baghdad, the capital of the old Abbasid Empire, in 1055. Their forces were unlike what is ordinarily thought of as an army. The first Seljuk troops were nomads who brought all their lives with them — families, dwellings (tents), animals and belongings. They were at home wherever the pastures were good for their sheep. Relatively soon after their arrival so many Turks had come that the region to the southwest of the Caspian Sea, Azerbaijan, was Turkish. Large groups of Turks were also spread over other regions of Iran and Iraq.

The nomads did not stop once Iran and Iraq were conquered. They were soon raiding into the Byzantine Empire, which lay to the west of Iran, in Anatolia. In 1071, the Byzantine defeat to the Seljuks in a great battle at Manzikert opened Anatolia to Turkish settlement. Over the next two hundred years the nomads kept moving into Anatolia in great numbers. Although the Turks themselves did not use the term, Anatolia had become Turkey. Many other peoples remained there. Greeks, Kurds, Armenians, and others shared the land, and many of them adopted the Turkish language, converted to Islam (forced conversion was almost unknown), and became Turks themselves. Because the Turks had no concept of "race" that would exclude anyone, they accepted those who wished to be Turks as Turks. The Turkish people were thus made up of the descendants of the Turks of Central Asia and those who had become Turks.

The Turks who first came to Anatolia accepted rule by tribal and local leaders, loosely united under the leadership of the Turkish emperors of Anatolia, the Rum (their name for Rome, since this had been part of the Roman, later the Byzantine, Empire) Seljuks. Under the successors of the Rum Seljuks, the Ottoman sultans, the Turks expanded into Europe. There once again new waves of Turks settled and local people transformed themselves into Turks. Unlike in Anatolia, a majority of the Ottoman subjects in the Balkans and Central Europe retained their language, customs, and religion. Nevertheless, large Turkish communities took root in

---

[1] Sultan, a term for a secular head of state in an Islamic empire, roughly corresponding to "emperor."

what is now Bulgaria, Greece, and other countries of Southeastern Europe. As Turks had in all the areas they settled, the European Turks adopted or retained many local customs, remaining Turks all the while.

Nineteenth and early twentieth century refugees added to the numbers of Turks in Anatolia. The descendants of the Turks who had lived for five hundred years in Europe were forced from their homes. Large numbers of these Turks were either killed or exiled when the countries of the Balkans rebelled against the Ottoman Empire and became independent. They were joined in their exile by Bosnian Muslims, Bulgarian Muslims (Pomaks), and others who were forced to flee to what remained of the Ottoman Empire. Russian invasions of the Ottoman Balkans and the creation of new Balkan states resulted in the expulsion of more than a million Turks. The exiles eventually settled in Anatolia and Eastern Thrace (the European part of Turkey).

The Russians were also responsible for the immigration of more than two million Turks and other Muslims from the Crimea and the Caucasus Region. Both regions were overwhelmingly Muslim in population. The Crimean Tatars were Turkish-speakers who had lived in the Crimea for centuries. The Caucasians, primarily the peoples known as Circassians, Abhazians, and Laz, were not Turks, but were Muslim peoples who had lived on their lands since the beginning of history. These groups and others were forced to flee their homelands by Russian armies or laws. They too came to what today is the Turkish Republic.

From 1800 to the 1920s more than three million refugees came to what is now Turkey. Many of the immigrants were already Turks in culture and language. Others, such as the Circassians and Bosnians, kept many of their ethnic traditions, but became Turkish in language and loyalty. The ethnic Turks of modern Turkey thus are descendents of those who came from Central Asia many centuries ago. A number are also descendants of peoples whose ancestors were Hittites, Phrygians, or other early peoples of Anatolia. Others descend from the peoples exiled from their homes by Russians and others taken in by the Turks of Turkey.

Peoples are often defined by the unique states to which they belong. This is especially true of the Turks, who were tied to one of the greatest empires of history, the Ottoman Empire, then to one of the first successful "developing" countries of the modern world, Turkey.

Partly because the poetry, art, and other aspects of the Turkish character are little known to the West, Europeans and Americans have usually thought of Turks as soldiers and administrators. While there is much more than this to the Turks, it is true that Turks rank among history's great empire-builders and rulers. Under the Ottomans they conquered vast territories in the Balkans and the Middle East and ruled for six hundred years. The Ottoman Empire was founded at the end of the thirteenth century by a Turkish military leader, Osman, and his son Orhan. They and their successors conquered in Europe, Asia, and Africa. One sultan, Selim I, took what today are Egypt, Jordan, Israel, and Lebanon in one campaign. His son, Süleyman the Magnificent, expanded the empire by taking Iraq and Hungary. When Süleyman died in 1566 the Ottoman Empire stretched from the borders of Poland in the North to Yemen in the South and from near Venice in the West to Iran in the East. For centuries, the Ottoman Empire was the primary homeland of the Turks.

> Tolerance and administrative ability were not enough for the Empire to last forever.

The Ottoman Turkish administrative genius lay in retaining and governing what they had conquered. The survival of any government for six centuries is in itself a testimony to greatness. The Turks proved to be adaptable to new circumstances. They managed to turn their system from a nomadic state whose members were more naturally wanderers than statesmen to a settled empire with laws, land registers, taxation systems, and economic might. Their system was not without troubles, but revolts and sometimes poor politicians could not bring it down. The state was based on tolerance of differences among its subjects. Christians and Jews were allowed to keep their religious practices and their means of gaining a livelihood. This was good for the Ottomans, because satisfied subjects did not rebel. It was also good for the subjects.

Tolerance and administrative ability were not enough for the Empire to last forever. In the 1600s and 1700s the Ottomans could not cope with the new power of Europe. The Europeans were translating the benefits of the Renaissance, the Scientific Revolution, and the discovery of the Americas into military and

economic advantage. Europeans began to dismantle the Empire, taking Ottoman lands for themselves, causing the great exile of Turks and other Muslims mentioned above. Nationalist leaders of ethnic and religious groups, such as the Bulgarians and Greeks, became affected by European ideas of nationalism. In the nineteenth century they revolted, relying on European military might, especially that of Russia, to create their new nation states, once again expelling many of the Turks that lived within their new borders.

As the Ottoman Empire compressed, the Turks also began to develop a national consciousness. Driven into Anatolia, the Turkish exiles and the Turks of Anatolia began a slow process of thinking of themselves not only as a religious group, Muslim, or the mainstay of an empire, Ottoman, but as the Turkish People. Turkish philosophers and politicians called upon the Turks to think of themselves as a nation.

The ultimate push toward Turkish nationhood came after World War I. Following Ottoman defeat in the war, the Arab and Muslim provinces had been stripped from the Empire. Anatolia, Istanbul, and a small portion of Europe were all that was left to the Turks. Then, in 1919, Anatolia was also invaded. Aided by Britain and France, the Greek army landed and took control of Western Anatolia and Eastern Thrace. The European Allies took Istanbul themselves. Many Turks already had been driven from both Europe and Asia into Anatolia, and Anatolia seemed about to be lost also. Drawing on their old military skills, the Turks organized to save what remained. They rallied under the leadership of General Mustafa Kemal, defeated the Greeks, and created a new state, the Turkish Republic, in Anatolia and Eastern Thrace.

The identity of the modern Turks was forged in the Turkish Republic under the tutelage of Mustafa Kemal, who became the first president of the Republic. Once again the Turks proved adaptable to change. Mustafa Kemal devised political, economic, and social reforms that would bring Turkey into the modern world. Radical change was legislated covering most facets of life. Soon after the founding of the Republic,

> **Turkey became a secular state... Women were given the vote and elected to parliament. The Turkish language began to be written in Western characters, not the Arabic letters used previously.**

Turkey became a secular state. Islam remained the religion of most of the people, but the state was not religious. Other changes followed quickly: The veil and the fez were banned and Western styles of clothing appeared. Women were given the vote and elected to parliament. The Turkish language began to be written in Western characters, not the Arabic letters used previously. Laws were based on Western legal codes. Schools followed Western models. In short, Turkey became rapidly Westernized under Mustafa Kemal. As a symbol of change, Mustafa Kemal's government required all Turks to change the habits of centuries and adopt family names, as in the West. Mustafa Kemal himself was given the name Atatürk ("Father Turk") as his surname. An entire culture began to be altered. Nevertheless, study of the history and traditions of the Central Asian Turkish ancestors of the Turks of Turkey was stressed, as well.

Why follow the ways of Europe and America? Atatürk and the Turkish reformers felt that Western ways could not be adopted piecemeal. They believed that copying the industries and economies of the West was not possible unless one also accepted Western schools, business practices, and social customs. It was the whole of the Western culture that allowed Europe to develop economically, Atatürk felt, and he wanted his country to develop, so the country had to Westernize. Accepting the ways of the West meant accepting democracy. Atatürk kept authority in his own hands, but he deliberately schooled the people in the forms and ideas of a democratic society. In the 1950s the Turks created a real democracy which, despite some obstacles, continues to this day.

Westernization is another facet of the Turkish makeup. While some Turks would prefer to go back to old ways, the country as a whole has been committed since the time of Atatürk in the model of the West. Turkey has been a full member of NATO since 1952 and an ally of Europe and America in the Gulf War with Iraq and the reform of Afghanistan. Turkey is a candidate to join the European Union.

Who are the Turks? They are the descendants of the nomads from Central Asia and the refugees from the Balkans and the Caucasus, brought together in the

Turkish Republic. Most of the Turks are Muslims, following the prayers of Islam in the mosque, but living in a secular state. They are also the inheritors of the governmental traditions of the Ottoman Empire and the democracy of Atatürk and the West.

The citizens of today's Turkey do not come from one ethnic group, no more than do the citizens of the United States. As in the United States, the ancestors of today's Turkish citizens come from many different places and many different cultures. The majority are ethnically Turkish. That is, they speak Turkish at home and feel themselves to be a part of the great ethnic tradition that goes back to Central Asia. Some others are "Turks by adoption." They speak Turkish as their first language, but their ancestors came to Turkey, primarily in the nineteenth century, speaking other languages. Others are Turkish citizens but do not speak Turkish at home. This too is similar to the United States.

Of those who are Turks by adoption, the majority are the descendants of refugees from the Caucasus and the Balkans. The refugees were driven from their homes by Russian and Balkan armies and settled in what today is Turkey. Peoples such as the Circassians and the Laz have kept some of the folk traditions from their old homeland. However, they seldom speak the old languages. They have become part of the Turkish "melting pot."

The largest concentration group of non-Turkish speakers, the Kurds, is centered in Southeastern Anatolia. Other Kurdish-speakers live in Iraq, Iran, and other parts of what was the Soviet Union. Many Kurds now also live in cities all over Turkey, integrated into the general society. Groups of Arabic speakers live in provinces that border Syria. Of late, large groups of Persians have come to Turkey, refugees from the regime in Iran. There are also numerous smaller groups who have come from all over Europe and Asia.

The Jews in Turkey are both distinct and integrated. Today, their primary language is Turkish, but they have a separate language, Judeo-Espanol, which is also used. Most of the Turkish Jews are descended from those who were expelled from Spain in 1492. Although they are economically and politically completely integrated into Turkish life, the Turkish Jews retain a strong sense of ethnic and religious identity.

By no means do all the ethnic Turks originally come from Anatolia and Eastern Thrace, the area of modern Turkey. The ancestors of many, more than two million, were exiles from the Balkans and what today is the Armenian Republic. Other Turks were forced out by the Soviets in the 1950s. Still others came in large numbers in the 1980s when the Bulgarian State first discriminated against them, then allowed them to emigrate to Turkey.

All of these groups make up the citizenry of the Turkish Republic.

Part of the old city of İstanbul, where the Bosphorus Strait empties into the Marmara Sea. Sultan Ahmet Mosque is in the foreground, and diagonally back of it, the Topkapı Palace of the Ottoman Sultanate perches above the point of the shoreline behind Hagia Sophia. Hagia Sophia was the great church of the Byzantine Empire, later a mosque, and today a museum. Some of the newer sections of the city can be seen across the water and stretching away to the north.

Traditional and Modern:

Top: A bakery in Trabzon.
Right: Miss World 2002, Azra Akın, a Turk.
Bottom left: A cafe in Beyoğlu.

Photo by Ersin Karabudak.

**City Scenes,
Traditional and Modern:**

Left: Copper craftsmen at work.
Below: A pepper seller.
Bottom: Scene at a sidewalk cafe.

Photo by Ersin Karabudak.

Photo courtesy of *Hürriyet.*

City Scenes, Traditional and Modern:

Top left: Produce at a local market.
Top right: Metro riders.
Bottom: The saddler's shop.

Photo by Ersin Karabudak.

Photo by Pınar Korun for *Time Out.*

Photo by Ersin Karabudak.

Photo by Pınar Korun for *Time Out*.

Land of the Old and the New:

Top: Modern towers and shopping.
Bottom: Theatre at the Roman city of Ephesus.

Photo courtesy of *Hürriyet*.

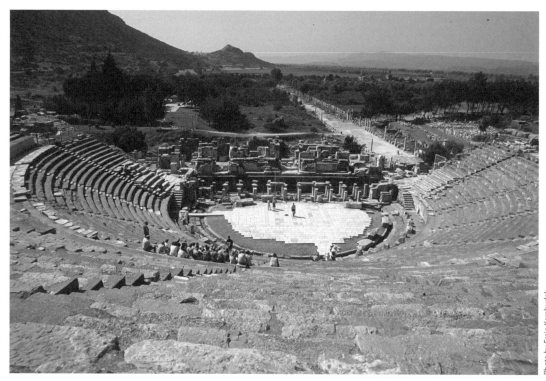

Photo by Ersin Karabudak.

Land of the Old and the New:

Top: Byzantine cisterns under Istanbul.
Bottom: Ottoman houses in Arnavutköy, and a hillside village.

The subway.

Haydarpaşa Railway Station.

Sailing off the Turkish coast.

Bust of Antiochus and other monumental sculptures at the Nemrut Dağ National Park, Adıyaman, 1st century B.C.E.

The Ottoman Imperial palace, Topkapı Sarayı.

A Turkish resort.

Rock climbers.

Buildings in Levent, Istanbul.

Students at Boğaziçi Üniversitesi (Bosphorus University). This English-speaking university has a spectacular location overlooking the straits, next to the 15th century fortifications of Rumeli Hısarı.

Hanging out with friends.

Soccer fans.

Soccer players.

Graduation Day.

The Turks' Westward Movement

This lesson will introduce students to the concept of movement across vast geographic regions. The Turks, a people who originated in Central Asia, followed patterns of movement across the Eurasian regions, conquering and incorporating many peoples as they moved westward.

Aim How did the Turks' westward movement change the lands they encountered?

Performance Objectives Students will be able to:
1. Identify and trace the migration routes of the Turkish people.
2. Explain the relationships between the Turks and other established groups in the Middle East.
3. Create a hypothesis as to the results of Turkish expansion into the Middle East.

Springboard/ Development ▷ Teachers distribute reading: *Origin of the Turks* (**Worksheet 1**)
   ◆ Allow students approximately 15 minutes to read selection and complete exercise.
   ◆ With entire class, create an organizer debriefing the reading:

THE NOMADIC LIFE OF THE TURKS	
Advantages	**Disadvantages**

   ◆ Why did many other people feel the nomadic Turks were both a nuisance and a threat?
   ◆ If you had lived at that time, would you have enjoyed this life? Explain your answer.

   ▷ The change from nomadic life to sedentary life took place over a long period of time.
   ◆ Teachers will distribute **Worksheets 3, 4, and 5**.
   ◆ Based upon all the information presented in the timeline and maps, how did Turkish life change over a period of time?

▷ Students are arranged in groups of four. Using the timeline and maps:
- Each group will create a storyboard of four panels describing what they feel are the four most important events of Turkish westward movement.
- Place the finished storyboards on the walls. A representative from each group will explain their storyboards to the class.

▷ Compare the westward migration of the Americans in the 19th century with that of the Turks. Create an organizer as shown below:

19TH CENTURY AMERICAN WESTWARD MIGRATION AND TURKISH WESTWARD MIGRATION	
Similarities	**Differences**

We have looked at two westward migration patterns in different countries at different times in history.
- What other examples from history can we add?
- How does this show us that in many ways the cultural patterns of the Turks were part of a world-wide movement?

Application ▷ Distribute **Worksheet 2**:
- How does the Talat Halman reading help us better understand the origin of the Turks? Explain your answer.

Origins of the Turks

If the sky above did not collapse and if the earth below did not give way, oh Turk people,
who can destroy your state and institutions.
—ORKHON INSCRIPTIONS

IN THE BEGINNING OF THEIR RECORDED HISTORY TURKS WERE NOMADS. THEIR ORIGINAL HOME WAS IN CENTRAL ASIA, IN THE VAST GRASSLAND THAT spreads north of Afghanistan, the Himalayan Mountains, and China. The steppe grasses of their homeland best supported livestock and the Turks were primarily herdsmen. Because sheep devoured the grass in any one area fairly quickly, the Turks were forced to move from one pasturage to another in order to feed the flocks upon which they depended. Large groups would have quickly over-grazed the land and small groups could not defend themselves, so the earliest Turkish political units were tribes. Although the size of each tribe varied according to its environment and the success of its leadership, none could have been considered large or important.

The Turkish tribes became great conquerors when they merged their forces in confederations and accepted the rule of powerful chiefs, (called **hans** or **khans**). The first recorded Turkish writings, the Orkhon Inscriptions of the eighth century, celebrated the rule of one of the hans, but Chinese chronicles mentioned Turkish confederations in the fourth century B.C.E. Successive Turkish confederations ruled over Central Asia, often battling the Chinese and extending their rule into Europe. The most well known of these were the Huns, called the Hsiung-nu by the Chinese.

The Turks were among the major waves of invaders who attacked the Middle East. There was constant tension between the peoples of the steppes and deserts that surrounded the Middle East and the inhabitants of the settled areas. Nomads were viewed as a threat by both rulers and farmers. If they entered the Middle East, they could be expected to turn farm land into grass land to support their flocks. Nomad raids would disrupt trade, damage farming, and generally harm the tax base upon which rulers depended, while they themselves did not pay taxes. Nomad groups periodically succeeded in overwhelming the defenses of the Middle East. The Persians had been an early group of successful invaders, the Muslim Arabs another. After a period of upheaval, the nomads settled down and their rulers became the new guardians of the Middle East against the next group of nomads.

The Arab Muslims who conquered the Sassanian Persian Empire in the seventh century extended their dominion into the borderlands of Central Asia, across the Oxus (Amu Darya) River into the region called Transoxania. There they came into contact with the Turks.

Turks first came into the Middle East as traders and slaves. The latter were captured in Central Asian wars or by Middle Easterners. Because of their martial abilities, the slaves usually remained soldiers, now fighting in the armies of their new masters. Some rose to high position, occasionally revolting against their lords. In 868 one of the Caliphs Turkish generals, Ibn Tulun, took over Egypt, which his family ruled for the next forty years. But the Turks only came into the Middle East in great numbers when they were brought in by local rulers who used them as mercenaries. Unlike the earlier Turkish slave-soldiers, the new Turks arrived in the Middle East as military units under their own leaders. The tribes had previously been part of the Oğuz Confederation north of the Oxus River. Now they rented their military services to Middle Eastern rulers. But these Turks also soon revolted and created their own empires. The Karahanids created an empire in Transoxania and Central Asia. The Ghaznavids

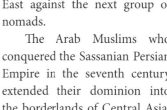

> Successive Turkish confederations ruled over Central Asia, often battling the Chinese and extending their rule into Europe. The most well known of these were the Huns, called the Hsiung-nu by the Chinese.

ruled in Afghanistan and Northern India. Another group of the Oğuz, the Seljuks, took Iran and Iraq in the eleventh century. They entered Baghdad, the capitol of the derelict Abbasid Empire, in 1055.

The power of the **Seljuks** was founded on an army of nomadic Turkish warriors. The first Seljuk sultans can themselves be considered to have been traditional nomad leaders. However, the Seljuk sultans soon decided to create a more stable and regularized state. They built an army, a tax system, and a bureaucracy. Partially successful attempts were made to settle the nomads by awarding lands to their leaders — lands that could be used to support the leaders and men as the sultan's soldiers.

Most important for future history, the Seljuks expanded Turkish rule to the West. They encouraged the nomads to raid into the Byzantine Empire, which was on their western border. The benefits of directing the nomads westward were great: nomads who raided the Byzantine lands were not causing trouble in the Seljuk domains. Moreover, they were weakening the Byzantines, an enemy of the Seljuks. The Byzantine emperor, Romanus Diogenes, realized the nomad threat. He mobilized his army and moved east across Anatolia. The Seljuk sultan, Alp Arslan, in turn mobilized his own forces and moved west. The two armies met at Manzikert in 1071, where the Byzantines were completely defeated.

The way into **Anatolia** and the **Byzantine Empire** was now open to the Turks. Since soon after the time of the Prophet Muhammad Muslims had attempted to defeat the Byzantines. After taking Syria and Egypt, the Muslim armies had been unable to conquer the remainder of the Byzantine Empire in Anatolia and the Balkans. For 400 years Anatolia had resisted Muslim incursion. All that was now ended. The Byzantine Empire remained alive. For long it retained land in Western and Northern Anatolia. The Turks had begun to move in, however, slowly turning Anatolia into Turkey.

The Turkish nomad chiefs in Anatolia organized under their own leaders, families of proven lords who set up small capitols in various Anatolian cities. They loosely came under the overlordship of a branch of the Seljuk family known as the Rum Seljuks (The "Seljuks of Rome," called that because they ruled part of what been the Roman Empire.)

There were many opportunities for war for the Turks in Anatolia. The Byzantines remained for centuries. Crusaders from Europe came, fought the Turks, and went. Tribes of nomads came from other parts of the Middle East and from Central Asia to fight for booty and the chance to expand the rule of Islam. These warriors, called *gazi*s ("fighters for the Faith") attached themselves to the campaigns of the Rum Seljuks and other Turkish lords. Some were awarded lands where they themselves might rule. One of these, Osman, was by tradition given lands bordering the Byzantine Empire by the Rum Seljuk sultan. He and his successors were to create the great Ottoman Empire.

Based upon the reading above, complete the following questions:

▷ Several words in the reading are in **bold** print. Define each of these words.
▷ Where did the Turks originate?
▷ According to this reading, the Turks were nomadic people. Write a short paragraph describing the life of nomadic people.
▷ How did other groups react to the movement of the Turks into their regions? Explain your answer.

E Pluribus Unum:
Diversity and Unity
in Turkish Culture and Literature

"I AM A TURK," PROCLAIMED THE NATIONALIST POET MEHMED EMIN YURDAKUL IN THE EARLY 20TH CENTURY, "MY FAITH AND MY RACE ARE mighty." This poetic line of effusive pride apotheosized **"din"** (religious faith: Islam) and **"cins"** (ethnic stock: Turkishness). It reflected a mood prevalent at the time.

These two components, however, did not always hold equal power in the fifteen centuries of the recorded history of the Turks. At the outset, tribal culture shaped their identity. Islam started to gain ascendancy in their consciousness after the 9th century. In the Seljuk and Ottoman periods, Turkishness was relegated to a lesser status than religious and dynastic allegiance. In the Turkish Republic, secular nationalism rather than Islam has played a dominant role in government and education.

Patriotc pride aside, Turks point, with some justification, to several truisms or objective facts:

* Few nations have been sovereign so long (about a thousand years) without interruption.
* Few have had a broader geographic spread (from China and inner Asia through the Middle East and the Balkans to the Westernmost reaches of North Africa, virtually from the Pacific Ocean to the Atlantic Ocean).
* Few have experienced a similar diversity of religious life (pagan beliefs, "sky religion", shamanism, Buddhism, Manichaeism, Judaism, Christianity, Islam, secularism, etc.)
* Few have lived in a greater variety of political systems (tribal organization, nomadic confederacy, principalities, small states, empires, republics.)
* Few have employed more systems of writing for essentially the same language (The Göktürk, Uighur, Arabic, Latin and Cyrillic scripts).

The story of the culture of the Turks, whether they live in the Republic of Turkey or in such recently created Asian republics as Azerbaijan, Kirghizia, Turkmenistan, Uzbekistan and others or as guest-workers in Germany and other European countries or as minorities in Bulgaria and Iraq or as the majority in the Turkish Republic of Northern Cyprus — is one of diversity, change, disparity, and sometimes cataclysmic transformation. Yet, it is also a story of unity, even uniformity, and certainly solidarity.

One can make, with impunity, one more generalization — that few nations have undergone so much change and preserved an authentic identity and cultural personality.

The population of the Turkish Republic (close to 60 million in 1992) is comprised of the descendants of three masses:
1. Natives of Asia Minor since antiquity
2. Migrants from Central Asia since the 9th century
3. Immigrants from the Middle East, the Balkans, and the Mediterranean basin since the 15th century.

The territory of present-day Turkey (often referred to in classical times as Anatolia or Asia Minor) has by and large remained under Turkish control since the 1070s. This dominion, now in its tenth century, has witnessed one of history's most extensive and sustained processes of miscegenation. Seljuk and Ottoman ethnic groups intermingled. Conversions and mixed marriages frequently occurred. Although most non-Muslim communities maintained their cultural autonomy under the "millet" system and some isolated rural communities and nomadic tribes remained cohesive, Anatolia created a vast melting pot which has been inherited by the Turkish Republic. Consequently, it would be foolhardy for any "Turk" living in Turkey today to claim ethnic purity.

The definition of the "Turk" is certainly untenable in terms of race, blood, or ethnic background. The only valid criteria are the Turkish language and presumably the emotional commitment to "Turkishness." There are those who insist on the Islamic dimension as a *sine qua non*. This, however, contradicts the constitutional imperative of secularism — and the Republic has many non-Muslim Turkish-speaking citizens although more than 99 per cent of the population belong to the Islamic faith, mostly of the mainstream Sunni persuasion.

In cultural terms, the diversity of the heritage of the Turkish mainland is astonishing. Anatolia, inhabited with an unbroken continuity for nine millennia, was truly "the cradle and grave of civilizations"— Hattian, Hittite, Urartian, Phrygian, Lydian, Lycian, Carian, Greek, Hellenistic, Roman, Byzantine. It was a peninsula of countless cultures, cities, religions, cults. It nurtured its own myths, epics, legends — and an amazingly broad spectrum of styles, native and foreign, flourished in architecture and in all creative arts. Asia Minor produced a diversity that stands today as a marvel of archaeology.

Into the heartland of Anatolia's life of civilizations the Turkish exodus from Asia brought the dynamics of nomadic culture, rich in oral literature, music, dance, decorative arts. The incoming culture had its autochthonous norms and values. New converts to Islam, the Turks embraced not only the Islamic ethics but also the Arabo-Persian esthetics whose achievements held sway in the areas into which they moved wave upon wave, conquest after conquest. Yet, they clung to their own Turkish language for identity, for state affairs, and for literary expression. Especially in the rural areas, their ethnic/folk culture, with their Asian roots, remained alive.

The Seljuk state, which controlled much of Anatolia from the middle of the 11th century to the latter part of the 13th, embodied the new Islamic orientation and the region's enchorial traditions while perpetuating the basic forms of Central Asian Turkic culture. This amalgam was to culminate in the grand synthesis created by the Ottomans.

The Ottoman state, growing from a small mobile force in the closing years of the 13th century into an empire within two hundred years and the world's leading superpower in the 16th century, enriched the synthesis by adding to it the features of the cultures of its minorities, "millets", conquered or subject peoples and the technology and the arts of Europe. Central Asia, ancient Anatolian cultures, Islamic civilization, Middle Eastern and North African creativity, and a Turkish spirit and style coalesced into a unique synthesis.

> During its life span of more than six centuries (from the late 13th century until 1922), a single dynasty —the House of Osman—reigned in unbroken continuity.

During its life span of more than six centuries (from the late 13th century until 1922), a single dynasty — the House of Osman — reigned in unbroken continuity. Islam was not only the religious faith but also the political ideology of the theocratic state. The Empire was multi-racial, multi-national, multi-religious, multi-lingual. Its ethnic diversity may be likened to the composition of the U.S. population. Although minorities and subject peoples were allowed to speak their own languages, Turkish served as the Empire's official language, its lingua franca, and its vehicle of literary expression.

—TALAT S. HALMAN, PH.D.

Gök Medrese, Sivas. Built in1271.

A Timeline

NOTE: The dates for many of these empires and confederations, especially the early ones, are very approximate.

c. 200 BCE-216	Hun Empires/Confederations in Central Asia
c. 350-550	Hun Empire in Eastern Europe and Western Asia
434-453	Rule of Attila
c. 552-744	Göktürk Empire/Confederation in Central Asia
732-735	Orkhon Inscriptions, first discovered written records in Turkish
c. 620-1016	Khazar Kingdom in Western Central Asia, today's southern Russia and Eastern Ukraine
9th Century	Oğuz Confederation of Tribes north of the Jaxartes (Syr Darya) and in Transoxania
868-905	Tulunid Empire in Egypt and Syria
992-1211	Karahanid Empire in Transoxania and Central Asia
977-1186	Ghaznavid Empire in Afghanistan and Northern India
1038-1194	Great Seljuk Empire
1071	Battle of Manzikert
1077-c.1307	Rum Seljuk Sultanate
1220	Jenghiz Khan first invades the Middle East
1243	Mongols defeat Rum Seljuks at Kösedağ
1250-1517	Mamluks in Egypt and Syria
1256-1353	Il Khanid Empire (Mongols) in Iran
1258	Mongols capture Baghdad
1281-1923	Ottoman Empire

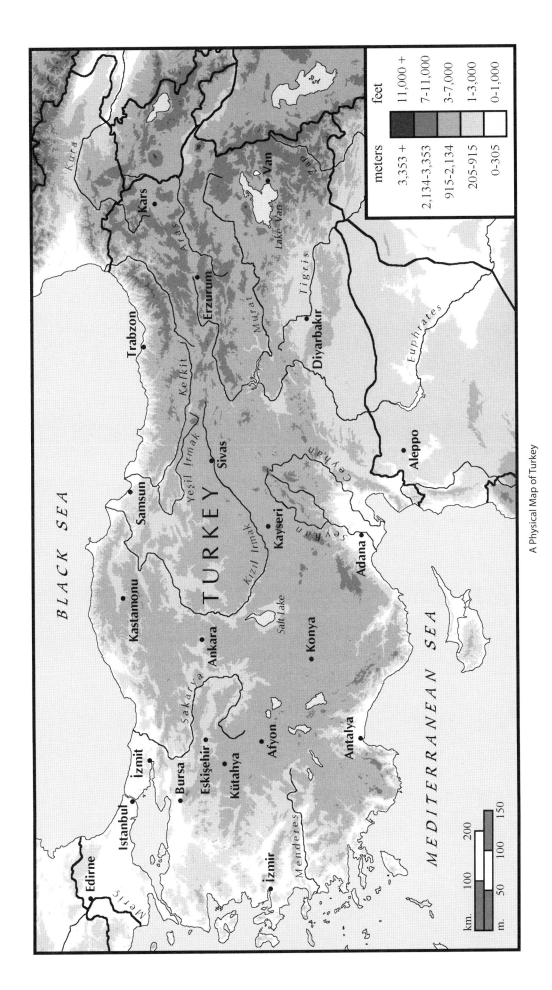

A Physical Map of Turkey

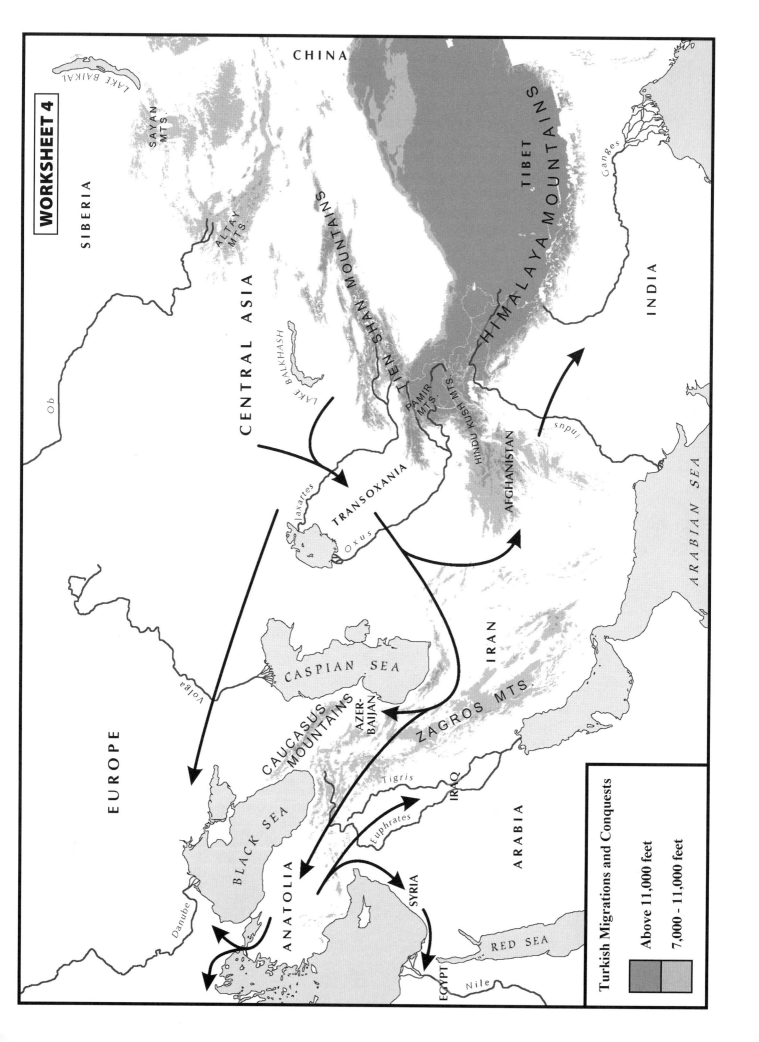

WORKSHEET 4

Turkish Migrations and Conquests

Above 11,000 feet

7,000 - 11,000 feet

Can We Consider the Ottoman Empire a Great Period in History?

In this lesson the students will try to get some sense of the extent and greatness of the Ottoman Empire. Many of the more traditional history books tend to denigrate the Ottomans or to castigate their system of ruling. However, in reality, we now know the Ottomans had a glorious empire and civilization and their culture touched the Middle East as well as many parts of Europe. There is a need to reappraise the significance of the Ottomans in world history.

Suggested Time   This lesson can take two or three days.

Performance Objectives
1. Students will define and discuss the Ottoman rise to power
2. Students will analyze the Ottoman system of governance as their role in "empire building."
3. Students will assess the Ottoman Empire and its great leaders vis-a-vis other historical empires and figures.

For Homework   Each student will read the **Homework** worksheet, *The Ottoman Empire: Historical Background.*

Springboard   Teacher will place the names of Empires on the chalkboard:
Empire of Alexander the Great, Roman Empire, Empire of Benin, Manchu Empire, Habsburg Empire, Mongol Empire.
- Why do we call each of these "empires?"
- How would you attempt to define each of these of these periods in history?
- Based upon your answers, what are some of the ingredients that we consider important to "make an empire?"

Strategy   Students will work in a jigsaw cooperative learning lesson. There are five readings. Each group of four will receive a worksheet giving some information about the Ottomans. Students will read the materials and answer the questions at the bottom of each worksheet. Class will reassemble and reporters will share their findings with the entire class.

Summary   Based upon what we have all read and shared, can be consider the rule of the Ottoman a great period in history?

The Ottoman Empire: Historical Background

THE OTTOMANS WERE THE MOST SUCCESSFUL OF ALL TURKISH STATES AT TURNING AN ARMY OF NOMADS INTO AN ENDURING SETTLED STATE. The first sultan, Osman, ruled over a small region around the town of Söğüt in Northeast Anatolia. Osman and his main general, his son Orhan, were fine military leaders who had the good fortune to rule on the border of the decaying Byzantine Empire. From there they could mount attacks on the Byzantine lands. These provided plunder and conquered new lands but, most important, brought **gazi** warriors to the Ottoman camp. These warriors fought to expand the rule of Islam, and were not adverse to collecting plunder. For plunder, glory, and expanding the rule of Islam, Christian lands had to be attacked. The Ottomans provided prime geography for attacks into the Byzantine lands, good generals, and a history of successful conflicts. The nomads rode in from all over the Turkish world, As the Ottoman victories increased, so did the size and power of their army.

> **Mehmet II's greatest conquest was of a relatively small piece of land, the city of Constantinople, the last remnant of the Byzantine Empire.**

Early Conquests

Orhan, the second sultan, expanded Ottoman rule to all of Northwestern Anatolia and a small part of Europe. The next sultans, Murat I and Bayezit I, conquered or made vassals of nearly all of Southeastern Europe, including most or all of what would become today's Greece, Bulgaria, Serbia, Kosovo, and Macedonia, as well as part of Romania. Bayezit I also broke tradition and attacked other Turkish states in Anatolia. But by advancing into Asia he came up against the imperial plans of the greatest conqueror of the day, Tamerlane, who ruled over Central Asia and Iran. Tamerlane defeated Bayezit at the Battle of Ankara (1402).

Bayezit died in captivity, leaving his four sons to contest for rule. Tamerlane had taken away Bayezit's conquests in Anatolia, but left the Ottomans their old Anatolian lands. European vassals of the Ottomans took advantage of their straitened circumstances to declare independence, but much Ottoman land also remained in Europe. Bayezit's four sons fought and conspired from 1402 until 1413, when one of them, sultan Mehmet I, took absolute control.

A New Empire

Only temporarily daunted by Tamerlane, the Ottomans staged an amazing recovery. Mehmet I consolidated Ottoman land and military forces. He and his successor, Murat II, rebuilt the Empire until it included all of Bayezit's European conquests south of the Danube and new territories in the western Balkans. They even retook much of Bayezit's previous conquest in Anatolia.

Murat's son Mehmet II, known forever to the Turks as **Fatih** ("the Conqueror") greatly expanded the Empire in both Europe and Asia. He added Bosnia, Albania, Montenegro, Southern Greece, and part of Romania. The Crimean Tatars, Turks who ruled over the Crimea and today's Southern Ukraine, became Ottoman vassals. All of Central, Western, and Northern Anatolia became Ottoman. His greatest conquest, though, was of a relatively small piece of land, the city of Constantinople, the last remnant of the Byzantine Empire. Muslim forces had tried to take the city since soon after the death of the Prophet, Muhammad. Bayezit I had been defeated by Tamerlane before he could attempt it. Fatih Mehmet was successful. Constantinople was strategically and commercially important. Its conquest united Ottoman Europe and Asia and secured easy lines of communication between both parts of the Empire. But the greatest triumph was the prestige that came with the Ottoman conquest of the onetime capitol of the Eastern Roman Empire and the greatest city of the Middle Ages, the city that was called the New Rome.

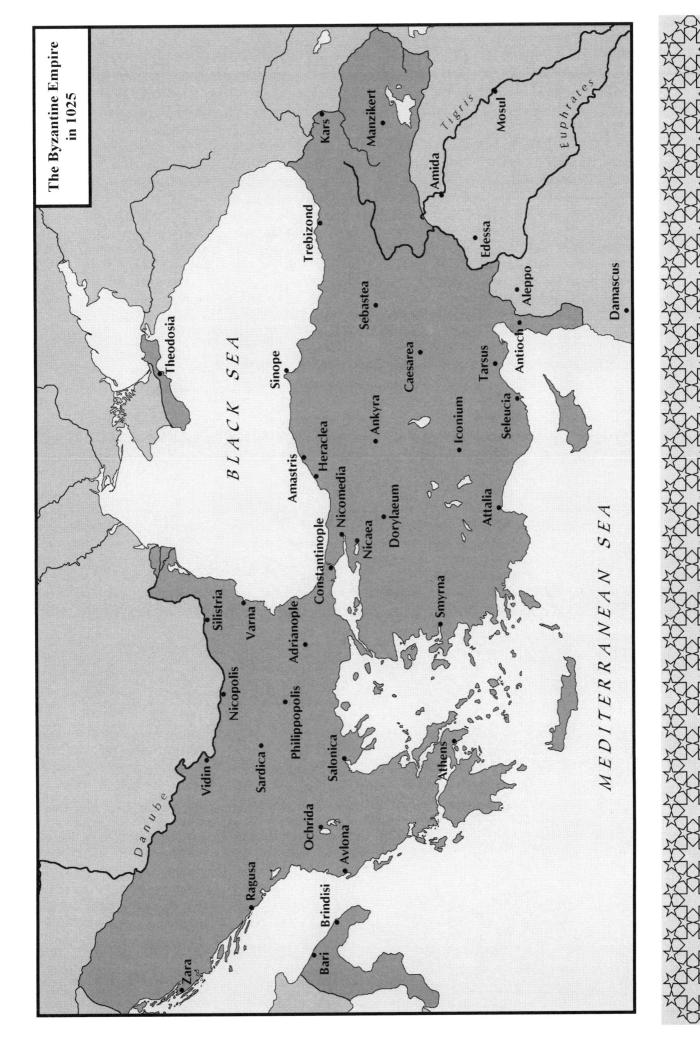

The Byzantine Empire in 1025

Danube

Zara
Ragusa
Brindisi
Bari
Vidin
Sardica
Nicopolis
Philippopolis
Ochrida
Avlona
Salonica
Athens
Silistria
Varna
Adrianople
Constantinople
Smyrna
Attalia

BLACK SEA

Theodosia
Sinope
Trebizond
Amastris
Heraclea
Nicomedia
Nicaea
Dorylaeum
Iconium
Seleucia
Tarsus
Antioch
Aleppo
Damascus
Caesarea
Ankyra
Sebastea
Edessa
Amida
Mosul
Kars
Manzikert

Tigris
Euphrates

MEDITERRANEAN SEA

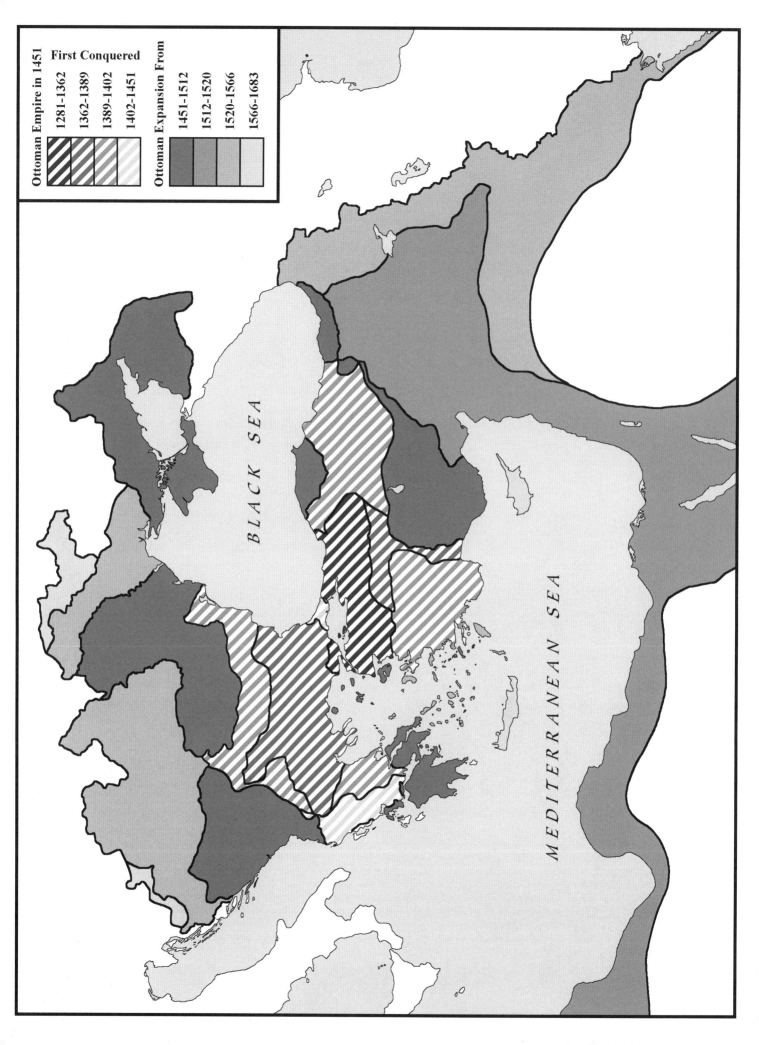

Ottoman Empire in 1451   **First Conquered**

1281-1362   1362-1389   1389-1402   1402-1451

Ottoman Expansion From

1451-1512   1512-1520   1520-1566   1566-1683

BLACK SEA

MEDITERRANEAN SEA

Mehmet followed his capture of Constantinople with conquest of Byzantine lands that had broken away from allegiance to Constantinople — the Empire of Trebizond in northern Anatolia and small states in Greece.

Crusades

The Christian states of Europe did not ignore the Ottoman advance. Popes and preachers delivered orations against the Turks. Voices were heard throughout Europe calling for a new crusade to defeat the Turks. Aggressive talk was abundant, but action was minimal. Constantinople was little helped in its death throes. Sympathy for the Byzantines was muted; many felt the Eastern "schismatics" were little better than the Muslims. The Europeans were more concerned with their own problems. The French and English were occupied with the 100 Years War. The Great Schism divided the Roman Catholic Church. Venice fought Genoa. German lords argued and fought over rule in the Holy Roman Empire. The effects of the Black Death were still felt everywhere.

Beset by their own internal conflicts, the European Christians were never able to mount a unified, powerful force to oppose the Ottomans. They took little advantage of the opportunity afforded by Tamerlane's defeat of the Ottomans to attack the Ottomans when they were weakest. They did, however, send forces at other times to aid the Christian kingdoms that were most threatened by the Ottomans. Buoyed by the European support, countries such as Serbia threw off vassalage and joined in attacking their Ottoman overlords. The Hungarian kingdom was a particular leader and focus for the European threat to the Ottomans.

The Ottomans managed to defeat all the crusades. Although Murat I died in the battle, the Ottomans defeated the crusaders at Kosova (Kosovo) in 1389. Bayezit I defeated another crusading army at Nicopolis in 1396. In 1444, crusaders from Poland and Germany gathered in Hungary, moved east along the Danube, and met Murat II's forces at Varna, where they were once again defeated. The crusader armies were badly mauled, and no further crusades were staged.

Conquest of the Arab World

Mehmet II's successor, sultan Bayezit II, made only small additions to the size of the Ottoman Empire. Instead of conquest, Bayezit consolidated Ottoman reign over new provinces. He built administrative systems, and provided civil peace and internal order that allowed commerce to flourish. After the almost constant wars of past sultans the Empire needed a break. The next two sultans would renew the conquests.

Bayezit's son, Selim I, overthrew his father in 1512. He was faced with two enemies in the Middle East — the Safavids[1] of Iran and Mamluks[2] of Egypt. The Safavids were defeated in 1514, but not conquered. The Mamluk lands of Syria (1516) and Egypt (1517) were taken into the Empire. With them came the acceptance of Ottoman sovereignty by the civil and military leaders of the Holy Cities of Islam, Mecca and Medina. The Ottomans were now the "Custodians of the Holy Places," the highest honor for Muslim rulers. The conquests of Syria and Egypt also brought with them riches from the trade and agriculture of new territories.

Selim only ruled for eight years. His son, Süleyman, took control of a powerful and rich empire. Süleyman himself conquered Hungary and Iraq. Ottoman rule now stretched from the borders of Austria to Yemen in South Arabia. All of the major ports of the East-West trade with India and China were in Ottoman hands (see "The Ottomans and International Trade" below). The cities of the Prophet Muhammad, Mecca and Medina, accepted Ottoman rule. The Ottomans had become the richest and most powerful rulers in Europe and the Middle East, perhaps in the world.

---

[1] The Safavids, a Turkish family that, like the early Ottomans, depended on an army of Turkish nomads, ruled over Eastern Anatolia, and Iraq. They instituted the Shia form of Islam as their state religion. This set them religiously as well as politically against the Sunni Ottomans. The Ottomans were able to dislodge them from Eastern Anatolia and Iraq, but the Safavids remained in control of Iran.

[2] The Mamluk state seems an odd form of government to most. It was made up of military slaves who were organized in households. Each household purchased slaves and trained them in military skills. The slaves became rulers, but remained slaves of their households, not slaves belonging to any individual. The Mamluks, as well as the Ottoman Janissaries, illustrate the fact that slavery in the Middle East was quite different than slavery in the United States and elsewhere. Slaves in the Middle East could rule, become rich, and even own slaves themselves.

The Ottoman System of Government

As seen in their own time, the early Ottomans would have appeared as but one of many Turkish principalities, rising from the Turkish nomadic tradition, dependent on Turkish nomad soldiers. Like the Seljuks and other Turkish rulers, the Ottomans faced the problems inherent in dependence on nomad forces. The nomads were great fighters, but poor subjects. An empire needs administration, not only conquest. It needs taxes and a bureaucracy. No settled state can rely on the plunder from conquest for its support. Few states managed to resolve the contradiction between dependence on nomads and the need for a settled state. The Great Seljuks had ultimately been defeated by their own nomads. If the Ottomans hoped to create a lasting empire, they had to retain the nomads as a military force, but keep them under control.

Mehmet II

The Genius of the Early Ottomans

The Ottomans managed to rule for more than 600 years by a policy of "divide and rule," by making themselves part of the culture of the regions they ruled, and, especially, by a pragmatic openness to borrowing from political and cultural traditions other than their own.

To offset the power of the nomads, the Ottomans created an army of soldiers from slaves of the sultan (see below). They also settled nomadic Turks on conquered lands, allowing them to live off proceeds of the land rather than raiding, but keeping them available to fight in the Ottoman wars. Where there had been one source of military power, the nomads, there were now many — the nomads, the slave army, and the settled Turks. Diplomacy and cleverness kept each group divided even within itself, each leader vying for the sultan's favor.

The early sultans also became part of the life of domestic power groups in Anatolia. Groups such as merchant and craft guilds, Islamic mystical brotherhoods, and local defense organizations had been the real unifying forces in the Turkish culture of Anatolia when civil order broke down at the end of the Rum Seljuk Empire. The Ottomans were a part of these organizations. They were themselves tied to mystical religious organizations, in which at least some sultans were believers, practicing mystics. They also joined or favored guilds. Each of the early sultans was trained in a craft, such as leatherwork, goldsmithing, or crafting armaments. Where other Turkish leaders had been purely military men, the Ottoman sultans were also intimately a part of the culture of their people. The Ottoman sultans were not foreign occupiers; they were a part of the place and the people they ruled.

In the end, the Ottoman success cannot be explained without acknowledging that the first sultans were extraordinary men. They were distinguished for both their military prowess and their diplomatic abilities. Sultans managed to use the armies of defeated enemies to fight for the Ottomans against other enemies. Bayezit I used Turkish armies to fight against Christian states in Europe, then used the armies of Christian European vassals to fight against Turks in Anatolia. They borrowed administrative systems from their enemies. Because Christian tax-collectors and bureaucrats best knew how to tax newly-conquered territories, the Christians were retained in their jobs. They purchased the best weapons from whoever could provide them. The largest cannons used by Mehmet II to breach the walls of Constantinople were purchased from a Christian cannon-maker. They balanced forces within their supporters so that no one threatened the sultan's rule. Murat II relied upon Turkish lords as administrators, but his son, Mehmet II, felt the Turkish lords had become too powerful, so he relied on administrators and advisors drawn from his own slaves. Most important of all, the sultans learned from enemies and friends alike. Mehmet II battled the Byzantines, but he listened to the consul of Byzantine princes. Bayezit I also depended on the consul of Christians — those who best knew the lands he had conquered.

The Ottoman System

Turkish states were often named for the families of their rulers. Thus the Seljuk Empire was named for the father of the first Seljuk sultans. The Ottoman Empire was named after Osman. In Turkish it was named the Osmanlı ("those with Osman") state. The state was not tied to one region, like France or England, nor to one people. Not until very late in the Empire's history was the Ottoman Empire considered "Turkish." The rulers were culturally Turks, but non-Turks could learn their customs and join them. Albanians, Arabs, and other Muslims could easily join the rulers. It was an Islamic state that *belonged* to the sultan. The two emblems of the state were religion and the sultan.

The duties of the sultan were to protect and, if possible, expand his empire, protect and foster Islam, and provide justice for his subjects. He was assisted in this by his advisors and subordinates, often called the "ruling class" (not a term used by the Ottomans, themselves.) In turn, the sultan and his followers had the right to exploit the revenues of the Empire. In other words, to protect and collect. This was, in fact, the reality of most pre-modern governments. What counted to the subjects in any land was how well the duties of protection and justice were carried out. Were the roads safe for commerce? Was banditry suppressed? Were foreign armies kept at bay? Did the imperial armies conquer new territories that could be exploited and bring home much booty? Did the tax collector leave enough for a reasonable life? Those were the real questions of government. Political theories meant little to subjects.

The sultans and their government were for centuries very good at carrying out their duties and at enjoying their perquisites. To succeed they had to be both good generals and good administrators. They created a system that borrowed from the traditions of all those with whom the Turks had come into contact — Persians, Arabs, Byzantine Greeks — and blended them with Turkish traditions to create a distinctly Ottoman system of government. It was always a state that thought of itself as military. What is called the Ruling Class simply called themselves "the Military" (**Askeri**).

It is traditional to describe the Ottoman Government as it was in the time of sultan Süleyman the Magnificent. Government was different from that standard both before and after Süleyman's time, but the Turks themselves felt that Süleyman's reign had been the high point of government and a template of proper rule.

Administration of the Ottoman state was led by an official who was both chief administrator and head general, the Grand Vezir. He met in council with other vezirs to advise the sultan. There were not departments of state as known in modern governments (e.g.., State Department, Finance Ministry, etc.), in which departments each have specific duties. The duties of individual vezirs might change often. A bureaucracy of scribes kept records. To them fell the all-important duty of keeping the government books of revenues and expenditures, in addition to recording the activities of government.

> The sultan encouraged division and competition among his officials, keeping them at each other's throats, rather than at his.

Originally, members of the Ruling Class arose out of what are called the "Turkish notables." The Turkish notables were descendents of the leaders of the Turkish nomads who had fought alongside Osman and Orhan, the first sultans. Their power base was land granted them by the sultans, called timars. They used taxes from their timars to support themselves and their armed men, making up part of the Ottoman army. The other group were the **devşirme** (literally "those who had been turned.") These were soldiers and officials who had been taken from Christian villages as children, converted to Islam, and educated in the Ottoman system from an early age. It was felt that, unlike the Turkish notables, these devşirme would have no loyalties to any region or group of the population. Their only loyalty would be to the sultan. The two groups competed for power and the sultan's favor, as did individual members of both groups and their supporters.

Successful sultans realized that they could retain their power by balancing the power of interest groups within their administration. If any groups within the class of rulers became too powerful, they could become the real power in the Empire; the sultan would become a figurehead. To prevent this, the sultan used his considerable power and wealth to given benefits to one group, then to another, making sure that all stayed dependent on him and none grew too powerful. The sultan encouraged division and competition among his officials, keeping them at each other's throats, rather than at his.

A third group of the Administration was the **ulema**, the group of Muslim religious scholars, administrators, and judges. In Islam, all law was supposed to be Holy Law, based on the Quran and the traditions of the Prophet Muhammad. Because they applied this law to the circumstances of life and made court rulings, the ulema had considerable power. Even sultans were expected to abide by Holy Law, and they were expected to obtain rulings of legality (fetvas) from a religious scholar before they made major changes in state practice. In practice, they usually agreed with the sultans, who named their leader (the Şeyhülislam) and paid their salaries, but the sultan always had to reckon with their prestige within the Muslim Community and could not push them too far.

At its height, the Ottoman system was thus a balance of powers. Until the reign of sultan Mehmet II, the conqueror of Constantinople, the grand vezir was a member of the Turkish Notables, balancing the power of the devşirme and their close identification with the ruler. Mehmet changed that, and future grand vezirs were devşirme. The power of the devşirme gradually increased and was to become a problem to the sultan's own authority. The system was always fluid, however, and the sultan always remained at its head.

▷ List 3 to 5 important pieces of evidence about the Ottoman Empire from this reading.
▷ Discuss how the Ottoman system helped make the Empire strong.
▷ Can we consider the Ottoman Empire a great period in history? Explain your answer with examples.

Vestibule of Uskudar Mosque

The Military, the Ottomans as a "Gunpowder Empire"

Like the Administration, the structure of the Ottoman Army changed over time. It began as an assemblage of nomad warriors. This was never a stable source of power. Nomads were fine cavalrymen, but they were too independent and often proved unwilling to adopt the latest military techniques. The Rum Seljuks had never conquered the independent spirit of the nomads. Their leaders had held the real power in the Rum Seljuk Empire. The Ottoman sultans responded to the problem by settling the nomads and making their leaders parts of the power structure. As seen above, these leaders were given lands, timars, where they and their troops could lead a more comfortable life, yet be ready to fight when the sultan's order came. They served as the main cavalry of the Empire. Bows and spears were their main weapons, so they lost their usefulness as muskets became the weapons of enemy armies.

The Ottomans added a slave army, the **Janissaries** ("new troops") to their forces. These troops were taken as children, as told above, and trained to act as parts of a disciplined unit. The most talented among them were trained further and made generals and devşirme administrators. The Janissaries were taught to use the latest weapons. Never a large force, 10-30,000 at the height of their effectiveness, their discipline and use of the latest gunpowder weapons made them a formidable force.

The Janissaries were primarily an infantry force. Other slave soldiers were part of the Ottoman cavalry. Slave soldiers also made up most of the specialized units of the army.

As the Ottoman Empire grew it came up against military obstacles that were impervious to cavalry attacks. Fortified cities could hold off cavalry attacks for many years. If they could be supplied by sea, they could stand for decades. A cavalry force did not have the siege machines necessary to breech a city's walls, nor did nomads have the patience to camp outside a city's gates

for months while the population was starved into surrender. The second sultan, Orhan, was only able to take the Ottomans' first real capitol, the city of Bursa, after 5 years of siege. To remedy the defect, the Ottomans organized a cannon corps. They added a wagon corps to carry supplies. The nomads had carried their own.

Nomads remained as part of the Ottoman forces for the first Ottoman centuries. They were gradually relegated to raiding and leading wild cavalry charges that demoralized the Ottomans' enemies. The bulk of Turkish soldiers soon became those who were settled on the estates of the Turkish notables. In the early days of the empire, Turks had been enrolled as salaried members of the army, as both foot soldiers and cavalry. Christians also served. By the time of Süleyman, however, the military was completely Muslim and most of the Turkish soldiers had been absorbed into the timar system.

The Ottoman Empire began as a land power, and the army remained the most important military force throughout the Empire's history. However, any empire with as much sea coast as the Ottoman Empire needed a strong navy. Until very late in the Empire's history, most of the Ottoman sailors were Christians, often Greeks from the Aegean islands and ports. Their ships were galleys, rowed by slaves or sailors whose villages provided rowers in lieu of paying taxes. What would today be called marines (azabs) were stationed on the ships. Galleys fought by ramming other ships and coming close enough for soldiers on the ships to fight hand to hand, so the marines were essential.

The navy was led by a Grand Admiral (kapudan paşa). As the importance of the navy increased, whole islands and provinces were given to the Grand Admiral as timars to support the fleet.

The main exceptions to the Christian character of the Ottoman navy were pirates. Like the Christian states of the time, the Ottomans encouraged pirates who preyed on the shipping of enemies. The pirates were Muslims. Their leaders might take high positions in the Ottoman navy. The most famous Ottoman admiral, Hayrettin Barbarossa, was a pirate chosen by Süleyman to lead the navy.

In the time of Süleyman the Black, Aegean, and Red Seas were under firm Ottoman control, but control of the Eastern Mediterranean, the Gulf, and the Arabian Sea were fiercely contested with Christian powers. The navies of the Habsburgs, Venice, and others fought the Ottomans in the Mediterranean, neither side gaining a real advantage. (See below for Ottoman activities in the southern seas.)

In their best days, the Ottomans were willing to innovate. No less than their government, the Ottoman military system was an amalgam of Turkish and foreign ideas and technology. Recently, historians have begun to classify states such the Ottoman Empire as "gunpowder empires," because they depended on gunpowder weapons to conquer their lands. While such generalities hide many essential differences between states, it is true that the Ottomans relied on new gunpowder weapons. They freely adopted the latest military technology in their great days of conquest.

The Janissaries were probably the first standing army to uniformly adopt gunpowder weapons, armed with early forms of the musket. Murat II, had already organized a cannon corps in his army. The Ottoman forces often won their battles because of superior firepower, not only superior training and dedication. The Ottomans accepted that they were not at the forefront of technology in artillery. They therefore bought artillery from the Christian Europe, often duplicating it

in Ottoman armories. For example, Mehmet II, the conqueror of Constantinople, realized he needed great cannons to breach the city's walls. He bought cannons made by Christian and even imported Christian experts, who were well paid to aid in the conquest of a Christian state.

The Ottoman generals and sultans were practical men. The old traditions of Turkish warfare can be called chivalric — nomadic soldiers led by their chiefs, riding horses into battle, shooting their arrows, and often engaging in single combat. Ottoman foes such as the Safavids retained much of this tradition. Selim I, the conqueror of Eastern Anatolia, Syria, and Egypt, met the traditional methods of the Safavids, and later the Mamluks, with cannon. The Safavids learned their lesson and reformed themselves into another gunpowder empire.

Relying on its military innovations and administrative competence, the Ottoman state became one of three great Muslim empires that ruled from Burma to the Atlantic Ocean, the greatest military powers of the sixteenth century — the Ottoman, Safavid, and Mughal Empires — the Gunpowder Empires. Each used its military might to bring together Islamic lands that had previously been independent. The Mughals and Ottomans expanded their power into regions in India and Southeast Europe that had never been ruled by Muslims. The rule of Islam had never been greater, and was never to be as great again.

> ▷ List 3 to 5 important pieces of evidence about the Ottoman Empire from this reading.
> ▷ Discuss how the Ottoman system helped make the Empire strong.
> ▷ Can we consider the Ottoman Empire a great period in history? Explain your answer with examples.

Mehmet the Conqueror and Süleyman the Magnificent

EACH OF THE FIRST TEN OTTOMAN SULTANS NUMBER AMONG THE GREATEST OF RULERS. THE TWO AMONG THEM WHO ARE OFTEN THOUGHT to have been the greatest are Mehmet II and Süleyman I.

Both Mehmet and Süleyman were fortunate in their fathers. Mehmet's father, Murat II, had insured Ottoman power by defeating the last true threat from Europe, crusades. He defeated Christian crusades at Varna in 1444 and at Kosova in 1448. As important, he left behind a well functioning administrative system and a solvent treasury. Mehmet was left with few overly powerful external or internal enemies, so he could devote himself to conquest. Süleyman's father, Selim I, had defeated a grave threat from the Safavids of Iran and had added Syria and Egypt to the Empire. Selim had left the great wealth from his conquests to be spent by his son.

Mehmet II was able to take advantage of whatever he needed to bring victory. In his intellectual life he was eclectic, willing to learn from friends and enemies alike. He did not hesitate to borrow military technology. He was also willing to borrow intellectually. He read Greek as well as Middle Eastern languages and kept Greek books in his library. Once he had conquered Constantinople he retained the Greek Orthodox Church, but made it into an instrument of his own power. He named an anti-Western scholar, Gennadius, to be patriarch and put the Church firmly in the patriarch's hands. In fact, the Greek bishops exercised more power over their flocks than they had in Byzantine times. With the clergy under his thumb and the people represented by the clergy, Mehmet brought acceptance of Ottoman rule where there might instead have been opposition and civil war.

The rule of Mehmet II was shaped by the sultan's early conquest of Constantinople. The prestige that ac-

> **The rule of Mehmet II was shaped by the sultan's early conquest of Constantinople.**

companied that victory made him virtually invincible within the Empire. Opposing "the Conqueror" the leader who had brought such a great prize under the rule of Islam, was nearly impossible. He was willing to use this power as he saw fit, even violating Muslim Holy Law when he felt it was needed. He always needed money. Wars were expensive. To pay for them and for his rebuilding of Istanbul. he seized properties that had been willed to pious foundations. These had been given by rich Muslims to provide for various good causes, but also to preserve the properties from the tax collector, since taxes could not legally be collected from the foundations. The grantor could also name the administrators of the foundations, insuring jobs for friends and family. The properties were by law inviolate, but Mehmet simply seized them. His power and prestige overrode religious objections. He also seized lands belonging to old Turkish families, often without any cause but his need for money.

Mehmet had a sense of the grandeur that must be a part of a great empire. When he took Constantinople the city was dilapidated, with many neighborhoods in ruins. The shrinkage of the Byzantine Empire and the final battle for the city had left behind a sorry memory of past greatness. Mehmet set about immediately to change this. He built new religious buildings, such as mosques, hospitals, and schools, endowing them with land and markets whose rents would insure their upkeep. Because religion organizations supplied what we would consider today to be public services, these provided an economic and social infrastructure for Mehmet's new city. The sultan made it known that other government officials were expected to follow his lead. Soon grand buildings were under construction all over Istanbul. At its fall, Constantinople was greatly depopulated. Realizing that a large population was needed for a great capitol, Mehmet imported people,

Rumeli Hisarı, the fortification completed in 1452 by Mehmet the Conqueror, is situated on the European side of the Bosphorus, at the narrowest part of the straits. Together with another fortification built across on the Anatolian shore, he gained control of the waterway before taking Constantiple the following year.

especially artisans and craftsmen, from other parts of his empire, whether or not they wished to come. Thousands of others came on their own, because the newly built city created economic opportunity. Constantinople grew and changed. The new buildings and new population changed it into what was to be called Istanbul, an Islamic and Ottoman city.

Mehmet was a practical man, ruthless and intelligent, but always practical. When he ascended to the throne, for example, Janissaries revolted against him. He put down the revolt in a bloody fashion, then increased the pay of loyal Janissaries. All learned he was a fearsome opponent who rewarded loyalty magnanimously.

Mehmet was also a skilled military strategist. One of his most dangerous enemies was Venice, supported by the Papacy. The city-state could make use of its navy to attack various parts of Ottoman Europe in rapid incursions that could not be quickly countered by the slower moving land forces of the Ottomans. The threat was doubled when Venice made a treaty in 1472 with the Ak Koyunlu ("White Sheep") Turks who ruled the land to the east of Ottoman Anatolia. Beset by enemies on two fronts, Mehmet built a fleet to protect the sea approach to Istanbul, then moved his army east. He defeated the Ak Koyunlu, then sent the army to Europe. Venice could defend itself by sea, so Mehmet attacked by land. When the Ottoman raiders reached the outskirts of their city, the Venetian leaders sued for peace. They were forced to cede cities and islands to the Ottomans and pay a large tribute. The sea lanes secure, in 1480 Mehmet sent his forces by sea to Italy to punish the pope. The pope fled from Rome as the Turks advanced, but Mehmet died unexpectedly, at age 49, before Rome could be taken, and the Turkish army returned to follow the wishes of the new sultan. Had Mehmet II lived longer, the Ottoman Empire might have included both the New Rome, Constantinople, and Rome itself.

Mehmet's aim was to advance his Empire, which he did by whatever means were needed. He was a conqueror and a builder. At his death, the Empire was militarily strong and, for the first time, geographically unified.

> The Ottoman imperial system and government are traditionally described as they were under Süleyman, as the template of proper Ottoman rule.

Süleyman was the image of what Kipling called "more than Oriental splendor." European contemporaries called him "The Magnificent," more for the glory of his court than for his power. No European king's palace could approach the grandeur of the sultan's court. Looking at Süleyman's rule, one gains the impression of a man who was more concerned with rule than conquest. He was a conqueror, seizing both Hungary and Iraq, but he also ordered the imperial system. The Ottoman imperial system and government are traditionally described as they were under Süleyman, as the template of proper Ottoman rule. He codified the Ottoman administrative legal system, for which the Turks gave him the title "Süleyman the Law-Giver." Law was more important to the Turks than the magnificence of Süleyman's court. For centuries after his death, Ottoman subjects looked on his rule as the height of proper government. This neglected more than a few failings, but there was much truth in the assessment.

Although the days of a sultan riding at the head of an army of nomad troops were long over, Süleyman was nevertheless a warrior sultan. He was the commander in charge of a vast army of Jannisary and other slave troops, the forces of the Turkish notables, vassal armies, and even the remaining nomads, who now formed feared units of raiders. The army contained quartermaster and cannon corps and other specialized units. All this was needed, because Süleyman faced formidable enemies. In Asia, he faced and defeated the Safavids, who had recovered from the defeat handed them by Selim. In Europe, he faced the armies of the Habsburgs, the most powerful forces in Europe, seizing Hungary and nearly, but not quite, taking Vienna. Süleyman's naval forces fought their enemies to a standstill in the Eastern Mediterranean and the Arabian Sea.

The military task facing Süleyman was immense. The Ottoman Empire had grown so large that its armies took many months to reach their enemies from their headquarters in Istanbul. It was effectively impossible to fight on more than one front in any one year. Throughout his early years of rule, Süleyman and the army were off to battle nearly every year. It was no wonder that he eventually tired of war. The Ottoman Empire had reached its practical limits. Only small territorial gains would be seen in future years. The Ottomans might be stronger and better organized than their enemies, but the enemies fought closer to home. The Ottomans took wearying months to reach the battles.

Like Mehmet II, Süleyman was a builder. His construction in Istanbul was perhaps more notable than that of Mehmet. In particular, Süleyman caused one of history's great architects, Sinan, to construct the vast complex that bears his name, the Süleymaniye. Its centerpiece was a great mosque that this author feels to be the most beautiful in the world. Attached to the mosque was the highest level school in the Empire. The leading jurists and scholars of the Empire were trained in and taught in the Süleymaniye. The complex also contained a hospital, a medical college, schools, a soup kitchen for the poor, and residences for students, religious leaders, and scholars. Lesser but impressive edifices dotted the city and the Empire.

Süleyman was a great sultan because he managed to effectively rule and even expand such a far flung empire. Moreover, his modification and codification of the administrative system allowed the Empire to live on when lesser men became sultans. As a man, Süleyman was complex — an administrator, a warrior, a great patron of the arts, a calligrapher and a poet.

Both Mehmet and Süleyman left behind mixed legacies.

The worst part of Mehmet's legacy was fiscal imprudence and cavalier rule. Mehmet's successor, Bayezit II inherited a much enlarged but nearly bankrupt empire. Bayezit spent his reign replenishing the treasury. He also returned lands taken by Mehmet and soothed the egos of notables wronged by Mehmet. Both the treasury and the notables were to be essential parts of future conquest and rule.

Sultan Ahmet Mosque, Istanbul.

Süleyman began a tradition of sultans who removed themselves from the day-to-day running of the Empire. Wearied by years of war, he spent his final years largely in his harem, coming more and more under the influence of court politicians. One of the most active of the politicians was his much beloved wife, Hürrem (called Roxelana in the West). Süleyman wrote her beautiful love poems, but he also killed his best Grand Vezir and his most able son at her wish, leaving behind Hürrem's less able son, Selim II, to succeed him. While the Empire had the good fortune to have Mehmet succeeded by a sultan who could correct Mehmet's excesses, it was not so lucky when Süleyman died and left behind Hürrem's son to rule. There were still more than 300 years of life left to the Ottoman Empire. Good and bad sultans were to follow. But the age of the greatest sultans had passed.

> ▷ List 3 to 5 important pieces of evidence about the Ottoman Empire from this reading.
> ▷ Discuss how the Ottoman system helped make the Empire strong.
> ▷ Can we consider the Ottoman Empire a great period in history? Explain your answer with examples.

Ottoman Rule of a Great Empire

THE FIRST FACT TO CONSIDER ABOUT OTTOMAN GOVERNMENT WAS THE SIZE OF THE EMPIRE. IT STRETCHED FROM CENTRAL EUROPE TO ERITREA and Southern Arabia, from the borders of Iran to Morocco. The Empire's borders contained most or all of today's Bosnia, Kosovo, Montenegro, Macedonia, Hungary, Moldova, Romania, Bulgaria, Albania, Greece, Turkey, Syria, Lebanon, Israel, Jordan, Iraq, Kuwait, Yemen, Egypt, Libya, Tunisia, Algeria, and in some periods parts of Croatia, Slovakia, Poland, Ukraine, Russia, Georgia, Armenia, Saudi Arabia, and Iran. A government messenger travelling from Istanbul on horseback would take more than 600 hours of constant travel to reach Basra in Southern Iraq, more than 400 hours to go from Istanbul to Jerusalem, and this was time spent on his horse, not counting rests and sleep.

> **A government messenger travelling from Istanbul on horseback would take more than 600 hours of constant travel to reach Basra in Southern Iraq, more than 400 hours to go from Istanbul to Jerusalem**

In an age of poor communications it was not possible for rulers to watch closely such a massive empire. Governors and military leaders were sent from the capitol or chosen from local notables. It was these who ruled the provinces. Because of distance, only the most important decisions could be made in Istanbul. Modern states depend on rapid means of communication and transportation to direct local affairs. The Ottomans did not have modern methods of communication and transportation.

The educational level of the Empire and the difficulty of collecting and compiling information also forced the Empire to be decentralized. A modern system of taxation depends on an educated bureaucracy and the computers used by bureaucrats, but there were no computers in the Ottoman Empire (even paper was very expensive) and few trained in accounting. In fact,

as in the rest of the world until recently, only a small portion of the population was literate. In the sixteenth century the Ottomans were at the forefront of census-taking and the keeping of financial records. This information was necessarily incomplete and took many years to collect, however. It was useful, but always out of date. How could a government collect taxes in such a situation? Taxes could be collected in lands close to Istanbul or easily reached by sea, not so easily collected in remote regions.

The answer was to decentralize. Some government lands were given to administrators and military officers. The administrators used the proceeds from the lands to pay themselves, pay their officials and workers, and provide services. The military leaders would use proceeds from their lands to feed and outfit their soldiers. They provided local security and went to war when the sultan called. Other government lands were auctioned off to "tax farmers." These agreed to pay a set fee to the sultan, then were allowed to collect the taxes from local areas. For example, a rich man in Beirut would pay for the right to collect the surplus crops grown by villagers in some villages in Syria, then send out his representatives to collect the surplus during the harvest. In theory the sultan's government insured that the tax farmer would not collect too much and leave the villagers destitute. This was not always the case, but it is hard to see how else the government could have collected the taxes.

Decentralization created problems. Governors in far provinces were almost rulers, often little affected by the attitudes of the central government in Istanbul. If something went awry in a province, it might take months for the news to reach Istanbul, weeks for a letter demanding an explanation to reach the governor (delivered on horseback), weeks for the governor's response to arrive in Istanbul, then weeks more for an order to stop doing whatever he was doing to reach the governor. By that time, an independent-minded governor could have organized a revolt. It would then be many months before the Ottoman army could reach him.

The Ottomans met the challenge of decentralization with flexibility. To keep local officials from thoughts of disobedience or even independence, they named officials to watch each other. The system changed, but there most often was a governor, a high judge, and a military commander. Each was expected to keep an eye on the other and report back to the central government. When necessary, the central government also tolerated a great degree of autonomy in the provinces. This was a matter of political calculation: a local rebel knew that the Ottoman army could defeat him, if it was sent. The government, however, would rather use the army to defend the borders or attacks its foreign enemies. Both sides came to an accommodation. The rebel was named governor, with the understanding that he would rule in the name of the sultan and send enough tax money to Istanbul. If they thought it would work, the central government might support the new governor's enemies, attempting to ensure that his time in office was short.

The system of rule in the far-flung Empire was flexible and indefinite — a political art, not a political science — but it worked. Despite periods of autonomy in many provinces, no major province ever permanently broke away from the Ottoman Empire on its own. Those that became independent did so because foreign armies took the province or forced the Ottomans to abandon it.

▷ List 3 to 5 important pieces of evidence about the Ottoman Empire from this reading.
▷ Discuss how the Ottoman system helped make the Empire strong.
▷ Can we consider the Ottoman Empire a great period in history? Explain your answer with examples.

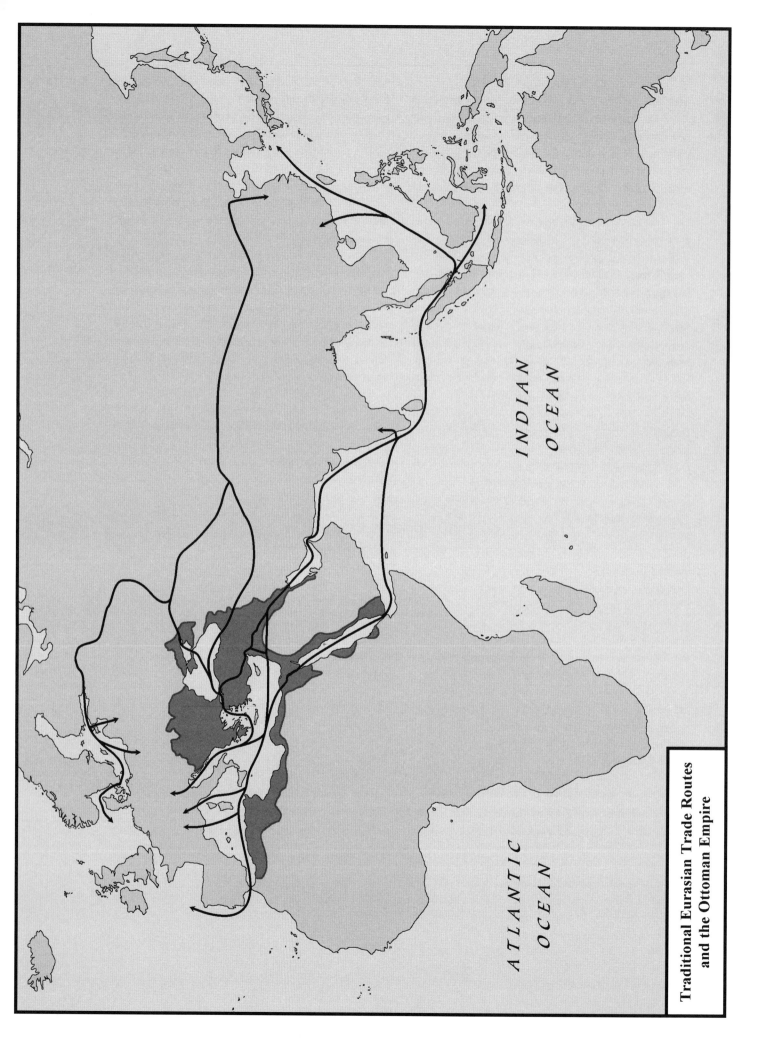

Traditional Eurasian Trade Routes and the Ottoman Empire

ATLANTIC OCEAN

INDIAN OCEAN

The Ottomans and International Trade

THE OTTOMAN GOVERNMENT UNDERSTOOD THE VALUE OF TRADE. IT WAS THE BASIS OF WEALTH FOR SUBJECTS AND GOVERNMENT ALIKE. Fortunately for the Ottomans, their Empire lay astride the main world trade routes of the time – the routes between Europe and the Orient. Unfortunately for them, technology was soon to displace the importance of the traditional routes.

Merchants had brought the goods of the East westward since antiquity, both by sea and by the Silk Road. In 1500 the long distance trade routes were roughly what they had always been: The main land route went from China, across Central Asia, to Western Iran and on to the Ottoman Empire. Some merchant caravans traveled across Anatolia to Istanbul, some went north to the Black Sea and on to Istanbul by boat, and others traveled west to Aleppo. Another land route went north of the Caspian Sea, eventually reaching Istanbul. By Sea, the goods of China, Indochina, and the Indian sub-continent were transported to Iraq or Egypt, then taken by caravan to Istanbul or to the Mediterranean coast. Goods passed to Europe from the Mediterranean ports or Istanbul by sea, usually on Italian boats. The primary goods were silk and spices, lightweight, easily transportable merchandise with a high profit margin.

Selim I's conquest of Syria in 1516 and Egypt in 1517 gave the Ottomans control of the international trade routes, all of which now passed through Ottoman territory. Once Süleyman had conquered Iraq (1533), all the main ports for goods from the East were also Ottoman. Ottoman subjects transshipped the goods for Europe, and the Ottoman tax man took a sizeable cut of the profits. The taxes on silk alone might provide 1 to 2 per cent of Ottoman state income.

> ## Not since the height of the Abbasid Empire had one government so controlled the trade routes.

Not since the height of the Abbasid Empire had one government so controlled the trade routes. The sultans intended to insure that success. They provided military guards for caravans, bought off Bedouin nomads who might attack merchants while they crossed the desert, made sure that accommodations, warehouses, and the like were available for caravans and merchants. The government supported guilds of merchants and craftsmen and sent its inspectors to insure that weights and measures were honest.

None of this solicitousness could protect the Ottomans from the results of the European Age of Discovery.

In a voyage in 1487-88, the Portuguese explorer Bartolomeu Dias rounded the Cape of Good Hope. Vasco da Gama first traveled around Africa in 1497, journeying all the way to the Indian coast. He returned in 1501 with 20 armed ships, intent on shutting down Muslim trade in the Indian Ocean in favor of the Portuguese. Successive Portuguese governors and admirals continued to attacked Muslim traders and open bases on the sea lines.

The Portuguese never succeeded in stopping the trade of Muslim merchants. There were too many hard-to-catch small boats carrying goods, but they did limit Muslim trade and kept Muslim rulers from stopping Portuguese boats. Security of transport and lack of significant rivals allowed the economies of sea transport to emerge. It was simply much cheaper to move goods to Western Europe entirely by sea. The alternative, older route, had meant loading goods in the East, unloading them in the Middle East, travelling by caravan across deserts, reloading the goods at Mediterranean ports, then unloading them once again in Europe. At each step new groups of merchants and new sets of tax collectors took their percentage of the profits. Desert raiders or bandits might seize the goods. The all-sea route was cheaper and much safer.

The Ottoman government was not oblivious to what was happening in the southern waters. Süleyman appointed the great sailor Piri Reis as Grand Admiral of an Indian Ocean Fleet. Piri Reis fought the Portuguese to a stalemate, but his successors were less successful. The Portuguese, with bases at Muskat and Hormuz, managed effectively to close the Gulf to Muslim shipping. The Indian Ocean was simply too far away from the center of the Empire for the Ottomans to project power there. Their navy was occupied fighting battles with the Venetian and Habsburg fleets closer to home, in the Mediterranean. What resources were available were needed for the Mediterranean naval wars, which were more essential to the survival of the Empire. Nevertheless, the Middle Eastern trade with the East did not disappear. The trade that went through the Red Sea to Egypt remained fairly strong.

It was not until new and stronger foes appeared that the Middle Eastern transit trade virtually disappeared. The fleets of England and the Netherlands replaced those of Portugal in the seventeenth century. The European boats were in effect large floating gun platforms that could not be opposed by Muslim navies. They were matched by the commercial might of Western Europe which, again, the Muslims could not match. The Middle Eastern merchant economy that depended on international trade then virtually disappeared, never to return.

▷   List 3 to 5 important pieces of evidence about the Ottoman Empire from this reading.

▷   Discuss how the Ottoman system helped make the Empire strong.

▷   Can we consider the Ottoman Empire a great period in history? Explain your answer with examples.

To What Extent Did the Turks Create a Tolerant Community?

The Turks take great pride in the tolerance that was evident throughout their community and their empire. Many different ethnic and religious groups lived under the Turkish flag but all were allowed rights and privileges even if they were not among the ruling majority.

Performance Objectives

1. Students will define the many diverse religions, sects and groups who lived in the Ottoman Empire.
2. Students will discuss the rights and privileges accorded each group under the millet system.
3. Students will analyze the extent to which the Turks created a tolerant community, provided stability and protection for all groups and benefited the empire as a whole..

Springboard

All students receive the background essay, *Turkish Toleration,* for **Homework** reading. Teacher will debrief the students on this reading. The teacher will place the following question on the chalkboard: According to the essay that you read for homework last night, "the tradition of Turkish tolerance came from both religious belief and practicality." Explain.

Procedure

▷ Today, we are first going to examine some of the strategies used by the Ottomans to ensure religious tolerance. Distribute **Worksheet 1**: *The Non-Muslims of the Empire.* Students will read the selection and answer the following questions:

- Why are Jews and Christians called the People of the Book?
- Why was toleration of other religions necessary to the Ottomans?
- How did the Ottomans attempt to solve this problem?
- Define the millet system.

▷ Teacher will divide students into cooperative reading groups of three: Distribute worksheet. Each group will complete the same reading and will work together to develop answers to the questions on the worksheets. Teacher will create the following organizer on the chalkboard.

GREEK ORTHODOX	ARMENIANS	JEWS

- From your reading and the class discussion, do you think that the millet system was beneficial to the people who lived under Ottoman rule?
- Although religious tolerance under the Ottoman rule was noteworthy, it was not perfect. Refer back to the introductory background essay and find

evidence to support the statement: "Ottoman tolerance was not Ottoman equality."

- ◆ Ottoman tolerance can best be appreciated when compared to tolerance in other countries of the time. How did Ottoman toleration of non-Muslims compare to European toleration of non-Christians?

- ▷ Distribute **Worksheet 2**: *How Lucky*. Teacher will read story aloud. Discuss the following questions:
  - ◆ In what three ways can you explain why Aziz feels lucky?
  - ◆ Why did Aziz start having doubts about his good fortune?
  - ◆ Have other children felt the same way about their religion and people as Aziz felt about his? Is it human nature to feel this way?

Application/ Homework: America has frequently been described as a land of immigrants. For homework, write a brief essay explaining how newly arrived immigrants are treated in your school or neighborhood or city or state. Do you think they would be better off living under the Ottoman system? Explain.

Turkish Toleration

ONE OF THE MOST NOTEWORTHY ATTRIBUTES OF Ottoman Turkish rule was Ottoman toleration of different religious beliefs. The Turks of the Ottoman Empire were Muslims, but they did not force their religions on others. Christians and Jews in the Empire prayed in their own churches or synagogues, taught their religion in their own schools and seminaries, and went about their business, sometimes amassing great fortunes. At that time, Ottoman toleration was unique.

The tradition of Turkish tolerance arose from both religious belief and practicality.

Turks were Muslims and were tolerant of other religions because of that. From its beginnings Islam had accepted the existence of other monotheistic religions. Jews and Christians had lived in lands ruled by Islam since the time of the prophet Muhammad. Certain rules had evolved to order the relations between Muslim and non-Muslim: Islam was to be dominant; rulers were to be Muslim. Muslims were not allowed to convert to other religions, nor could non-Muslims attempt to convert Muslims. Non-Muslims were to wear distinctive clothing. In various places at various times non-Muslims were also restricted in certain ways. Perhaps the most important of the special regulations was the demand that Christians and Jews pay a special tax, the jizya, that was not paid by Muslims. This tax was paid by adult Christians and Jews who lived in Islamic states. By common belief, it was based on an agreement forged between Christians and Muslims in the first days of Muslim conquest. In return for tolerance of religious practice and the protection of the Islamic state, the non-Muslims agreed to pay the tax and to accept the restrictions on their clothing, etc.

For those Christians who believed, as did the Muslims, that their own religious group should always be in control, the pact of toleration between Muslims and Christians was a disaster. However, for many Christians and for the Jews, the acceptance of Muslim rule was a real benefit. The Byzantine leaders who had ruled much of the Middle East before the Arab conquest often persecuted those Christians they considered not to be Orthodox in belief. To the Muslims, all the sects were simply Christians, all bound by the same laws, and none subject to persecution. Jewish life was to flourish in many Ottoman lands.

In practical terms, the extra tax paid by non-Muslims can be viewed as a military exemption tax. Non-Muslim males did pay an extra tax, but they also remained on their farms or at businesses when the Muslims went off to war. For many, this would not have been a disadvantage.

As Muslims, the Ottoman sultans and Turkish generals kept to the laws of Islam regarding non-Muslims.[1] When the Ottoman Empire was founded in the early fourteenth century Islamic tolerance had already lived for six hundred years. The Ottomans continued and built upon that tradition.

Ottoman tolerance was based on cleverness as well as on good will. It was in the interest of the Turkish Muslims to be tolerant of other religions. The Ottoman conquerors came upon a vast area where the population was primarily Christian, especially in the Balkans. To these people, religion was the most important element of personal identification. Kings and emperors came and went, borders changed, but Christianity remained. The government was the property of rulers, often leaders who taxed the villagers into poverty and whom the people did not particularly like. But religion was the property of the people and of God. By allowing Christians and Jews to practice their religions, the Ottoman Turks defended against the most likely cause of revolt. Farmers were unlikely to revolt in favor of a foreign king they did not care about, but they would readily revolt in defense of their religion. On the other hand, the Ottomans rightly assumed, if religion were

---

[1] The one major exception was the taking of Christian youth to serve in Ottoman Janissary Corps. These young men were converted to Islam whether they wanted to be or not.

secure and taxes were not too high, people would be satisfied with their situations.

For the Ottomans, religious tolerance became a sound basis for government. In almost all Christian states until modern times only one form of religion was accepted. This was obviously not true in the Ottoman domains. There are many forms of Christianity that flourished. By the nineteenth century, when Christian sects had proliferated, Istanbul held churches for Bulgarian Orthodox, Greek Orthodox, Greek Catholic, Armenian Apostolic, Armenian Catholic, Roman Catholic, Assyrian Chaldean, Anglican, Congregational, and other Christians, as well as synagogues for both Sephardic and Ashkenazi Jews. In earlier times there were three dominant non-Muslim religious groups — Greek Orthodox, Armenian Apostolic, and Sephardic Jews. The members of each of the religions preferred to associate with members of their own group. The Ottomans organized governmental life around divisions. Each religious community (**millet**) kept its own courts, schools, and welfare system. Members of the millet even built roads, water fountains, and communal buildings for their own neighborhoods. The members of millets were pleased to have these functions in their own hands and the Ottoman government was relieved of the necessity of providing them itself. Had the central government provided for these schools, welfare establishments, courts, etc. of the millets, taxes would have had to be raised and the members of the millets would have been restive at the costs and at the loss of communal control over their own lives. It was a good system for all.

Ottoman religious toleration was not perfect. The Ottoman Empire was definitely a Muslim state and gave preference to Muslims in many parts of government. Only in the last decades of the Empire were non-Muslims allowed to gain high office.[2] Muslims undoubtedly felt more a part of the state than did Christians. Just as the king of England had to be an Anglican Christian or the king of Germany a Lutheran Christian, the sultan

> **Each religious community (millet) kept its own courts, schools, and welfare system. Members of the millet even built roads, water fountains, and communal buildings for their own neighborhoods.**

of the Ottoman Empire had to be a Sunni Muslim. Official toleration did not mean that prejudices disappeared among Ottoman Muslims, Jews, or Christians. Muslims were undoubtedly the first subjects in the Empire, with greater rights and responsibilities than non-Muslims. Ottoman toleration was not Ottoman equality.

Why, if it was imperfect, was Ottoman religious toleration so noteworthy? Historical comparisons can be made to ideals. Compared to an ideal of a democratic government of complete equality for all citizens, the Ottoman Empire was deficient. Comparisons can also be made to modern times. Compared to today's governments in Western Europe or North America, religious toleration in the Ottoman Empire was also deficient. Such comparisons help us evaluate history, but they are surely not fair criteria to use to praise or damn peoples of other times. To truly evaluate the Ottomans they must be compared to others who lived in their own time. It is in that comparison that Ottoman toleration is shown to be exceptional and laudable as it was. Ottoman toleration was not so notable because it was perfect. It was notable because it was so much better than what existed elsewhere. The benefits of Ottoman rule are seen when one compares Ottoman practice with what was occurring in Europe at the time. In Europe only one religion was tolerated and conversion, exile or death was the rule for those who dissented. An example was Spain which, when conquered by Christian rulers, expelled the Muslims and Jews who had lived there for centuries. The Ottomans took them in. While Jews lived through ages of pogroms in Europe they lived in peace among the Turkish Muslims. In their time, the tolerance of the Ottomans was remarkable.

The practicality of Ottoman toleration was also remarkable. The system of the millets was pragmatic and useful, as well as moral. Yet it was exceptional that any government of the time would so set aside its prejudices to benefit the country. No Western government would have accepted the millet system and left

---

[2]Although even then, it should be noted, the Ottomans were relatively unique. An Ottoman Greek Christian, for example was foreign minister of the Empire. Would Britain, France, or Germany have named a Muslim or a Jew to be foreign minister?

so many ordinary functions of government out of its own control. Imagine a Western government in, for example, the fifteenth century that allowed non-Christians to run their own schools, to leave money to their children according to their own laws (not those of the state), to collect taxes to support welfare for its own group, to organize and police its own neighborhoods, to punish transgressors according to its own laws in its own courts. In fact, imagine a European government that allowed non-Christians to live in peace at all. The reality is reflected in the well known fate of the Jews in Europe. One cannot speak of the status of Muslims in much of Europe, because they were expelled when Christians took power. The ultimate intolerance for Muslims of Sicily, Spain or Portugal was exile from their homes and confiscation of their lands. The Otto-mans were exceptional in realizing that a diverse group of peoples could actually assist their Empire. Upon hearing that the Spanish king was forcing out Jews, Sultan Bayezit II, who welcomed the Jews to the Ottoman Empire, is reported to have said that if the Spanish king was mad enough to exile the most industrious of his subjects, the Ottomans would be glad to take advantage of his madness.

The success of Ottoman tolerance can most easily be seen in the fact that large Christian and Jewish communities existed in the Ottoman lands until the end of the Empire. Then it was European intervention and European-style nationalism, not internal failure of the system, that destroyed the centuries-long peace between religions that had characterized the Ottoman system.

Please complete the chart below and bring to class for discussion.

TURKISH TOLERATION
Three Examples of Tolerance in Islam
1.   2.   3.
Three Practical Benefits of Toleration
1.   2.   3.

The Non-Muslims of the Empire

To the Ottomans, religious tolerance was both a practical and a legal necessity. Islamic law absolutely mandated that Christians and Jews (called **dhimmis** or "**People of the Book**," the book being the Bible) be allowed to practice their religions. The non-Muslims were legally bound to pay a special tax in lieu of military service, but could worship in their churches and keep schools, religious organizations and other elements of their religions. As an Islamic Empire, the Ottoman Empire necessarily conformed to this Islamic law. There also was a practical basis for tolerance. The Ottomans ruled over a vast territory populated by members of different Christian sects. Even if they had wished to do so, forced conversion might have been beyond possibility. It surely would have caused revolt. As long as his subjects accepted his rule, it was in the interest of the sultan to leave them in peace.

Throughout Middle Eastern history, religious institutions had provided many of the public services that modern citizens expect of the State. Religion was considered to be the most important thing in life, so schools naturally were religious schools, teaching that which was important. No matter their religion, all agreed that relations between people should be governed by God's wishes (though that differed by which religion interpreted God's plan). Therefore, how one treated his or her family, business associates, and neighbors should conform to religious ethics, and was often decided by religious courts. God had commanded that people love and help one another, so charity was a thing of religion as well, organized into welfare systems operated by the Church. In short, religion was the essential factor in the actions that were most important to humans, so religions were integral to public welfare. Thus many functions of government were carried out by religion.

The Ottoman Empire took the religious traditions of the Middle East and Balkans and codified them into law. Each religious group was named as a **millet** (literally "nation"). The millets were in charge of the education, welfare and personal law of their members. Their leaders represented the needs of their people to the sultan's government. Sometimes as was the case with the Greek Orthodox, the place of the millet was specifically recognized by law. Other millets, such as the Jews, simply were recognized by tradition. As the centuries passed, more sects were officially recognized (such as the Greek Catholics or the Bulgarian Orthodox, who were recognized late in the Empire's history), but the millet system was an essential element of Ottoman government from an early date. Even before individual millets were officially recognized, they had a de facto separate existence.

Because Islam was the official religion of the Empire one cannot really speak of a Muslim millet. Nevertheless, the Muslim community functioned in much the same way as the Christian communities, providing welfare, schools, places of worship, and the other functions provided by the Christian and Jewish millets for their own people. The Muslim organization undoubtedly had advantages. It drew a certain power from the fact that the leading members of government, including the sultan, were among its members. The state was committed to the benefit of Islam. Thus in disputes between Muslims and members of other religions Muslim law took precedence, although the Muslim by no means always won the case.

Greek Orthodox

When the Byzantine Empire fell in 1453 the center of the Greek Orthodox Church was shaken. The Church had been closely entwined with the Empire, each supporting the other and each a symbol of Greek identity. The state was now lost, but Mehmet the Conqueror had no wish to lose the centralized church. Immediately upon his conquest of Constantinople he named a new Patriarch, Gennadius.

Gennadius was actually given more authority than previous patriarchs had held. Many of the powers given to the new Greek Millet had previously been held by the Byzantine State or shared between Church and State. In the Greek tradition, which was very different from Roman Catholicism, the authority of each bishop was great; the patriarch had little juridical control over local bishops. This had been especially true since the Turkish invasion had begun, because local Greek Christian communities had been cut off from central Byzantine authority. Now the power of the Ottoman State stood behind the patriarch as he administered the Greek Christian millet.

Mehmet may originally have seen the Greek millet system as a way to systematize the administration of all the non-Muslims in the Ottoman Empire, but jealousies between the various Christian and Jewish groups would have made this impossible. Other groups soon had their own millets. The Greek millet included the Orthodox populations of the Ottoman Empire. Although called "Greek," many of its members were Slavs and Romanians. They were called "Greek" only because they were in the Greek Church. When the Arab Provinces were conquered by the Ottomans, Arab Orthodox Christians became members of the Greek millet, listed in later censuses as Greeks. To the Christians, Muslims, and Jews of the Middle East and Balkans, religion, not language, was the source of identity.

Armenian Gregorians

The Armenian Gregorian Church differed from the Greek Orthodox in that its members were all from one ethnic group, the Armenians. The original home of the Armenians was in Eastern Anatolia and the southern Caucasus, but they had been migrating to other parts of the Middle East and elsewhere for centuries, and a small Armenian kingdom existed in Cilicia. To the Armenians, their Church was a point of identification that kept them together through rule by various larger and stronger neighbors. The Armenian Church was considered to be heretical by both the Greek Orthodox and the Roman Catholics. It was, therefore, persecuted under the Byzantines, always surviving, partly because of the remoteness of the Armenian mountains. Persecution by other Christians surely helped cement Armenian separation.

In the formative years of the Ottoman Empire the bulk of the Armenian population lay in areas under the rule of others. (In the Ottoman centuries, Echmiadzin, the main center of the Gregorian Church and seat of the chief Patriarch, the Catholicos, was never under Ottoman control, except for very few brief periods.) Mehmet II organized the Armenian Community by setting up an Armenian Patriarch in Istanbul, to whom he

> **Throughout Middle Eastern history, religious institutions had provided many of the public services that modern citizens expect of the State.**

gave authority over the Armenian Church within the Empire. However, much of the Armenian Community lived far from the center of the Empire. Armenian regions and villages were often virtually independent in their mountains. They ran their own affairs naturally, whether or not the millet system was in place.

Jews

With the exception of Iran, the centers of Jewish life in the Middle East, such as Iraq, Palestine, Yemen, and Egypt, all eventually came under Ottoman rule. Even in the time of Mehmet the Conqueror a significant community of Jews were Ottoman, remnants of the Jewish Diaspora that had spread across the Mediterranean in Roman times. More than any other community, the Jews of the Mediterranean Region had traditionally governed their own affairs. When Christian governments gave them orders it was usually to the Jews' detriment. In Islamic areas, the separation of Jews, Christians, and Muslims was ordained by the laws governing their status as protected "People of the Book." Therefore, in all the areas eventually ruled by the Ottomans the Jews were already a separate community. The Ottomans did little to affect Jewish status, other than to offer them a tolerance they had not known under Christian rulers. There was no perceived need to systematize the millet rules for Jews and, indeed, no formal charter for a Jewish millet was drawn until the nineteenth century. However, the Ottomans treated the Jews legally much as they did other millets.

Under Muslim rulers, Medieval Spain had contained Muslim, Jewish, and Christian communities. Christian rulers had gradually conquered the Muslims until in 1492 the last Muslim stronghold, Grenada, fell. The Spanish then proceeded to create a country with one religion. Muslims and Jews were forced into exile or conversion. Those who were baptized but attempted to keep their own religious practices and beliefs in secret were persecuted by the infamous Spanish Inquisition. The expulsion of Jews came at the height of Ottoman power. If they wished to religiously unify their empire, the Ottomans had their best chance then. Instead, they welcomed into their Empire the Jews who had been expelled from Spain. From that day until this, the Jewish Community of Spain survived in Istanbul and elsewhere in the Ottoman Empire, speaking their own Judeo-Espanol language and keeping their religion.

Ottoman toleration drew Jews to the Empire from Eastern Europe and Spain and Portugal. The latter came in a great wave of forced migration when Ferdinand and Isabella of Spain and their successors forced conversion or exile on the non-Christians of Spain. Along with some Jews already in the Empire they formed the Sephardic Community. Ashkenazi (or European) Jews formed the other part of the Jewish Community.

"How Lucky" Aziz Nesin

This excerpt was written by Aziz Nesin, one of Turkey's most beloved writers. The following selection is an excerpt which deals with the problem of national pride and tolerance.

Mustafa Kemal[3] had not yet made the statement, "How fortunate is he who can say `I am a Turk!'" In those difficult, distressing days of my childhood, I felt quite pleased with myself. Every time I was all by myself, I would think:, "Its good that I was born of Moslem parents; its good that I'm a Moslem...Many thanks, Allah, for creating me a Moslem boy from Moslem parents. What if he had created me a Christian — then when I died, I wouldn't be able to go to Heaven; I would crackle and burn in Hell. How lucky that I am a Moslem!"

My feeling of good fortune didn't stop at this point. I thought too, "It was good that I was born a Turk. I could have been a Moslem born in another country. The Turks are a great nation, very old, very big...How beloved a servant of Allah that He created me both a Moslem and a Turk. How lucky for me I'm a Turk!"

There seemed no end to my happiness and good fortune! I continued thinking along the same vein, I could have been a Moslem Turk, but born in a village in Anatolia. However, I was born in Istanbul, the paradise of the whole world. What marvelous fortune to be born a Moslem, be a Turk and also be Istanbullu.[4]

I further thought: "Would I change my father and my mother? Would I like to be the child of another father and mother? Not for the world!"

> **"I was born in this world paradise, Istanbul... These doubts have, from my early years on, become an irritant to my mind and disturbed me."**

I considered other fathers and mothers none were as good parents as mine. Father wasn't rich, it didn't matter whether he was or not...He was good-hearted and I loved him very much; he was my father, he was the best father. My mother, especially my mother was the best of all mothers...

"How lucky for me! First, Allah created me a Moslem. Then I was born a Turk. In addition, I was Istanbullu. Then I was the child of such rare parents. I am Allah's most beloved servant. How lucky, how lucky for me!"

It was thus I well understood and adopted Mustafa Kemal's phrase, "Say, what a fortunate Turk I am!"

But later, afterwards? The doubts began. I was born a Moslem. Why? If being a Moslem is superiority, why was another boy born a Christian while I was born was a Moslem? What was that boy's offense? What is my superiority? Why should a Christian child, after death, burn in Hell, because he wasn't the child of Moslem parents?

Istanbul is a city with beautiful, big schools and hospitals. How about the boy born in a distant village? What's his fault? What is my superiority?

These doubts have, from my early years on, become an irritant to my mind and disturbed me.

FROM: *Yol (The Path) Istanbul Boy, The Autobiography of Aziz Nesin, Part II*, by Aziz Nesin, 1979)

---

[3]Later named Atatürk, the hero of the Turkish War of Independence and founder of the Turkish Republic.
[4]"Istanbullu" means someone who comes from Istanbul.

How did modern Turkey accept the Challenge of Modernization and Europe?

Performance Objectives

Students will be able to:
1. Create a hypothesis as to why the Europeans were able to dominate much of the Ottoman Empire.
2. Explain how the differences in the development of Europe and the Ottoman Empire led to its collapse.
3. Understand how nationalism among different subject groups within the Ottoman Empire led to instability.

Procedures/ Development

Part I.

▷ Students will be given three maps:
 ♦ Ottoman Losses
 ♦ The Ottoman Empire in 1789
 ♦ The Ottoman Empire in 1914

Based on these maps, what conclusions can we draw about the Ottoman Empire from 1700 to 1914?

▷ Distribute **Worksheet 1:** *Modernization and the Challenge of Europe*
 ♦ In groups, students will read the worksheet, and answer the questions at the conclusion of the reading.
 ♦ Using the chart below, teacher will debrief the class.

| OTTOMAN EMPIRE ||
Time Frame	Reason for territorial losses in the Ottoman Empire
1699-1778	
1779-1839	
1858-1899	
1912-1918	

▷ There are several statements in the reading. Select one of the topics below and turn to a neighbor to discuss the truth or falsity of this statement. Be prepared to discuss this with your classmates. Cite evidence to prove your position.

- ◆ The Ottomans were known as the "Sick Man of Europe" and this accurately described their position.
- ◆ The Ottomans had not shared in the scientific and cultural advances of Europe.
- ◆ The Ottomans were too overconfident.
- ◆ Change was difficult for the Ottomans.

Teacher will ask the students to report on their conversations.

▷ What explanation can you give for the difference in the rate of development in Turkey as compared with Europe or America?

▷ If you had a role of authority in Ottoman Turkey, what ideas would you have suggested to the leaders?

Part II.

▷ In addition to having major issues dealing with imperialism, the forces of nationalism were rising around the world.

Distribute **Worksheet 2:** *The Cataclysm*

This reading deals with the expulsion of Muslims in lands where they had lived under the Ottomans. Teacher will examine the reading with the class as a whole, specifically examining Muslim loss and expulsion, using maps, to show students how the Ottoman Empire was disassembled by Christian Europe.

- ◆ To what degree did the treatment of the Muslims in former Ottoman territory indicate serious religious conflict?
- ◆ In your opinion, why were the Muslims expelled?
- ◆ Many people believe the Ottomans were responsible for gross atrocities during this period. What is the position of this reading? How would you get another point of view?
- ◆ Can we say that the seeds to today's issues in the Balkans were planted at this time in history? Explain your answer.

Summary Pretend you were born in Istanbul in the year 1890. You are writing a letter to your grandchild trying to describe the changes you have seen in your lifetime. Using the materials in this lesson, describe to the child the changes you have witnessed.

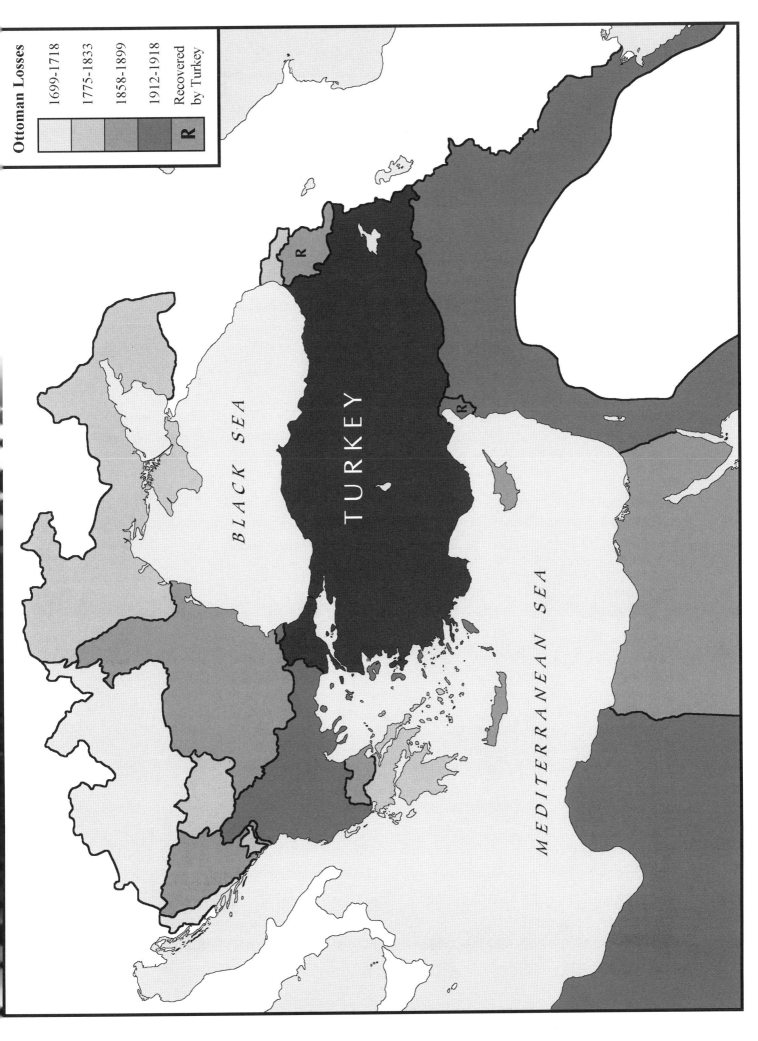

Ottoman Losses

	1699-1718
	1775-1833
	1858-1899
	1912-1918
R	Recovered by Turkey

BLACK SEA

TURKEY

MEDITERRANEAN SEA

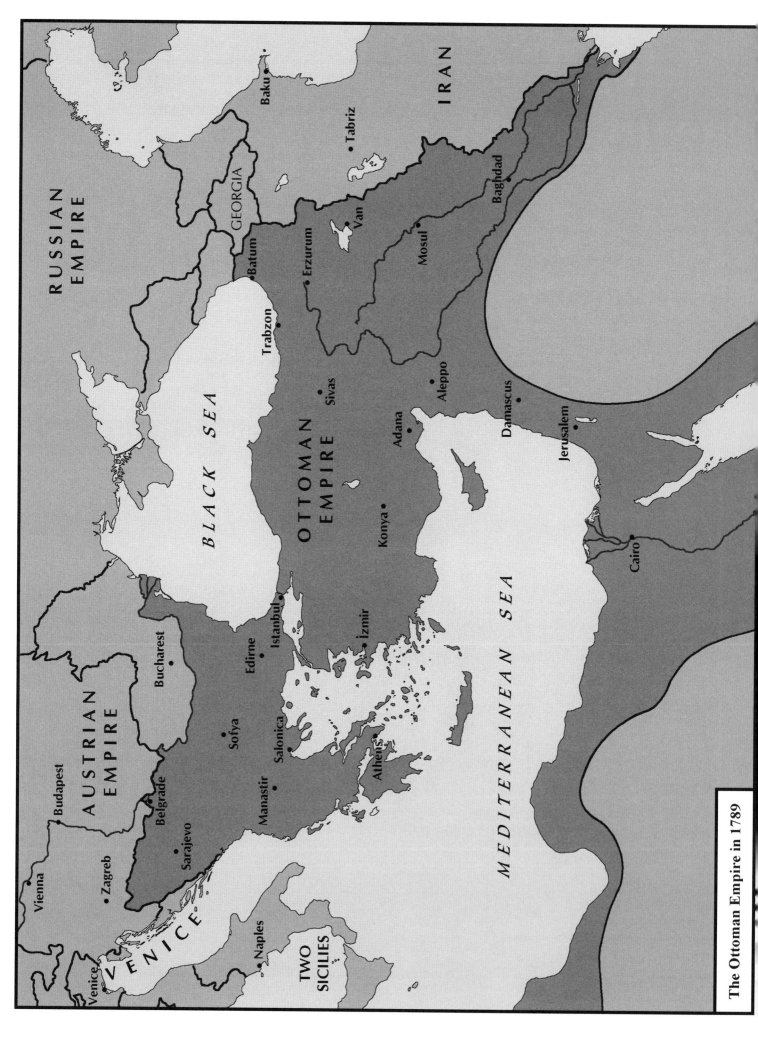

The Ottoman Empire in 1789

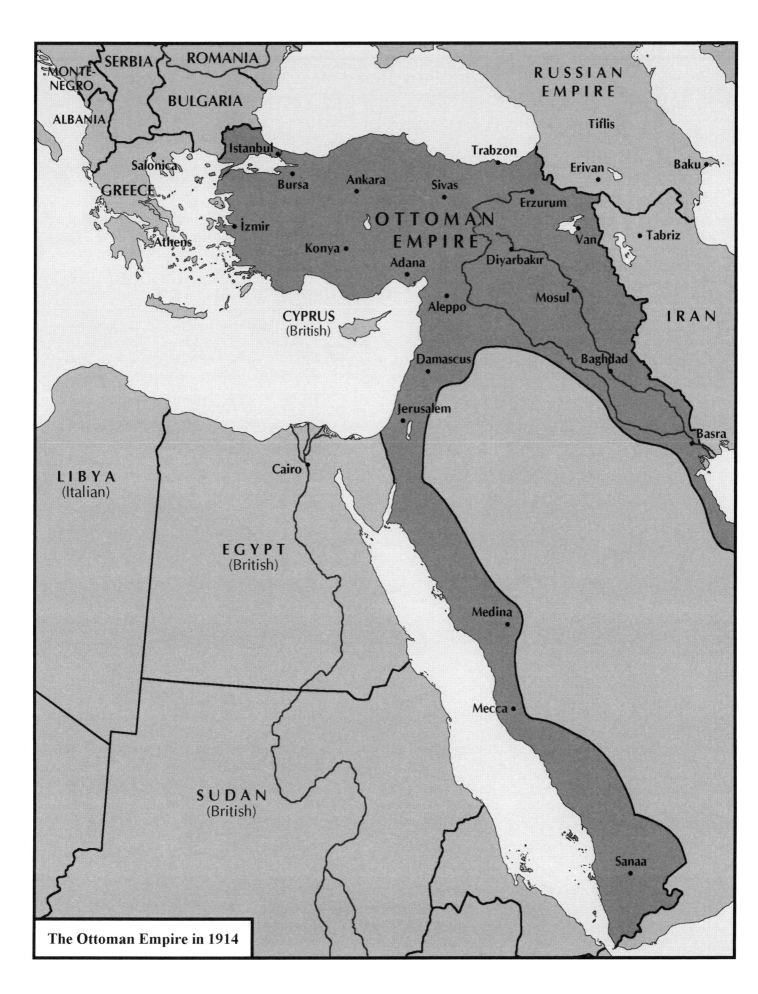

The Ottoman Empire in 1914

Modernization and the Challenge of Europe

The Ottoman Empire and Modern Turkey had the bad luck to begin modernization in the worst days of European Imperialism. In the nineteenth and twentieth centuries, all over the world Europeans were taking the lands of others. Modern techniques of warfare allowed the British, French, Germans, Austrians and Russians to create great empires. Few lands in Asia or Africa remained independent — Japan, Liberia, Thailand, Turkey and a few regions too remote for European power to reach. The success of Turkey in remaining its own master is not often appreciated. Nevertheless, Turkey was a success, because it survived.

Because it slowly lost the majority of its territory, the Ottoman Empire was known as the "Sick Man of Europe." The image was sadly accurate. Compared to Britain, France or Russia, the Ottomans were militarily weak. Without European education, European industry, or powerful European armies, the Ottomans were at a great disadvantage. They were forced to fight losing wars in defense of their empire. While they tried to copy Europe and reform their system, the Ottomans were buffeted by attacks from powerful neighbors, especially Russia. As they tried to reform, the revenues they needed to pay for modernizing were committed instead to hopeless defense. Russian armies detached Rumania and Bulgaria from the Empire. Britain took Cyprus and Egypt, Austria took Bosnia. Eventually Britain and France divided the Ottoman Arab lands between them. The worst calamity was the exodus of millions of Turks and other Muslims from the conquered lands into what remained the Ottoman Empire.

The Galata Bridge across the Golden Horn. Photo from the Library of Congress.

The Ottoman losses demanded enormous expenditures. Just as the Ottoman reform had begun to revivify their lands in Europe those lands were seized by others. Great sums were spent in modernizing regions, then more spent to defend them — all lost. The millions of refugees had to be housed, and they became a disruptive element when Ottoman poverty meant that the refugees could not be settled quickly. The Ottomans were forced to borrow at ruinous rates both to modernize and to defend themselves, until even the interest could not be paid.

How did this happen?

▷ **Europe had improved** economically and militarily. The Renaissance, the Scientific Revolution, the discovery of the Americas, and the development of commerce had made Europeans richer and more powerful. The Ottomans had not shared in these benefits. European development, whether it was caused by luck or good sense, was unique. No non-Europeans had taken part in the European changes. The industrial revolution was soon to make the gap between the West and the rest of the world even wider. The changes in Europe had made it possible for the Europeans to build better cannon and boats, pay for more soldiers and supplies, and organize their armies and navies better. Because they had neither the new ideas nor the money, the Ottomans could not compete

▷ **After centuries of power** the Ottomans had become overconfident. They did not feel threatened and so did not unite. Provincial governors had become almost independent. Political forces in the central administration fought for power among themselves. Sultans were not as well-trained as they had been and thus were worse rulers.

▷ **In the days before railroads or telegraphs** a great empire was inherently hard to rule and defend. Armies could not be on all threatened borders at once and they would have been forced to march hundreds of miles from one threat to another. This was not a great problem until strong enemies appeared in various regions — then defense became more than difficult.

▷ **In the early days of the empire**, the Ottomans had been eclectic, that is, they had borrowed ideas from Europe, Africa, or Asia, whatever would benefit them. Centuries of superiority had changed that. The Ottomans became unable to consider that their old enemies, weaker than them for centuries, could have something worth borrowing. This made it difficult for them to accept the new ideas coming from Europe. Moreover, the Ottomans did not have the European-type system of education and scientific investigation that was essential to running the new European system. By no means was there no borrowing. The Ottomans borrowed European weapons designs and made their own weapons on the models, but this became impossible when a sophisticated industrial establishment was needed to produce military hardware. Then the Ottomans were forced to buy their weapons. They had little money to do so, because they did not have a European-style economy.

For the Ottomans change was necessary, but it was difficult. Few people in the Ottoman Empire had enough knowledge of Europe to realize why the Ottomans were falling behind. For some time it was believed that the only real problem was that the Ottomans had fallen away from their own ideals. Reformers believed that if only the empire returned to the way it had been under Süleyman the Magnificent all would be well. At different times reforming sultans and grand viziers (prime ministers) stamped out corruption and brought government efficiency back to its old standard. It was never enough, because the Ottomans really needed to become more like Europe, not only go back to being better Ottomans.

Not until the nineteenth century did Ottoman leaders really understand that radical change was needed. Sultan Selim III (1789-1807) tried to reform the army and the administration, but he failed. Sultan Mahmud II (1808-1839) was more successful, organizing a European-style army and beginning to change the government. Mahmud realized that only the central government could lead and force through changes, because so few of the people understood what needed to be done.

One of the basic problems of the Ottomans was their isolation. Very few people in the empire understood European languages and few had been to Europe. Education was the only way to conquer this. In the period after Mahmud II's death, the great period of reform known as the **Tanzimat** ("Organization," 1839-1876) they began to attack that problem. European-style schools were built and teachers were even brought from Europe. It was slow work — elementary schools were needed before high schools could be useful, and universities and technical schools needed students trained in modern high schools. Teachers had

to pass through the system before new schools could be started. In addition, there were no science books written in Turkish, so students had to learn European languages before they could study. And new industries and new government depended on students with new knowledge. It was decades before a significant number of trained graduates was produced.

Another basic problem was economic. Money was needed to build schools, hire European teachers, and buy books. Modern industries might pay the bills, but they too demanded investments. Who would pay for new factories, European technical advisers, machines imported from Europe? One of the answers was borrowing. Money was also needed to build the highways, telegraph lines, roads, and railroads that were needed to improve the empire. European banks lent money to the Ottomans, but they charged for the funds. The Ottomans planned to borrow to build factories and roads, then to pay off the loans from the profits, but it was seldom so easy. Development took longer than the bankers would allow. More was borrowed just to pay the interest on old loans. Eventually, the Ottomans could not even pay the interest on the loans. Thus lack of money greatly hindered reform.

Many countries, such as the United States, built up their industries through a **protective tariff**. A protective tariff was a tax levied on manufactured goods coming into a country. It made imports more expensive and allowed local industries to compete with the stronger economies of Europe. The Ottomans could not use the protective tariff. Europeans forced them to keep an old system called the **Capitulations**, which allowed European goods into the empire with small customs duties. The Europeans thus protected their own exports and

Nineteenth century street scene.

their own industries. Militarily weak, the Ottomans were forced to see their industries destroyed by cheap imports.

The Ottomans were in a great predicament. They needed money to pay for new schools and industries, and they needed educated people and industries to make money. How could both be done at once? The very Europeans whom the Ottomans wished to emulate were hindering Ottoman development in order to protect their own exports to the Ottoman Empire. Nevertheless, despite all the roadblocks in their way, the Ottoman reformers did advance. Throughout the nineteenth and early twentieth centuries they built schools, until by the first world war there were 600,000 students in the empire's European-style schools. The government itself was centralized and improved. Government ministries and the legal system began to model themselves on European systems. Of greatest importance was the creation of a class of educated civil servants, men who often knew European languages and had plans for reform. They were able to build roads, railroads, and telegraph lines across much of the empire in the period from 1876-1914. This was essential for both defense and economic development. Unfortunately, economic reform was not so successful. Commerce with Europe increased greatly, but Ottoman industry languished, hurt by the factors mentioned above.

The worst problem was that the rest of the world did not stand still while the Ottomans reformed. Europeans, especially Russians, continued to attack the Ottoman Empire. The Ottomans would work and spend to develop a region of their Empire such as Bulgaria, only to have the Russians attack and seize it (1878). The Ottoman government was forced to spend half of its income on the military. This left much less for education or industry. Yet if they did not spend on the army there would be no empire left to reform. Russian conquests also resulted in an influx of millions of refugees into the Ottoman Empire. The refugees had to be fed and housed, further reducing the Ottoman chance to spend on development.

In the end, military losses destroyed the empire. Ironically, the end came just as Ottoman reforms were having their greatest success. A revolution in 1908 had taken real power out of the hands of the sultan (although the sultanate remained) and put it in the hands of reforming soldiers and bureaucrats (**The Committee of Union and Progress**). They made great strides in a short time, building on the work of earlier reformers. However, World War I destroyed their work. Justifiably fearing their old enemy, Russia, which was allied with the British and French, the Ottomans fought alongside Germany on the losing side. Millions of Turks died in the world war and the wars in Anatolia that followed, and large areas of Anatolia were laid waste. At the end of the world war the victorious Allies seized most of the Empire. The Allies decided that the Turks would be left only a small area in Northern and Central

Emirgân Middle School Boys

Emirgân Middle School Girls

Anatolia in which to live. All the great cities of the empire, in which reform had been most successful, were to be taken by the Allies and their friends. It seemed that reform had ultimately been a failure, defeated in war.

The Ottomans had indeed been sick, but they had not been allowed to cure themselves. Instead, those around them did what they could to insure that the illness resulted in death. Like other countries, the Ottoman Turks ultimately could not stand against the forces of imperialism. This is in no way exceptional. The remarkable fact is not that the Ottomans lost land to European imperialists. How many non-European countries did not lose land? How many survived at all? No, the remarkable fact was that the Ottomans held on so well. Ottoman loses to more powerful Europeans began at the end of the seventeenth century and went on for more than 200 years. Despite their military inferiority, the Ottomans survived European imperialism for more years than the United States has so far existed. The Ottoman Empire did finally succumb in World War I. Yet even at its end the empire held on amazingly well. Fighting against the English, the French and the Russians, the Ottomans lasted through almost four years of war. And after those four years the Turks regrouped to retain their independence.

Please answer the following questions:

▷ How do the Ottoman problems compare to the problems of developing countries today?
▷ What could the Ottomans have done to succeed, or were they doomed to fail by situations beyond their control?
▷ What was it about the Europeans that made them such a threat to the Ottomans?

The Cataclysm

IMPERIALISM AND NATIONALISM DESTROYED THE OTTOMAN EMPIRE. THIS WAS NOT SIMPLY A CHANGE IN POLITICAL BOUNDARIES OR THE CREATION OF new states from an old empire. The destruction of the Ottoman Empire left millions dead and millions more exiled from their homes. For the people of the Ottoman Empire, especially the Turks and other Muslims, the combination of imperialism and nationalism was one of the worst disasters in human history.

Muslims had lived in the Balkans since the first Ottoman conquests in the four-

بلغار مظالمه معروض قالامق ايجون ترك دار ودیار ابدن بدخت مهاجربنك استانبول
سوقاقلنده منظرهسی

Les émigrés rouméliotes fuyant les atrocités de l'armée bulgare.

Turkish refugees fleeing Bulgarian atrocities.

teenth century. They had lived in the regions south of the Caucasus Mountains[1] three centuries more. By no means were all the Muslims only descendants of the Turks who had first come to the region in the eleventh century. Many of the Muslims of both the Southern Caucasus and the Balkans were the descendants of those who had converted to Islam and had become Turks, as well as the descendants of the original Turks. Some of the Muslim peoples had lived in their homelands for more than 1,000 years. Others had been there as long as history recorded.

EXPULSION AND DEATH OF THE MUSLIMS						
Region	**Surviving Exiles**	**%**	**Dead**	**%**	**Remaining**	**%**
S. Greece, 1821-30	10,000	29	25,000	71	none	0
Bulgaria, 1877-78	568,000	38	262,000	17	672,000	45
Bosnia, 1875-78	245,000	35	dead and exiled		449,000	65
Balkan Wars, 1912-13	813,000	35	632,000	27	870,000	38
Crimea, 1772	100,000	*	*	*	*	*
S Caucasus, 1827-29	26,000	*	*	*	*	*
Crimea, 1854-60	225,000	*	75,000	*	*	*
Caucasus, 1864-67	800,000	*	400,000	*	*	*
S. Caucasus, 1877-78	70,000	*	*	*	*	*
Anatolia, 1912-21			2,736,000	19	11,619,000	81
S. Caucasus, 1914-20	273,000	*	410,000	*	*	*

*unknown

To Bulgarian, Greek, Serbian, and Armenian nationalists the Muslims would never belong. Part of the reason they opposed the Muslims was religious: For the nationalists, only their own people, defined as those belonging to their religion and speaking their language, had a place in their nation. Part of the reason they opposed the Muslims was purely practical; they felt that Muslims who remained in the new nationalist states would never be loyal citizens. Their allegiance of the Muslims, it was assumed, would always be to the Muslim Ottoman Empire. Moreover, the Muslims had much good land and other property that could be expropriated. To the nationalists, the new states would have no place for Muslims. The Turks and other Muslims would have to go.

The table includes only the largest incidents of mortality and forced migration. Many smaller expulsions, such as that of the Muslims of Central Greece or Serbia, are not included.

The expulsions of the Muslims of the Balkans followed a set procedure. At first, many were killed in what is called "exemplary violence." Those whose villages had not yet been reached by the Russian invaders or Balkan nationalists saw what they could expect, so they fled, taking only what they could carry. Once on the road they became prey to starvation and disease. Columns of refugees were attacked by their enemies.

Those who survived were never allowed to return to their homes. The same history was repeated in Greece, Bulgaria, Montenegro, Serbia, and elsewhere. In Southern and Central Greece, Serbia, and Montenegro, all the Muslims were expelled or died. In Bulgaria, less than half the Muslim community remained. Bosnia fared better, because it was taken by the Austrians, who were more humane. But Bosnia would suffer later when Serbian nationalists attempted once again to use the old tactics.

The Caucasian Muslims, the Circassians and Abhazians, lived on or near the Black Sea Coast. They died in great number because the Russians wanted their land.

> **Those interested could do no better than to read Tolstoy, who saw the carnage, reported it, and became a pacifist himself.**

(It must also be said that the Circassians had for centuries been involved in guerilla wars with the Russians and Ukrainians and in banditry.) The methods used by the Russians to dislodge the Caucasian Muslims are too gruesome to be described here. Those interested could do no better than to read Tolstoy, who saw the carnage, reported it, and became a pacifist himself. The Eastern Black Sea Region that had been the home of the Abhazians and Circassians was denuded of those Muslims by the Russians. After the Russians had murdered or expelled most of the Muslim population the land was left almost empty, waiting for settlement by Russians and their allies.

The migration of millions of Muslims had a negative effect on the security and the economy of the Ottoman Empire. The Ottomans felt that they were bound by religion and common humanity to take in the refugees. If they had not, those who were exiled would surely have died. As an example, the Russians expelled the Circassians and Abhazians of the Caucasus by forcing them from their villages to the Black Sea Coast. They were left there under the guard of the Russian Army, with little food and water. The Ottomans chartered every boat they could find to bring them to safety. They provided whatever food and medicine they could afford and gave land to the refugees. Where did the money for the rescue missions come from? It was taken from government funds that were sorely needed to develop a poor empire. It was also taken from funds that were needed by the military to defend against those same Russians, which must have been part of the Russian plan.

The Russians were also ultimately responsible for conflict between the Muslims and Armenians of the Southern Caucasus (today's Armenia, Azerbaijan, and Georgia) and Eastern Anatolia.[2] Until Russian armies arrived in the Southern Caucasus in the 1790s, Muslims and Armenians had lived together in the Southern Caucasus and Anatolia for 700 years. The lives of neither group were completely happy. Nevertheless, one fact indicates that the Christian Armenians could not have been badly oppressed — they were still there 700

---

[1] This region is sometimes called the southern Caucasus. The Russians called it Trans-Caucasia, because it was across (trans) the Caucasus Mountains from Russia.

[2] Anatolia is the part of today's Turkey that lies in Asia. The small portion of Turkey that lies in Europe is Eastern Thrace.

years later. The Turks and other Muslims had political and military control of the region. They were the majority of the population. If they had wished to eradicate the Armenians or force their conversion to Islam, they would have been able do so easily in 700 years.

Although it is seldom reported accurately, the conflict between Armenians and Muslims began not in the Ottoman Empire but in areas of Russian conquest south of the Caucasus Mountains. The Russians needed a local population upon whom they could depend. Although their real preference would undoubtedly have been to rule themselves, the Armenians were a minority who could never hope that the Muslim majority would let them rule. Given no other choice, many Armenians preferred Christian rulers, the Russians, to Muslim rulers. In addition, and perhaps more of an incentive, the Russians gave free land to Armenians and sometimes remitted Armenians' taxes.

When the Russians invaded what is now Azerbaijan in the early 1800s they enlisted Armenians in their cause. In wars Russia fought against the Ottomans and Persians from 1827 to 1829, Muslims were expelled from their lands in what today is Armenia, which then had a Turkish majority, and Armenians were brought in and given the old Muslims lands. The Russians felt the Christian Armenians would be reliable subjects of the tsar, something the Turks never would be.

The lines of battle were drawn. As the years went on and the wars became more deadly, Armenians increasingly felt they had to take the side of The Russians. Muslims knew they had to take the side of their government, the Ottomans. Both sides feared the other side would kill them if war broke out. Of such is built intercommunal war without quarter. The conflict was to last more than 100 years. It was surely not desired by the majority of either the Muslims or the Armenians, but imperialism and nationalism drew all into the catastrophe that followed.

In Anatolia, Armenian nationalists attempted to create an Armenian state during the last quarter of the nineteenth and beginning of the twentieth centuries, a task made difficult by the fact that the land claimed by the Armenian nationalists was three-fourths Muslim in population. They were opposed by local Muslims and the Ottoman state. Tens of thousands died, and the division between the two communities grew. The conflict came to a head during World War I, when both communities suffered terrible losses.

World War I began in Eastern Anatolia with grave Ottoman losses to the Russian Army. The losses were exacerbated by Ottoman Armenians who took the side of the Russians and carried on a guerilla war behind the lines. Armenian rebels attempted to seize major Ottoman cities, cut communications lines, assassinated officials, and forced the Ottomans to withdraw whole divisions of troops from the front to fight the internal enemy. The Armenian rebels were particularly successful in the City of Van, the largest city of southeastern Anatolia. They seized Van from the Ottomans and held it until the Russians arrived. The Ottomans, fearful of continued rebellion, deported Armenians from Anatolia to Syria and Iraq, away from the Russian invaders. (It is seldom reported that the large majority of those deported survived. Indeed a much larger proportion survived than did those Muslims and Armenians who were forced to live on a battlefield.)

World War I was not only fought by armies in Eastern Anatolia. It was a war of peoples. When the Armenians seized Van they killed every Muslim who could not escape. Those Muslims were mainly Kurds. The Kurds in the countryside retaliated by killing every Armenian they could find, just as Armenian bands killed all the Muslims they could. At the end of the war, retreating Armenians, who had finally lost to the Turks, killed all the Turks they could find on their line of retreat and filled the streets of the cities of northeastern Anatolia with corpses. In turn, the Turkish peasants who found Armenians killed them.

The Armenians of Anatolia, most of whom lived in war zones, lost 40% of their population. The Muslims in the war-torn provinces of the East lost almost exactly the same proportion of their population, 40%. Both Muslims and Armenians in the war zone died from war between the Ottomans and Russians, from starvation and disease, and by killing each other.

> **The Armenians of Anatolia, most of whom lived in war zones, lost 40% of their population. The Muslims in the war-torn provinces of the East lost almost exactly the same proportion of their population, 40%.**

Armenian losses in World War I are often cited, but Muslim losses are seldom mentioned outside of Turkey.[3] The horrible word genocide is often used against the Turks, even though no one has ever shown any real Ottoman order to deliberately eradicate Armenians. Claims against the Turks were believed in America because of prejudice against non-Christians, but mainly because the other side's story was never told. Even today, few know of the equal suffering of the Muslims in that terrible war. When only the deaths on one side in a war are known a mutual slaughter appears to be a genocide. It is far better to study and pity the inhumanity of those times than to lay blame on one side or the other.

> The sufferings of the Muslim populations of the Balkans, Anatolia, Turks and others, were among the most horrific in history. Yet they are little known in North America or Europe..

Also largely unmentioned in America are the Turkish losses in the Turkish Independence War. In direct violation of the armistice that ended World War I, the victorious Allies granted Southwestern Anatolia to Greece in 1919. Western Anatolia was also more than three-fourths Muslim, almost all of them Turks. The Greeks invaded, landing in İzmir on May 14, 1919, supported by the British navy. As they advanced, the Greek forces put into effect the same "ethnic cleansing" that had been perfected during the Balkan Wars. But this time the Turks were able to fight back and win. By war's end, 313,000 Greeks and 1,246,000 Turks (including a small number of other Muslims) in the war zones were dead. By treaty, the remaining Greeks in Turkey (excepting those in Istanbul) and the Turks in Greece (excluding those in Western Thrace) were exchanged.

The sufferings of the Muslim populations of the Balkans, Anatolia, Turks and others, were among the most horrific in history. Yet they are little known in North America or Europe. Sufferings of the Greek and Armenian populations in the same periods are well publicized, but Muslim suffering is largely ignored. One must ask why this is so. The only conclusion is that these people were not considered to be important, either by those who wrote in Europe at the time or by those of our own day. There are lessons to be learned from this — not only a lesson of the horrors caused by imperialism and nationalism, but a lesson of our own prejudices, as well.

دوچار سهالت اولان بدبخت مهاجرین قافلهلرندن بری

Un cortége d'émigrés roméliote.

فرطو: ؟ فرید

Turkish refugees.

---

[3] The issue of what transpired between the Armenians and Muslims during World War I is far too complicated and contentious to be considered at length here. Readers who are interested in the subject might wish to consult Richard Hovannisian's *Armenia on the Road to Independence* (Berkeley, 1967) and Justin McCarthy's *Death and Exile* (Princeton, 1995). The two books will give very different interpretations.

Mustafa Kemal (3rd from the left, front row) at Sivas
The Turkish Independance War

How did modern Turkey emerge from the collapse of the Ottoman Empire?

Performance Objectives

Students will be able to:

1. Discuss the emotional and physical impact of WW I upon the Turkish nation.
2. Understand how Atatürk helped create a national spirit.
3. Explain how nationalism, coupled with reform, helped Turkey become a modern world power.

Springboard

If you had to select one major American hero whose picture you would hang in your house, who would it be? Why did you make that choice?

(Students will mention, perhaps, Washington, Lincoln, or Martin Luther King, Jr.)

Every Turkish public place has a large photo of Kemal Atatürk and Atatürk died in 1938. What does it tell us about this man for the Turks?

Procedures/ Development:

▶ Many historians state that Atatürk is a product of the Turkish defeat and devastation in World War I.

▷ Distribute the reading **Worksheet 1**: *The End of the Ottoman Empire and the Creation of the Republic.*

The following five statements are from the reading:

1. "...but the Turks also found their salvation through war." (first sentence)
2. "...the Turks refused to be evicted from the only lands that remained for their people." (first paragraph)
3. "...reserving the worst punishment for the Turks." (second paragraph)
4. "Faced with imminent destruction, the Turks fought desperately." (fourth paragraph)
5. "The Turks triumphed by finding a national identity." (fifth paragraph)

With a neighbor, discuss the importance and the historical significance of **each** of these statements. Teacher will debrief with the class.

♦ Why do you think the Allies treated the Turks so poorly?
♦ What was the major population problem the Turks faced?
♦ How did the Turks manage to win a victory from such a terrible experience?

▶ The human cost of World War I was staggering for Turkey.

▷ Distribute **Worksheet 2:** *The Devastation that Remained*

♦ Based on the reading, who were the "real" victims in World War I? Explain your answer.
♦ How did this human devastation have some positive result?

▶ Atatürk emerged from WWI as the hero who reconstructed the Turkish nation. Look at Ataturk's own words to see his vision and ideas for the Turkish nation (**Worksheet 3**).

▷ Distribute **Worksheet 3**: Mustafa Kemal Atatürk in His own Words
Students will read the words of Atatürk
- Based upon your reading, what leadership qualities did Atatürk exemplify?
- Can we say that Atatürk was a catalyst for nationalistic change? Why?

▶ Atatürk established a model of government for the Turks.
▷ Distribute **Worksheet 4**: Reform in the New Republic
Class will work in cooperative learning groups and answer the questions at the bottom of the reading.
- Place quote on chalkboard:
  Above all, Atatürk's ghost can claim that he set about things in the right order. He started with the basics — a new sense of national identity for Turks without an empire, a new system of law, a reformed language, sensible hats instead of that embarrassing fez. He told the Turks that these things were necessary for the creation of a modern society, and they accepted his advice. To those foundations a multi-party system was added eight years after his death (to be thrice briefly interrupted, but never cancelled, by the too-privileged army). The economy began to be opened up to competition in 1980. All this continues to be done in Atatürk's name. Of Europe's three dozen countries, not many can claim that much steadiness of purpose over 70 years.
  — The Economist, "Survey on Turkey," December 14, 1991

Teacher will review the answers with the class to:
1. determine class attitudes about Ataturk's activities and actions.
2. assess the road taken by Atatürk.
3. analyze whether Ataturk's policies did modernize Turkey.

If you were living in a century moving toward modernization, would you want a leader like Mustafa Kemal Atatürk? Explain your answer.- How is Atatürk's influence still reflected among the Turks?

Application   You have just won a major contract to write a biography of Mustafa Atatürk. Based upon what we have discussed in class, develop the outline for this book.

The End of the Ottoman Empire and the Creation of the Turkish Nation

War caused the end of the Ottoman Empire, but the Turks also found their salvation through war. After the Ottoman defeat in World War I the Allies took all the Arab World for themselves. All except Arabia was seized by the French and the British. They also decided to divide up Anatolia and Eastern Thrace, where the population was overwhelmingly Turkish. Western Anatolia and Eastern Thrace were to be given to the Greeks, Northeastern Anatolia to the Armenians, and Southern Anatolia to the Italians and the French. The Turks were to be left only parts of Northern and Central Anatolia. Istanbul was soon seized by the Allies. But the Turks refused to be evicted from the only lands that remained for their people. When the Greeks invaded Anatolia in 1919 the Turks organized to defend themselves. Under the command of General Mustafa Kemal they drove out the Armenians in the East and the Greeks in the West. First the French and Italians, then the British accepted the defeat of their plans. The Turkish Republic was born.

At the end of World War I, the victorious Allies decided on brutal treatment for their late enemies, reserving the worst punishment for the Turks. The Ottoman Empire was to be divided with little land left for the Turks. The Allies promoted an Armenian takeover in Eastern Anatolia and a Greek takeover in Western Anatolia, in lands that were overwhelmingly Turkish in population. Allied warships landed troops and supplies for their surrogates. Istanbul, the Ottoman capital, was seized by the Allies themselves. The Turks were to be left only a small region in Central and Northern Anatolia, far too small for the Turkish population.

Where would the Turks go? Millions of Turks and other Muslims had been driven into Anatolia from the Balkans, the Crimea, and the Caucasus Region in the past 100 years. Now it was all too possible that the Turkish presence in Anatolia, land that had been theirs for 800 years, would be all but eradicated. No shelter remained.

Faced with imminent destruction, the Turks fought desperately. Led by General Mustafa Kemal (later Kemal Atatürk), they amazed the Europeans by defeating first the Armenians in the East, then the Greeks in the West. Even the Europeans, who would have been forced to fight a major war to enforce their plans for the Turks, capitulated and evacuated Istanbul. The Turkish Republic was born.

The Turks triumphed by finding a national identity. Under the Ottoman Empire, a sense of national identity had been discouraged. Turks were taught to see themselves as Muslims or Ottomans or subjects of the sultan, but not as Turks. Other Ottoman subjects — the Bulgarians, Greeks, Rumanians, Armenians, and others — adopted European nationalism and began to see themselves as "peoples" who should have their own countries, but it took disaster before the Turks saw themselves as members of a Turkish nation.

The result was amazing. After World War I the Turks literally had all the real power of Europe against them. Power was in the hands of the Allies who had won the war, and the Allies had decided to end the rule of the Turks. Those who the Turks could turn to for help were few. Moreover, the Turks had not organized themselves outside the Ottoman system for more than 500 years. The Ottoman government was prostrate before the Allies. Anyone estimating the chances of a disorganized people standing against the greatest powers of the world and winning would have come up with very poor odds. Yet the Turks won, and survived.

> **Anyone estimating the chances of a disorganized people standing against the greatest powers of the world and winning would have come up with very poor odds. Yet the Turks won, and survived.**

The Devastation That Remained

THE GREATEST LOSS IN WORLD WAR I AND THE TURKISH WAR OF INDEPENDENCE WAS THE HUMAN LOSS. MORTALITY OF BOTH MUSLIMS AND Armenians in eastern Anatolia had been approximately 40%. In some provinces, death rates had been much higher: 62% of the Muslims of Van province had died during the wars, for example. The mortality in western Anatolia, while not as bad as in the East, was still horrific, well above 10%.

10% of the population of Turkey were new immigrants — refugees who had arrived from the Balkans and Armenia with little or nothing. The people of Turkey were not the same as those who had been there in 1912, before the beginning of the Balkan Wars. Half the population of Turkey in Europe (not including Istanbul) had been born elsewhere, usually in regions of Europe lost to the Ottoman Empire. In the provinces bordering the new Soviet Union and in Western Anatolia, one-third of the inhabitants were new. They came to a country that was itself destitute. During the war more than one million Turks and Kurds had been forced from their homes by the Russians and the Armenians. 1.2 million Turkish refugees had fled the Greek invasion.

These figures cannot describe the suffering that accompanied the trauma of dislocation, starvation, and disease that was the refugees' fate. Both the East and West of Anatolia were largely in ruins. American observers reported that eastern cities such as Van, Bitlis,

> **62% of the Muslims of Van had died during the wars... 10% of the population of Turkey were new immigrants — refugees who had arrived from the Balkans and Armenia with little or nothing.**

and Bayezit had lost more than two-thirds of their population. More than 80% of the buildings in Van and Bitlis had been destroyed. In the West, Americans reported that cities such as İzmir, Aydın, Nazilli, and Bilecik had been totally destroyed. Villages in both the East and the West experienced similar destruction. Less than 10% of the buildings of Manisa, Alaşehir, Kasaba, and other cities remained. Less than one-half of the farm animals survived. In many provinces, all of the olive trees, essentials of both life and trade, were gone. The only thing that prevented mass starvation was the fact that there were many fewer people than before.

There is one positive factor to the mass migration of the Turks. The dislocation of so many Turks brought with it a new consciousness. Cultural and political conservatism had been the rule among the villagers who had never traveled far from their homes. They and their ancestors had been part of the world that saw little of the outside world. Once the Turks were forced to move, their horizons naturally broadened, even if what they experienced was often awful. The Turks had often learned brutal political truths from their experiences. They had seen the effects of the old ways and were not willing to accept radical change. That change was to be brought about by the hero of the Turkish resistance, Mustafa Kemal.

Mustafa Kemal Atatürk in His Own Words

THE REFORMS OF MUSTAFA KEMAL ATATÜRK LEFT FEW AREAS OF LIFE UNTOUCHED. PERHAPS MOST INDICATIVE OF RADICAL CHANGE was Atatürk's attitude toward women. He broke traditions of centuries with reforms that allowed women educational opportunities, political and legal equality, and other rights recognized as essential to a free society.

Friends, the Turkish nation has demonstrated in many important instances that it is a progressive nation with a liking for innovations. Even before recent years, our people attempted to follow the path of modernization, to achieve social reforms. But such efforts produced no real results. Have you asked yourselves the reasons for this? I think the reason was the failure to begin from the basis, from the very foundation...A society, a nation, consist of two sorts of people: men and women. How is it possible to elevate one part of society while neglecting the other half and expect the whole to progress? How is it possible for one half of a society to soar to the heavens while the other half remains chained to the very earth?

— Adapted from *Atatürk's Way*, Turhan Feyzioğlu, ed.

> **"How is it possible for one half of a society to soar to the heavens while the other half remains chained to the very earth?"**

NATIONALISM WAS ALIEN TO THE MIDDLE EAST. IT WAS IMPORTED FROM EUROPE, AS WERE MANY OTHER POLITICAL IDEOLOGIES. Mustafa Kemal used the ideology of nationalism during and after the Turkish War of independence to bind the Turks together into one nation. He was as much instructor as politician or general, teaching the Turks that they were a people with a noble common heritage.

...We are a nation which has been late and negligent in the application of ideas and nationality. Our nation especially has experienced the bitter results of inattentiveness to nationality. The various peoples within the Ottoman Empire, always holding fast to national principles, attained their goal through the strength of this national ideal. Only when we were driven out from among their midst did it dawn upon us that we were a nation both different from and alien to them. At the moment of our weakness they insulted and humiliated us. We realized that our shortcoming was our forgetting of ourselves. If we wish the world to respect us, we must show this respect to ourselves and to our nationality, emotionally, intellectually, in practice, through our actions and conduct. We must realize that those nations which cannot find their own identity are condemned to become the prey of other nations.

— Adapted from *Atatürk's Way*, Turhan Feyzioğlu, ed.

Please answer the following questions:

▷ What kind of change is Atatürk promoting in the first speech?
▷ Do you think this change is a good idea? Why/why not?
▷ According to Atatürk how did a lack of national identity hurt the Turks/Ottoman Empire?
▷ How would a speech like this second one affect a young person who had just experienced the aftermath of World War I?

Mustafa Kemal Atatürk

Reform In The New Republic

THE TURKISH SUCCESS DID NOT END WITH VICTORY IN WAR. ONCE AGAIN LED BY MUSTAFA KEMAL, THEY PROCEEDED TO RENEW THEIR country internally. In a space of twenty years Turkey was turned from an empire into a republic with new laws and a new philosophy of government. Education was reformed along Western models. Rights were guaranteed for women, who began to vote and were elected to parliament. Even the clothes on the Turkish backs were changed, from fezzes and veils to an approximation of European clothing. A whole society was being rapidly transformed. Many of the old ways remained, but very few cultures have been able to reform and modernize so quickly and so well.

The extraordinary fact of modern Turkish history is that the Turks managed to endure as a nation in their own state when so many others were falling under the imperial grasp of Europe. It is extraordinary that the Turks could survive militarily against all odds. It is also extraordinary that the Turks were able to modernize their society and economy along European lines and to keep their independence from the European powers. Despite the efforts of his neighbors, the Sick Man recovered and lives on.

Breaking with the Ottoman past, the Turks set up a new capital in Ankara, the city that had been the center of the resistance. Delegates from all over Turkey gathered in the Grand National Assembly (parliament), selected Mustafa Kemal as president, and set upon radical reform. The reforms touched the most basic parts of the lives of everyone in the country: Polygamy was abolished (1925), women were made the legal equals of men, and given the vote (1930). All families were obliged to take last names, something that they had not had before. (Mustafa Kemal took the surname Atatürk.) The past was largely discarded for new ways: Turkey was made a secular state (1928) and the old Arabic-based alphabet was abolished (1928) in favor of the Roman alphabet used in the West. The government was constructed to follow the European model of parliamentary democracy. New law codes were drawn up, copying Swiss, Italian, and German law statutes. Symbols were not ignored: Traditional styles of dress were discouraged. Wearing the fez was forbidden and the veil was strongly discouraged. The state radio began to play European music and European-style art was fostered and shown in exhibitions. The theory was that Turks should become more modern, more Europeanized in all aspects of life if they were to succeed in the modern world.

The Turkish Republic carried through to completion the Ottoman reforms of education. In the Ottoman Empire traditional Muslim schools had existed side-by-side with European-style schools. Now all students were to be enrolled in state schools or in private schools that met state standards and taught a basic curriculum. The number of students grew from 358,000 in 1923 to 1.1 million in 1940. However, despite great improvements many children in rural areas still did not have schools. The reason, as before, was lack of resources.

To improve the economy and increase the tax payments that supported the schools and government, the Turkish Republic attempted to reform industry. Like the Ottomans, the republic found economic reform difficult going. In the 1920s the resources of the state were committed to repairing the ravages of war. The

> The extraordinary fact of modern Turkish history is that the Turks managed to endure as a nation in their own state when so many others were falling under the imperial grasp of Europe.

1930s brought the greatest depression in modern history, the worst possible time to improve an economy. Like many other countries of the time, Turkey turned to state owned and operated enterprises as a solution. State enterprises in textiles, iron and steel, and other industries had some success, and did aid employment. However, private business and agriculture were less developed.

Atatürk and his followers believed in eventual democracy for the Turks, even though they had no wish to install it immediately. Instead, they set about a policy of education for democracy and Turkish nationalism. "Peoples Houses" (Halk Evleri) were set up all over the country. These taught the people practical subjects, such as adult literacy, with a strong dose of secularism and nationalism. The forms of democracy (elections, parliaments, legal equality for all, etc.) were taught in the schools. In fact, the most important training for democracy was in the schools, which educated an increasingly literate public that could understand the workings of government. Elections for parliament were held regularly, but except for a brief period Atatürk's Republican People's Party was the only national party. Atatürk obviously believed that the Turks needed education, economic development, and experience with the forms of democracy before true democracy could work. There was fear that reactionary elements would try to stall reforms, that ultra-nationalist elements would try to regain old lost territories at the expense of peace and reform, and that local separatists would weaken the unified nation. Fundamentalist religious sentiment was especially worrying. It was felt that time was needed to cement new traditions of secularism and the separation of religion and state. This policy of gradual transition to democracy, which has since been seen all over the world, has been debated from Atatürk's day to today. In the case of Turkey it did lead to democracy.

Compared to the record of the Ottomans or to that of other developing countries, the reforms of the Turkish Republic were a great achievement. Atatürk not only speeded the economic and political development of his country; he also educated and convinced

> One-fourth of the population of Anatolia had died. Whole regions in the East and West had been laid waste. Very few families had escaped terrible suffering

his people that reform should be a national ideology that continued after he was gone. He brought his nation from a state close to death to a functioning part of the modern world. How were they able to do it? Why were Atatürk and the modern Turks successful where the Ottomans had failed?

◆ The Turks were lucky to have a strong leader who possessed both good intentions and the power to direct reform. Atatürk was a "new man," the child of a bureaucrat, not an Ottoman aristocrat. He had no strong ties to the old ways. He was trusted as no one else could have been, because he literally had saved the country. Many of those who might have opposed his reformist ways had been discredited in the war. Perhaps most important, he was a strong-willed leader who knew how to get his way and how to properly use his power.

◆ Because of their military victory and the unwillingness of the Allies to fight a major war to defeat them, the Turks were now masters of their own country. They were able to set their own tariffs and taxes. The capitulations had been abolished during the war. When the Allies attempted to reimpose them after the war the victorious Turks refused, and there was nothing the Europeans could do about it.

◆ The specter of attack from outside was greatly lessened. Russia was now a communist empire with so many internal troubles that it did not again seriously threaten Turkey until after World War II. The other old enemy, the Austrian Empire (Austria-Hungary), had been dissolved after the war. The national strength and treasure that had been expended on the military could now be put to peaceful purposes.

◆ Atatürk and the parliament decided to accept the new borders of Turkey, rather than try to regain the Turkish territories seized previously. While many Turks naturally wanted to return to the homes taken from them, Atatürk was able to convince the people that they had to concentrate on building their new country and forget old wrongs. The national energy was not to be wasted in the quest for old glories.

- The Turks were able to build on the real successes of Ottoman reform. In particular, there was now an educated class of politicians, bureaucrats, teachers, and engineers who understand the modern world. At the beginning of the Republic the mass of the people did not understand economics or foreign policy, but the educated leaders did. It was thanks to the Ottoman reforms that those leaders existed.

Naturally, there were objections to Atatürk's actions and his reforms. The religiously conservative felt that the state should remain Islamic. They believed that Islamic law and Islamic traditions had been decreed by God and should never be changed. On the other hand, liberal thinkers objected to what they called one man rule and wanted more democracy. Some wanted to reconquer the lands taken from the Turks. The opposition never came close to success. Because of their differing views they could not unite. Moreover, there was little popular backing for opposition.

Atatürk's reforms could not have been undertaken if the Turkish people were unwilling to change. The Ottomans had often been stymied by the conservatism of the people. With little education and little experience of the world, the Turks of the Ottoman Empire had not wanted to exchange their old ways for new ways they did not understand. They had no reason to believe things would get better if they changed. War had changed that. One-fourth of the population of Anatolia had died. Whole regions in the East and West had been laid waste. Very few families had escaped terrible suffering. The Turks still might not know exactly which reforms had to be made, but they understood that change was needed. They had seen the result of the old ways and they were willing to let Atatürk and his fellow reformers try a new path.

Please answer the following questions:

▷ Atatürk established the forms of democracy and taught his people that democracy should be the basis of the Turkish government, but there was not true democracy in Turkey in his time. Instead, he stressed education and development for eventual democracy. Was this the right approach? Should democracy have been instituted immediately?

▷ Look at a map of Eastern Europe and the Middle East before the Russian Empire collapsed. What was the mutual advantage gained by Turkey and the West in the NATO alliance?

▷ Looking at the same map: Why was Turkish democracy so remarkable in that part of the world? Outside of Western Europe and the Americas, how many democracies existed in the world?

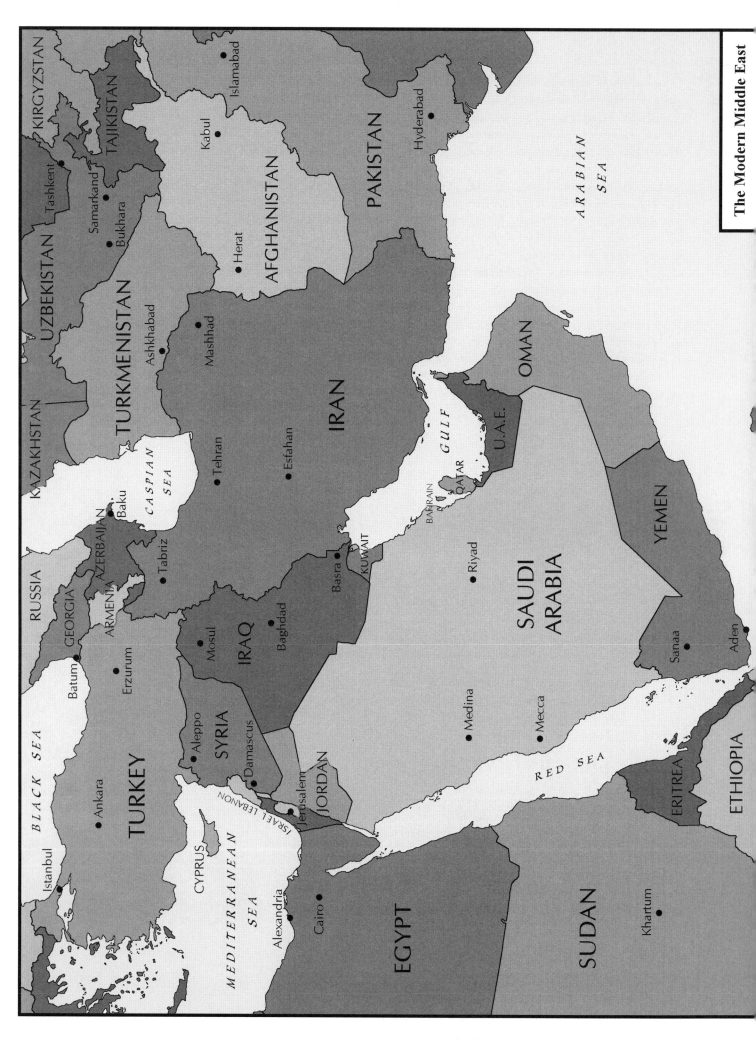

Eastern Anatolia

Turkish Society

An understanding of tradition and change can be obtained by studying the family and the role of women and their place in Turkish life.

Suggested Time	Two classroom periods.
Materials Needed	A class set of: Worksheet 1 Worksheet 2 Worksheet 3 Worksheet 4 Worksheet 5
Objective	An understanding of tradition and change can be obtained by studying the family and the role of women and their place in Turkish life.
Note to the Instructor	This chapter contains two different social studies lessons dealing with the traditional roles of women in Turkey. If time permits, both lessons should be taught so that students get a more complete and accurate picture of the lives of Turkish women.
Volcabulary/ Key Concepts	tradition gender roles change
Aim	To what degree did marriage customs in traditional (19th century) Turkey differ from contemporary marriage customs?
Major Idea	▷ In Turkey, marriage is considered an important milestone in a person's life. Traditional marriages were frequently arranged by the parents of the bride and groom. The concept of equality of mates, current in Western thinking, was not necessarily an important factor in a Turkish marriage. Since the beginning of the Turkish Republic these concepts have been changing. Turkish marriages today resemble marriages in Europe or America.
Performance Objectives	Students will be able to: 1. Define: extended family, nuclear family, polygamy. 2. Examine and discuss the characteristics of a good marriage in Turkey. 3. Compare and contrast Turkish marriages and Turkish families to the families of the students. 4. Compare and contrast traditional and modern marriages.
Development/ Procedure	Teacher should develop a semantic map as shown below:

Characteristics of a Good Marriage

- ♦ Allow students time to list the ingredients of a successful marriage.
- ♦ Ask students if these ideas come from their own families, from the movies, from books, or from T.V.
- ♦ Place check marks next to those characteristics which are determined by your culture.

▷ Distribute **Worksheet 1**: Marriage and Family.
Allow students time to complete reading and answer questions.
- ♦ What do you think of this kind of marriage?
- ♦ How did the Turks traditionally feel about:
  - ▷ equal marital partnerships?
  - ▷ men as "breadwinners'?
  - ▷ sexual purity among the young girls?
- ♦ How did the traditions change?
- ♦ Why do you think they changed?
- ♦ Compare your beliefs with traditional and modern Turkish beliefs.

▷ Although many of us may find older Turkish marriage customs different from ours, the Turks strongly advocated their policies.
Let us look at two points of view.
- ♦ Divide class into two groups.
  - ▷ Group 1: **Worksheet 2 and 3**
  - ▷ Group 2: **Worksheet 4**
- ♦ Allow students time to complete worksheet.
- ♦ Review definitions of polygamy, extended family and nuclear family.
- ♦ Based upon the reading, what reasons do the Turks give for traditional marriages?
- ♦ Do you agree with them that these marriages could have benefitted them in their time?
- ♦ Which type of marriage, traditional or modern, might be best for a family? Explain.

Summary/Application ▷ Imagine you are a Turkish parent living in the Ottoman Empire in the 19th century. You have either a son or a daughter. Write a letter to a close friend of the family discussing your concerns and hopes for your child.
Students will read letters and discuss.

Marriage and the Family

In the Ottoman Empire and even in some rural areas of Turkey today marriages were very different than marriages in modern Turkey or America. It is difficult for modern readers to understand traditional Turkish marriages. Young people today have difficulty when they look at the relations between their grandmothers and grandfathers. When Grandma married Grandpa during the time of the Ottoman Empire women were not treated as equals by men. Both men and women were bound by the cultural values they inherited. It is important to keep this in mind when we talk about Turkish culture long ago. But on the other hand, it should also be remembered that our ancestors in America and Europe were not too fair when it came to equality between the sexes.

As was true in all Muslim countries, every Turk was expected to marry. Ideally, the young were to marry at an early age, sometimes soon after puberty.

> **Traditionally, almost all marriages were arranged by the parents of the young people.**

The Turks were practical. They believed not having a sexual partner was unnatural but sex was only lawful in marriage. If the young did not marry, they would find trouble and that would cause all sorts of social and moral evils. For parents, the sexual purity of their daughters was essential.

Traditionally, almost all marriages were arranged by the parents of the young people. The first consideration was economic — a "good marriage" was to find a mate for your child of equal or higher social and economic standing. However, other such issues were also addressed. Mothers wanted their children to be happy. Physical attractiveness was not ignored. As a rule, men were respected for their abilities as a "bread-winner" and women for their skills in housekeeping and child caring. Strength was appreciated in a man; virtue was appreciated in a woman. These values were the same in most traditional societies.

Please answer the following questions:

▷ What does this reading tell you about the traditional (19th century) role of men and women?
▷ How did the parents help ensure their daughter's happiness?
▷ Why were parents concerned with the sexual purity of their daughters?

Traditional Turkish Families

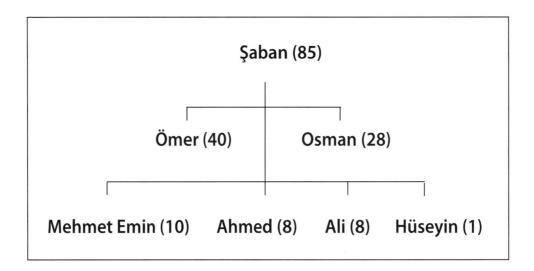

THE MODEL FAMILY IN MOST OF THE MODERN WORLD IS A NUCLEAR FAMILY — MOTHER, FATHER AND CHILDREN. THIS WAS NOT TRUE among the Turks of the Ottoman Empire. There the ideal was the extended family — a family with at least three generations lived together in the same household. The extended family allowed the members to work together and pool their resources. There was always someone to help with work in the fields or watch the children. Parents could leave for a while and know their children, their house, and their farm were safe.

Turkish extended families took many forms. Sometimes it was three generations of males, along with their wives and daughters, who lived in one house or on one compound of houses. Look at the family of Şaban, an elderly grandfather with two surviving sons who lived in the Black Sea region of Anatolia in the 1840's. He was a farmer. His two sons were married and part of Şaban's household. In all, there were seven males in the household and probably an equal number of females — wives and children. However, the Ottoman registrars did not include women in their records. This was considered a violation of the privacy of the family.

The idea behind the extended family was simple — sons did not move out of the family home. Instead, brides moved in with the husband's parents' family and, in most cases, these households remained like that until the death of the oldest male. Then a family might break into different households, each led by a son. Sometimes two or three brothers kept a family together but that was actually two nuclear families joined together. In some areas of Anatolia this form of extended family was common. Another reason for such families was the fact that women often brought up families of young children after the father died. The mother was in fact the head of the household as the children grew up and that arrangement remained the same even after the sons reached adulthood.

▷ Define: 1) nuclear family 2) extended family
▷ According to this reading, what were the benefits of the extended family?

Polygamy

ONE MAJOR DIFFERENCE BETWEEN MARRIAGE CUSTOMS IN ISLAMIC AND CHRISTIAN CULTURES WAS POLYGAMY (MORE PROPERLY polygyny, a husband having more than one wife). Islamic Law allowed a man to take up to four wives, although he was not allowed to obviously favor one wife over another. All wives were all to have equal living space, clothing, and time with their husband, at least in legal theory.

Polygamy seems to have been fairly rare among the Turks of the Ottoman Empire. Evidence shows that in normal times fewer than 5% of the women may have been in polygamous marriages. The reason was probably social — both men and women preferred monogamous unions and parents were not usually willing to give their daughter as a second wife. In the Turkish cultures of Central Asia, monogamy was the rule before coming into contact with Middle Eastern traditions.

Why then did polygamy exist among Turks at all? One of the reasons was surely the most obvious one, an assertion of male power and desire among those rich enough to gratify themselves. Such is seen in different guises in all societies. The most common type of polygamy in the Ottoman Empire, however, was part of the social welfare system that bound Turkish families together. When a man died it was the duty of his brother to look after the surviving family. Brothers often lived with their families in the same household. The wives of the two brothers had been companions, their children had played together. Since the family believed that all women of childbearing age should be married and they wanted to keep the inheritance in the household, the most natural solution was the marriage of the widow to the brother. This would keep the fabric of the family and society together. Polygamy also benefited society as a whole because it kept the birth rate high. At various times during Ottoman history, wars caused the death of a great number of Turkish males. If society were monogamous, many women would be without husbands and without children. The population would have declined, and the results would have been disastrous for the village and the society as a whole.

The Turkish Republic outlawed polygamy in 1925. With the end of the centuries of constant warfare, the social need for polygamy was over. That was not the reason it was abandoned. The leaders of the new Turkey rightly felt that polygamy was not modern and European. More important, it was argued quite correctly that polygamy denied the rights of women, who were emerging as equal citizens of the Republic.

> **In the Turkish cultures of Central Asia, monogamy was the rule before coming into contact with Middle Eastern traditions.**

▷ Define polygamy.
▷ According to this reading, what were the benefits of a polygamous family?

Changing Marriage Patterns in Modern Turkey

Marriages in modern Turkey no longer consistently follow the traditional pattern. This is especially true in cities, but rural areas have changed, as well. In the new pattern, marriages are not arranged. A man and woman meet, fall in love, and marry, just as in other parts of the world. The wishes of their parents are important to them, but it is the couple that makes the decisions.

As in Europe or America, schools and colleges are common places for couples to meet. Others meet at work or in their neighborhoods. Dating varies quite a bit. Very traditional couples might get together only in the houses of members of their families or with other groups of young people, and are not often alone. University students, on the other hand, often go to dances and movies in couples and groups. Single professionals, such as lawyers, business persons, or doctors, meet members of the opposite sex for dinner and the theater. Less wealthy couples might just walk together, look at shop windows, and talk of what they will buy when one of them strikes it rich. Young men and women are often seen drinking tea in pastry shops or talking quietly together on benches in parks. In short, couples do not act much differently in Turkish cities than elsewhere in the world.

Marriage ceremonies in many villages follow traditional customs. To look at the celebrations one might think it was centuries ago. The people prefer the old ways just as many Americans prefer the type of church weddings their great-great grandparents might have had. But today's village newlyweds might be off the next day for a job in Germany, where many Turkish villagers have gone to work, or they might have both returned to their ancestral village for a traditional celebration before they return to their jobs in Ankara or Istanbul. The lives of the newlyweds may be very different than those of their grandparents, even though the marriage ceremony is the same.

For middle class couples in cities, marriages are usually not at all traditional. The legal marriage itself is usually only a short visit to the equivalent of a justice of the peace to exchange marriage vows. The real occasion is the celebration, which is held in a special "marriage hall" or a hotel. Because marriage is a great event in the lives of families, as well as in the lives of the married, families hold great parties to celebrate. All of the families' friends gather to eat, drink, and dance, often until early in the next morning. It is this celebration that is photographed, kept in family albums, and remembered.

Families throughout Turkey help their newlywed sons and daughters to set up house. Families in the cities might chip in to buy an apartment for the couple or help them with their rent. In villages, all the relatives and friends get together to build a house. If money is tight, room might be added to a village house or one room of the family apartment in the city set aside for the newly married until they can afford a home of their own. In general, families assist each other more than is common today in America. Help from fathers, mothers, sisters, brothers, aunts, and uncles is especially important when children are born. New mothers depend on help from their families. Family always seems to be available to get the kids to school or watch them so parents can go out for an evening. Grandparents often live with their children or in nearby houses or apartments, and all believe that is the correct way to treat the elderly. It is a system that blends the best of the old Turkish tradition of the extended family with new ways.

Authority within the Turkish family has changed. Like other countries, Turkey has seen a gradual evolution from male-dominated families to families in

> **Very few countries outside of Europe and America can compare with Turkey's record on women's rights.**

which authority is shared between husband and wife. The change has been easier in Turkey than in other Muslim countries because of old Turkish customs that had always stressed women's power in the home.

Throughout history, Turkish women have been known for their strength and authority over their households. Nevertheless, in the Ottoman Empire the man was legally in charge of the family. Muslim law gave men precedence over women in theory, even though the wife might in fact be the equal of the husband in a marriage. The laws of the Turkish Republic changed all that. Women became equal to men in law. They began to attend universities in large numbers and ultimately entered business and the professions. Women of all economic groups routinely worked outside the home. Political and economic power translated into real equality. Of course, no country has yet allowed women complete equality, and Turkey is behind Western Europe and North America in this regard, but great changes have been made. Very few countries outside of Europe and America can compare with Turkey's record on women's rights.

> **They [Women] began to attend universities in large numbers and ultimately entered business and the professions.**

Some groups, particularly Islamist religious groups, do protest women's new position. They are in a distinct minority in Turkey. As girls and boys see their mothers working outside the home, voting, and sharing in household authority, the idea of women's real equality spreads. It will surely continue to do so. Even Islamist political parties have highly-places female members. One can often see a women, clad in extremely modest attire, her hair completely covered by a scarf, delivering a passionate political speech for an Islamic party. In this way, some Turkish women of today hearken back to the earliest days of Islam, when the wife and daughter of Muhammad had high political place and authority.

The Turkish family is changing rapidly. Some families still follow the old traditions. Others are completely converted to new ways. The majority are in between, keeping some of the old customs and taking some of the new. As time passes, new family traditions more and more take the place of old.

> ▷ How is the modern Turkish family different than the traditional Turkish family?
> ▷ Are there benefits to continuing some of the old traditions?

Contemporary Turkey

In the nineteenth century the Ottoman government began to adopt the ways of the West. Ottoman reformers realized that if the Ottoman Empire kept its traditional system the Empire would eventually be defeated and swallowed up by the Europeans. At first, the Ottomans tried to copy only European technology and technical education. They were interested in building their economy and national strength, not in becoming like the Europeans. It soon became evident that technology alone was not enough. European strength was based on more than the presence of factories. European factories depended on European colleges for ideas. The colleges depended on the secondary and elementary schools. An economically developed nation had to be literate and dedicated to scientific knowledge. Therefore, the Ottomans began to build schools like the European schools, even sending students to Europe to study. Students in the upper schools were taught European languages.

However, European-style education was not enough. The economy improved, but the Empire still lagged far behind Europe. The relative weakness of the Ottomans ultimately meant that the Empire was defeated and dismembered in World War I. Before the war, Turkish reformers had begun to believe that the real basis of European economic superiority lay in European culture. What was needed was a whole nation dedicated to new ways, not just an educated elite that understood European technology. The reformers began to suggest political and social reform, the beginning of the path to democracy. The disaster of World War I convinced the Turks that such changes had to be made.

Under the leadership of Mustafa Kemal Atatürk, the Turks began a policy of radical Westernization and Modernization. Atatürk was a war hero whose leadership had saved Turkish independence and who had become president of the new Turkish Republic. Now he used his prestige to effect change. Schools were built all over the Republic. They taught a modified European curriculum. Laws of countries such as Italy and Switzerland were substituted for the Ottoman laws. "Peoples Houses" were set up to teach adults to read and to understand new ways. Atatürk's government even changed the clothes Turks wore, discouraging the veil for women and outlawing traditional headgear for

men. Most important, a start was made on transforming the political culture of the Turks. People's Houses and schools taught the principle of equality of all citizens in place of the idea that a ruling class deserved to rule. While he lived, Atatürk kept power firmly in his own hands, but he planned and prepared for democracy.

Like all such changes, Atatürk's reforms sometimes went slowly. Many times they were frustrated by the natural human desire to keep what is familiar and avoid change. Nevertheless, the reforms bore fruit. After World War II the Turkish Republic became a true democracy, with different parties contesting elections. Economic reform went more slowly, but in the 1950s and 1960s Turkey began to advance rapidly in that area, as well. Neither politics nor the economy always went smoothly. The army intervened when officers believed that politicians were deviating from Atatürk's path of reform. In the 1970s, civil unrest between leftists and rightists, and high inflation caused a stagnant economy. The 1980s saw a major change, however, and Turkey had the highest rate of economic growth of any country in the Middle East, North Africa, or Central Asia, despite the fact that it had little oil.

> # The 1980s saw a major change, however, and Turkey had the highest rate of economic growth of any country in the Middle East, North Africa, or Central Asia, despite the fact that it had little oil.

Perhaps, the best example of the changes in Turkish society is the status of women. Women's participation in society, politics, and the economy is a key indicator of success in development. Women's freedom is also one of the most difficult aims to achieve. The place of women in Middle Eastern societies had developed long before the Turks arrived from Central Asia. It was based on the need to protect women and children in dangerous times. The survival of the family depended on the tradition of men going off to war (and its corollary, politics) and women maintaining the family. It was a system that worked, but it was attuned neither to the needs of a modern society nor to the equality that is a necessary part of democracy.

From an early date the ideology of the Turkish Republic was committed to equality. Overcoming social and religious obstacles, polygamy was abolished in 1925. Laws were amended to offer women equal rights of divorce and inheritance, which they had not held under Islamic Law. Women voted in municipal elections in 1934. In the latter year women were also elected as deputies in the Parliament. The scope of this achievement is indicated by the fact that in the United States the 19th amendment recognizing women's right to vote was only ratified in 1920. Since 1934 women in Turkey have been politicians and members of Parliament, and they have been cabinet members since 1971. One Turkish female politician, Dr. Tansu Çiller, served both as head of her political party and as prime minister.

On the law books, women in Turkey have been equal for more than half a century. However, reality has not always matched the law. Turkey is not the only country to find women's equality a difficult goal to attain, Tradition dies hard, especially in the rural areas of Turkey, where women usually fill more traditional roles. In the work world, women have done best in professions, as is the case in Europe and the United States. They are commonly physicians and university professors. On the other hand, in commerce and industry women find it easier to enter the work force than to rise to the top. In the home, the majority of house work is still done by wives and daughters. Yet a great number of educated women actively oppose this situation. In general, improvements in the Turkish economy have been matched by improvements in the status of women.

All of this has left great variance among women's lives in modern Turkey. The life of a typical village woman is different than that of a middle class woman in the cities. The daughters of many urban families dress in clothes that might be seen in Paris, Rome, or London. Some families have followed an Islamic revival (most have not) and women in these families are relatively secluded. Economic need has forced women to work outside the home when they and their spouses would rather they did not. Some politically active women call for a return to traditional values. Although Turkish society is generally more conservative than Western European or American society, descriptions of women's position and women's problems are remarkably similar.

The Era After Atatürk: an Example of a State "Coming of Age?"

In this lesson, we will attempt to look at some of the transition steps taken in Turkey after the strong leadership of Atatürk disappeared. Turkey maintains it is a democracy but, at the same time, it also states it suffers from the excesses of democracy and those attendant problems.

Performance Objectives

Students will be able to:
1. List the achievements of Turkish democracy after Atatürk.
2. Determine the degree to which these changes forwarded the course of democracy in Turkey.
3. Evaluate Turkey and the Turkish achievements in nation-building in the second half of the 20th century.

Springboard

Pretend you have been appointed an Ambassador to a newly "emerging" nation and your job is to assist the people of this country with democracy-building.
- What suggestions would you make to them?
- How would you prioritize those suggestions?
- What mechanism would you establish to determine if you are successful.

Teacher will poll the class and establish a chart culled from the student responses. Examples should include:
(a) voter turnout
(b) political parties
(c) access and equality, etc.

Procedure:

▷ Distribute **Worksheet 1**: *Democracy — Successes and Problems*
Students will work in pairs to determine if Turkey's democratic processes are in line with the chart the students have developed.
- Where are they the same?
- Where are they different?
- What is the role of the military in Turkey? How do you feel about this in a democratic country? Give examples to prove your position.
- The reading states that Turkey suffers from "an excess of democracy." Do you agree or disagree with that statement? Give examples.

▶ One of the major concerns for Turkey in the last half of the 20th century was economic. It was important that a new economic course be established.

▷ Distribute **Worksheet 2**: *Bringing Turkey into the World Economy*
Students will read this aloud with the teacher and cite each example taken by the Turkish government to make the Turkish economy viable in the world economy. Teacher will list these on the chalkboard.
- How would you assess the role of the government in changing the economic face of Turkey?
- How successful has Turkey been?

Students will be assigned research projects to examine the role of the Turkish economy internally and on the world scene.

Summary Let's return to your role as Ambassador. You have now been recalled to the United States but before you leave you wish to develop a report for your successor on Turkish democracy and the Turkish economy.

For Homework Students will review their material and their readings and determine the effectiveness of the Turkish government in nation-building. These reports will be used for the lesson on the following day.

The Grand National Assembly Building, where the Turkish Parliament meets.

Democracy:
Successes and Problems

ATATÜRK DIED IN 1938. HE WAS SUCCEEDED AS PRESIDENT BY İSMET İNÖNÜ. İNÖNÜ TRANS-LATED ATATÜRK'S POLICY OF EDUCATING AND planning for democracy into reality. As president of a country that had accepted one-party rule, İsmet İnönü could easily have retained all rule in his own hands. Instead, he accepted and encouraged opposition within his own party and in new parties. By no means was İnönü's toleration of dissent accepted by all in the Republican People's Party. It was difficult to relinquish power. President İnönü's personal prestige and authority were essential if democracy was to succeed.

In 1946 the first strong op-position party was formed, the Democrat Party. It won the elections of 1950, defeating Atatürk's and İnönü's party. From that point on, democracy has been the rule in Turkey, but there have been difficulties. The Democrat Party's victory in 1950 reflected the people's desire for change. The Turkish population had tired of deprivation during World War II, which was somewhat unjustly blamed on the ruling party. Businessmen opposed burdensome regulations and an entrenched bureaucracy. The Democrat Party promised a liberalized economy and an improved standard of living, both of which it provided, at first, once in power.

The government of the Democrat Party demonstrated the growing pains of a new democracy. Its leaders, President Celâl Bayar and Prime Minister Adnan Menderes, had been members of the Republican People's party, Menderes as a parliamentary deputy and Bayar as Atatürk's last prime minister. They had not completely abandoned the political traditions in which they had been schooled. Like the previous government, the Democrat Party government began to lose support because of the economy. After the Democrats won a second election in 1954, economic growth diminished

> **Military interventions in government have not been unusual in history. What is atypical in Turkey is the military's actual dedication to civilian rule.**

and inflation increased. Inflation especially hurt civil servants, teachers, the military, and others who were on fixed incomes. The response of the Menderes government was repression of the very liberal ideas that had brought it to power: Censorship of the press was increased. Bureaucrats were brought under tight political control. Price controls were instituted. Even though it had engaged in some vote-rigging, the Democrat Party lost much support in elections held in 1957, losing its majority in parliament, although, as largest party, it still led the government. Political conditions worsened. Student protestors were suppressed. Meetings of the Republican People's Party were hindered, and even the much respected İnönü was harassed.

On May 27, 1950, a committee of military officers (the National Unity Committee) overthrew the Menderes government in a bloodless coup. Some members of the Committee wished to institute what would have been a military government, but they were silenced. The Committee instead caused a new constitution to be written, held a referendum on its acceptance, and held elections for a civilian government in October, 1951.

The leaders of the 1950 coup asserted a standard of military intervention in government that was to become part of Turkish politics. The military never stated that it had a right or duty to rule, but it did identify itself as a defender of Atatürk's principles and what it believed was proper democrat government. Briefly put, the military believed that when politicians ruled improperly the military should step in to return to proper democratic government. Military interventions in government have not been unusual in history. What is atypical in Turkey is the military's actual dedication to civilian rule. The military was to intervene again in Turkish politics in 1980, when it reacted to virtual civil war between leftists and rightists and domestic terrorism, exacerbated by economic collapse. Once again, a new constitution was drawn up and government returned to civilians. In 1974, the chiefs of the military had demanded that a nonpartisan government of "technicians" be installed to reform the state, although they staged no coup. The chiefs intervened again in 1997 with a warning that the coalition government led by the Islamist[1] party of Necmettin Erbakan (which had won 21% of the vote) was straying from Turkey's and Atatürk's principles of secularism. In reaction, the parliament created a new coalition without the Islamic party. The military remains powerful in Turkish government.

To a large extent, the power of the military in Turkey has been based on popular respect, not only their armed might. In opinion polls, three-fourths of the Turks routinely stated that they had more respect for and confidence in the military than in politicians. For Turks who feel the military, never elected, has no place in politics, and for Europeans who, it must be said, often have little understanding of conditions in Turkey, any place of the military in politics is always unacceptable. No one can doubt that the experience of military governments in most countries has been negative, nor that in a democracy those who are elected should hold ultimate power. Other Turks think that such beliefs are utopian, that democracy is never perfect and the military has generally acted with democratic principles in mind. Many support the military as a bulwark against the possibility that an Islamic political party might someday take power and change the Turkish state into an Islamic government. Still others feel that this could never happen, that a majority of the Turks would never accept an Islamic state, that they only wish to gain more religious expression in politics. The debate will surely continue.

> Like some European countries, such as Italy, Turkey has a large number of political parties and an electoral system that encourages political diversity.

In some ways, Turkey's politics have suffered from an excess of democracy. Unlike the system in the United States, the electoral system has been designed to reflect the varying shades of political opinion in Turkey. Like some European countries, such as Italy, Turkey has a large number of political parties and an electoral system that encourages political diversity. Voters are able to choose among many alternatives, and do so. The result is many different parties in parliament and coalition governments. It is often difficult for the parties to agree on a national agenda. For example, 8 parties gained votes in the 1999 Turkish general election. Of these, 5 parties each took more than 10% of the vote, the percentage needed to take seats in parliament. The vote was fairly evenly split. It therefore took a coalition of three parties of very different political ideologies to form a government. A prime minister can be selected without any political mandate in such a system. This occurred in Turkey in 1996, when the Islamist-oriented Welfare (Refah) Party assumed the prime ministry, even though it had earned only 21% percent of the vote (the most ever gained by an Islamist Party.)[2] Ironically, even the most democratic system can lead to results that do not represent the will of the people.

Democracy has been the rule in modern Turkey. There have been difficulties: Politics have never been stable; there have been 57 governments in the Turkish Republic. An armed Kurdish separatist movement disrupted civil order in Southeastern Anatolia. Turkey has also seen conflicts between radical leftists and radical rightists, both of which wished to take power, neither of which succeeded. The Turkish political achievement is best understood in context: In the years since 1950, in the whole of Eastern Europe, the Middle East, and North Africa, the only country with more years of democratically elected government than Turkey is Israel.

---

[1] "Islamist" is used here to denote those who feel that Islam should have an important place in government and society. Islamists generally oppose a strict separation of religion and state, which in Turkey usually means they oppose Atatürk's secularism. Islamists do not agree, however, on all political and social matters. They range from those who wish to see Islamic morality applied to public life to those who wish to see Islamic Law made the Law of the Land. The term "fundamentalist," often applied to this group, is at best a misleading reference from Christianity.

[2] A new moderate Islamist party, the Ak ("white") Party, was elected in November of 2002.

Bringing Turkey into the World Economy

Turgut Özal, who led Turkey first as prime minister and later as president, brought about changes second only to those of Atatürk. His party, the Motherland Party (Anavatan Partisi), was the first to come to power after the 1980 military coup. Özal was a technocrat who had worked in the World Bank and private industry before returning to government. He had campaigned on a policy of liberalized economy and openness to world markets.

Turkey's economic policy, set first by Atatürk, had been called "statism." It was a mixture of socialism and protectionism, created in reaction to the Great Depression of the 1930s. Most basic industries were in the hands of the state — mines, steel mills, the largest textile producers, railroads, the telephone and telegraph system, and other industries. In addition, domestic industries were protected from foreign competition by high customs duties. Goods imported from other countries could easily double in price and importers faced a host of bureaucratic rules that made it difficult to import. Even if a buyer was willing to pay twice as much as the goods cost, he found it very difficult to import them.

Government ownership and protectionism were by no means unique to Turkey. Major industries had been nationalized all over Western Europe. Of course, the Communist countries had almost completely socialist systems. In the Depression, the United States and European countries had led the way with protectionist tariffs. European consumers were denied Turkish goods just as surely as Turks were denied European manufactures. By the time Özal took power, however, these practices were being disowned by the Europeans. Led by Britain, nations began slowly to dismantle government ownership of industry. Western Europe created the Common Market (later the European Union), which cut tariffs and encouraged trade. World leaders created the General Agreement on Trade and Tariffs (GATT) to stimulate trade between countries. They had decided that trade and private ownership would lead to enrichment of their countries. While this was not always the case for less developed nations, it definitely proved to be the case for the Europeans.

Özal set Turkey firmly on the European path.
Turkey's currency had been protected by an artificially high exchange rate that made Turkish goods more expensive overseas. Özal's government began the transition to a completely exchangeable currency (completed in 1990), one in which the value of the Turkish Lira was set by the world market. To support the government, he adopted the European system of Value Added Tax.[2] Customs duties were greatly reduced and free trade agreements negotiated with other countries. Imports began to arrive in great number in Turkey. Exports also grew rapidly. The government began a policy of favoring "export-oriented" industries. Export industries were subsidized and excused from paying customs duties on goods needed for exporting industries. Bureaucratic hurdles were greatly lessened. Tourism was also favored. Modern hotels began to spring up, especially along Turkey's Mediterranean coast and in Istanbul. Both exports and tourism brought in foreign currency, which in turn made it possible to buy foreign goods.

Privatization of government industries, which was a key part of European economic reform, was not very successful in Turkey. Investors simply did not want to buy the old-fashioned government companies. Instead, the government ended the monopolies that had kept the government industries in business. Private companies soon began to produce everything from beer to textiles. Investor-owned airlines carried Turks across the country. Where before there had been only state television, Turks now watched multiple independent stations.

---

[2] A tax levied at each stage of production. Income tax, which was often avoided by those who could do so, was not a sufficient source of income for the Turkish Government.

Like any radical change, the Özal reforms had a negative side. As business improved and great amounts of money were made by entrepreneurs, the gap between the rich and the poor grew. Devaluation of the currency led to constant inflation, which savaged the salaries of those on fixed incomes. The presence of new money inevitably led to in increase in political corruption as businessmen bribed government officials for favors and political parties increasingly became dependent on donations. Lack of effective oversight of the financial industry led to first the creation of banks that were poorly-run or, worse, illegally diverted funds to their owners. (In the late 1990s, during an economic crisis, these banks failed at a great rate.) The danger increased of citizens who felt the state was not theirs, but the property of the rich. This has not been unknown in other countries.

Despite such problems, the Özal years were resounding economic successes for Turkey. The gross domestic product rose by an average of more than 5% a year. Exports increased five-fold. When the Özal Government began its reforms Turkey primarily exported agricultural goods, but by 1990 three-fourths of Turkey's exports were industrial goods.

The Özal government revived Turkey's long moribund application to become a member of the European Union. This was the beginning of a long process, but it showed Turkey's commitment to become part of Europe and the West. Turkey had altered the economic policies of Atatürk to meet a new age, but it had kept his commitment to acceptance as a European state.

Istanbul Stock Exchange

Turkey in the 21st Century:
An Analysis of Domestic Issues

Performance Objectives

Students will be able to:
1. Survey the current state of affairs for Turks at home and abroad.
2. Assess the successes, failures and challenges which confront Turkey today.
3. Develop a "plan of operation" to assist Turkey move forward at home and abroad.

Springboard

We have all watched TV programs like *The West Wing* as well as followed the course of Presidential elections and the development of party platforms and party strategy to meet the complex problems that face both pre- and post-industrial nations. The leader of the nation needs to be very well informed about multiple issues. This "briefing" is accomplished through a group of experts.

For the next few days, the class is going to take on the role of researchers, specialists and advisors for the President of Turkey. They have been given the task of determining what has been accomplished in the Turkish Republic, what problems still face the nation and what action plans can be developed to help the state grow.

Procedure

▷ The teachers will divide the class into at least 15 groups. Some of the groups will deal with **domestic issues**; other groups will focus on **international issues.**
   ◆ Each group will be a **special interest group** and they will be given the task of doing some in-depth research on a topic (either foreign or domestic).
   ◆ The group will prepare a preliminary report for the President.
   ◆ After presenting the first report, the group will write an "action plan" to help Turkey move ahead.

We have provided you with worksheets which deal with both foreign and domestic concerns. **These are not all the possible topics.** There is little about Turkish education (both compulsory and higher education), youth culture, and other significant issues. Students will decide which groups they want to join and then commence to read the assigned material, **do additional research both online and in print** (good online sources can be found in the Web Sites listing in the appendix as well as through *google.com* or *askjeeves.com.*

Day 1: Student groups will form and begin the research process after the teacher has spoken with the class.

Day 2: Student groups will develop first draft of paper for President and other advisors.

Day 3: Students will meet as a group with the President and present the first draft of their report.

Evaluation ▷ The teacher will reassemble the class. Each group will be asked to re-form quickly and, based upon the reports presented to the whole body and other gathered information, the groups will the develop a Five Step Action Plan. Each plan will be written on poster paper and hung around the room. Class will then respond to these plans, determining the feasibility of the plan, etc. Class will then assess Turkey today.

Tourism is an important industry for modern Turkey. With its wealth of history, monuments, cruisine, coastlines and sunshine, it is a favorite vacation destination for many Americans, as well as for Europeans.

International Concerns:
The Turkish Republic and the West

AFTER WORLD WAR II TURKEY CONTINUED THE ALIGNMENT WITH THE WEST THAT HAD BEGUN A CENTURY BEFORE. WHILE COMMITTED to Western values, Atatürk had favored neutralism, a policy dictated by the need to recover from the wounds of World War I and fear of the dominant ideologies in Eastern Europe in the 1930s, fascism and communism. Both fascism and communism tried to lure Turkey into its camp. However, after World War II the situation had altered. Stalin and Russian Communism were supreme in Eastern Europe. Turkey opposed them and allied with the United States. It fought alongside America in the Korean War. Turkey joined as a full member of NATO in 1952 and remains a military ally of the United States and Western Europe. It has been an important ally of the United States and Western Europe in both Desert Storm and Afghanistan.

Economically, Turkey has turned to market capitalism. It has allied itself with the West economically as well as politically and militarily. Atatürk had experimented with state ownership of major industries, with mixed results, but beginning in the 1950s the private sector became increasingly dominant. This was particularly true in the 1980s and 1990s, as trade and industrial policies were liberalized. Economic difficulties surely continued. Labor was restive, the East of Turkey developed much more slowly than the West, rapid population growth strained resources, and inflation and other difficulties remain. Nevertheless, in the 1980s and 1990s the Turkish economy was among the fastest growing in the world. (Gross National Product rose an average of over 5% a year in the 1980s.) In the 1990s Turkey continued its economic opening to the West: The national currency, the Turkish Lira, became completely convertible with other currencies. Taxes were changed to conform to European models. Free trade in most commodities and industries began with the European Union countries. Indeed, Turkey became one of the foremost champions of free trade.

As they received European television, radio, and movies, the Turks began to adopt many aspects of European culture. A walk down the shopping streets of Ankara or Istanbul revealed Turks who dressed like Europeans and bought and sold European-style goods. Some of these were imported, but many were made in Turkey. Bookstores sold European and American books to a public eager to be part of the European intellectual tradition. Schools teaching English sprang up all over the country, as did universities that used English as the medium of instruction. Great numbers of European tourists brought their culture with them to Turkey. The tourists also saw the changes in Turkey; they felt at home. Admittedly, not all of Turkey changed quickly. Villages and smaller towns changed more slowly than major cities. Nevertheless, an unstoppable Europeanization was advancing. The Turks did not abandon their own cultural traditions. They adapted them to coexist with European ways, just as had all the other countries of Europe.

The opening to Europe begun by Mustafa Kemal Atatürk has obviously been a success.

> **Turkey joined as a full member of NATO in 1952 and remains a military ally of the United States and Western Europe.**

International Concerns:
Turkey at the Crossroads

THE TURKS ARE BEST KNOWN AS ALLIES OF THE UNITED STATES. THEY HAVE BEEN PARTNERS IN NATO, FOUGHT ALONGSIDE AMERICANS IN Korea, and were allied with America in the Gulf War. While this is important, it represents little of the history and life of the Turks. There is much more to the Turks than their friendship with America.

The greatest success of the Turks, their history as administrators, has been little appreciated in the West. For six hundred years the Ottoman Empire ruled successfully over a great land, an imperial record that can stand with that of the Romans. The Ottomans created an empire of unique toleration, where many peoples and religions kept their own traditions at a time when religious persecution was the rule elsewhere. It was an empire of laws, held together by rules as much as by the personality of the sultan. It is no accident that the great sultan Süleyman, known to the West as The Magnificent, was known to the Turks as The Lawgiver, a sign of his, and the Empire's true success.

If the achievements of the Turks in politics and law are little known in America, those in the humanities are even less so. Yet Turkish music, art, architecture, and poetry were their crowning glories. Coming as they do from a different cultural tradition, the beauty of Turkish poetry may only be fully appreciated in Turkish and Turkish classical music may not perfectly match what is expected by Western ears, but the beauty of Turkish art can easily be seen. The grace of Turkish calligraphy, the colors of Turkish miniature paintings, and the geometric forms of Turkish porcelain tiles are known to be high art by anyone who has seen them. The great mosques of Istanbul, especially Sinan's Süleymaniye Mosque, rival any buildings in the World.

> For six hundred years the Ottoman Empire ruled successfully over a great land, an imperial record that can stand with that of the Romans.

The accomplishments of Modern Turkey have been in a different context. The task of the modern Turks was to create a democratic, independent society. In a time of imperialism, Turkey was one of the few nations to keep its independence, despite great odds against it. Turkey was almost unique outside of Western Europe and North America in its sustained drive to gain democracy. First noted under Mustafa Kemal Atatürk for its campaign to educate and develop its people to live in the modern world, Turkey now is an economic success and a multi-party democracy. It is one of the few countries of its region that have significantly raised itself up economically, without oil revenues to depend on. Much remains to be done, but the success is notable.

Today, Turkey is a bridge between the Middle East and the West, as well as a bridge between the West and the newly freed lands of Central Asia. It is a state whose people are overwhelmingly Muslim, yet also a state that is thoroughly secular in its laws and government. The great tradition of Islam is not forgotten, nor is the tradition of western philosophy, government, and technology.

The success of Turkey is all the more remarkable because, as has been said, "Turkey is in a rough neighborhood." Those who justifiably bring up Turkey's failings must also look to what Turkey might have been —- a dictatorial state like some of its neighbors, a religious state turning its back on the West, like others, or a state that adopted Communism and its economic defeats. The Turkish experiment in democracy has sometimes been interrupted and its economic development has not been perfect. Nonetheless, Turkey has been the envy of those who can only wish their nations had taken the same path.

International Issues:
Turkey and the War on Terrorism

F EW COUNTRIES SUFFERED AS MUCH FROM TER-
RORISM AS MODERN TURKEY. TERRORISTS STRUCK
AT TURKISH TARGETS BOTH OUTSIDE AND WITHIN
Turkey's borders.

Armenian terrorists who aimed to create an Armenian state in Eastern Turkey began to attack Turkish targets in the 1970s. Their aim was to draw world
attention to their cause. The most dangerous of the
groups was ASALA ("Armenian
Secret Army for the Liberation of
Armenia," formed in 1975). Its overall philosophy was both Marxist and
nationalistic. ASALA was part of the
international terrorist network of
the 1970s and 1980s, cooperating
most famously with the Abu Nidal
faction. It looked favorably on the
Communist Block and particularly
on the Communist government in
the Armenian SSR. Its headquarters were initially in
Beirut and later in Syria, which supported ASALA as
a way to put political pressure on Turkey. Political elements in Greece also supported ASALA for the same
reason.

ASALA first appeared in world news with an
attack on the World Council of Churches office in
Beirut, but its main terrorist efforts were directed at
Turkish diplomats and Turkish offices in Europe. It's
worst single attack was the bombing of the counter of
Turkish Airlines at Orly Airport in Paris in 1983. Eight
were killed and 55 wounded. Other offices of Turkish
Airlines were bombed as well. Swiss and French objectives were also attacked to force those governments to
release imprisoned members of the organization.

Many other Armenian terrorist organizations were
founded in the 1980s. Some of these were splinter organizations from ASALA. The most active of the other
organizations, however, was the JCAG ("Justice Com-
mandos for the Armenian Genocide," also called the
"Armenian Revolutionary Army.") JCAG was the military wing of the Dashnak Party, a long-standing Ar-

menian political organization. It has been thought that
JCAG was founded as an outlet for Armenian terrorism that did not threaten traditional Armenian politics.
Unlike ASALA, it did not have a Marxist doctrine and
did not declare that its aim was to revolutionize Armenian politics as well as threaten Turkey. It is thought to
have been established in 1984 in Los Angeles. In addition to foreign targets, JCAG attacked Turkish targets
within the United States, in Califor-
nia and Boston, both centers of large
Armenian communities.

From 1973 to 1994, 36 Turkish
diplomats or their wives were assassinated by Armenian terrorists.
Armenian terrorists also engaged in
car bombings, taking hostages, and
bombing or burning Turkish tourism, and commercial offices.

The ASALA terrorists were
never a threat to the internal security of the Turkish
Republic. Attacks by Kurdish separatists in the East of
Turkey was a grave threat to the security of the Southeast of Turkey.

The PKK ("Kurdistan Workers' Party") was formed in
1978 by Abdullah Öcalan. It began a terrorist onslaught
against Turkey in 1984, intending to create a Marxist
Kurdish state. The PKK conducted a particularly gruesome war of intimidation against all those who might
oppose its program. Its victims included thousands of
ethnic Kurds, as well as ethnic Turks. Particular targets
were those who stood for the authority of the state, a
group that included policemen and government officials, but also teachers. "Village Guards," Kurds who
were charged with defending their villages, and their
families, were particular targets. Villages populated
by Turkish peasants who lived in areas claimed by the
PKK were destroyed, as were Kurdish villages that too
obviously supported the government.

The PKK aimed at the infrastructure of the provinces of southeastern Turkey to induce economic collapse of the region. They destroyed businesses, bridges,

> **Few countries suffered as much from terrorism as modern Turkey.**

highways, and communications lines. With these terrorist activities came a political campaign, aimed at the sentiments of Kurds who felt the Turkish Republic had tried to suppress their ethnic identity (see **Worksheet 5**). However, the PKK made enemies of Kurds, as well, through their tactics and advocacy of Marxist revolution. The Kurdish political organizations of Northern Iraq were among those enemies.

The PKK also carried out a program of attacks on Turkish establishments in Europe, especially Germany. In Turkey, but outside of the Kurdish region, the PKK attacked trains, buses, and boats. Foreign tourists were abducted in southeastern Anatolia. In short, the PKK attempted to disrupt Turkey in every possible way.

The Turkish military eventually defeated the PKK. Thousands died; many more suffered. For security reasons, the army relocated villagers from rebel-infested regions. It was a dangerous and vicious war. Civil liberties suffered, as is always the case in guerilla wars.

Few countries aided Turkey in its fight against the PKK, although the United States did identify the PKK as one of the 30 main terrorist organizations in 1997. Syria provided the main support for the PKK, assisted by Greece. As they did with ASALA, these two countries used their support of the PKK to bring political pressure on Turkey. Syria finally renounced its support only in 1998, when the Turks threatened war if support of the rebels continued. Deprived of his base, Öcalan, the PKK leader, was eventually captured by Turkey. His final journeys illustrate international cooperation in terrorism. Öcalan fled from Damascus, Syria in October, 1998 for Moscow. He left Moscow in November for Rome, where the Italians refused to hold him. His next haven was the Greek Embassy in Nairobi, Kenya. Turkish agents, reportedly aided by Israeli Intelligence and the CIA, captured him in Nairobi in February, 1999.

Turkey effectively defeated the PKK at a great price. The government counted 4,630 civilians, 5,314 soldiers and police (including 1,200 village guards), and 340 officials (including 7 city mayors, 105 village mayors, and 111 teachers) killed by the PKK. The number of PKK followers who died is unknown.

> **Turkey... was one of the first nations to offer support to the United States in its War on Terrorism. It was one of the few nations to join the United States and Britain in the eradication of the al-Qaeda terrorists in Afghanistan.**

From its own experience, Turks knew that terrorism must be combated, even if the terrorists' targets were not Turks. The members of ASALA who killed Turkish diplomats may have been Armenians, but they were part of a worldwide terrorist network, seemingly separate organizations that supported each other and trained each other's members in terrorist tactics. ASALA and the PKK had cooperated with each other and with other terrorist organizations against Turkey. The anti-Turkish terrorists were supported by governments of other states. All the bases of terrorism — international terrorist organizations, support from governments, and the terrorists — had to be opposed and defeated. Turkey, therefore, was one of the first nations to offer support to the United States in its War on Terrorism. It was one of the few nations to join the United States and Britain in the eradication of the al-Qaeda terrorists in Afghanistan. On June 20, 2002, Turkey assumed command of the international security force in Afghanistan, sending 1,400 soldiers to Afghanistan as part of the allied effort there. As NATO's only Muslim member, Turkey's participation was an effective sign that the U.S. and its allies were making war on terrorism, not on Islam.

International Concerns:
The Turks in Europe

In 1961, Turkey signed an agreement with what was then West Germany to facilitate German hiring of **GASTARBEITER** (literally "guest workers") to work in Germany. While some of these Turkish workers were skilled craftsmen, most took up low-paying jobs that Germans did not wish to do. These workers were not allowed to become German citizens, but usually attained "permanent resident" status. By 1970 there were nearly 500,000 gastarbeiter, by 1975 more than 800,000. Most of the Turks had been recruited in villages and from recent migrants from villages to Turkish cities by German firms. They arrived willing to work, but with a different culture and religion than German citizens.

Economically, the experiment in mass migration was a success for both Germany and Turkey. The German economy soon depended on the work of the Turks. Turkey gained some release from population pressure. Those who returned from Germany also brought with them skills that were needed in their homeland. Most important, Turks in Germany sent home money. Their remittances made villages richer and helped balance the foreign exchange deficits that resulted from Turkish imports of Western goods.

The social situation of the Turks in Germany was not so successful. At first, the Turkish workers had been young males. The Germans expected them to work, then return to Turkey. Instead they stayed and brought their families. Germany soon had a large Turkish minority. Because of German law, the Turks could never become integrated into the political life of the country. Very few were able to become German. Due to the wishes of the Turks, themselves, and German cultural prejudices, the Turks as a group also did not become socially integrated into German life. Turkish

> **[In Germany] anti-Turkish prejudice became widespread... Turks who migrated to other countries have experienced fewer problems.**

newspapers, mosques, and restaurants became a prominent feature of German cities, a fact that had a negative effect on German nationalists. All the arguments always seen whenever there is immigration surfaced: The Turks were supposedly taking German jobs. They supposedly could not ever understand German political and social life. The Turks were "different," which was not considered a good thing. A small number of radicals carried their antipathy farther and attacked Turks, killing some. Most Germans would have nothing to do with this sort of reaction, but anti-Turkish prejudice became widespread.

While the second generation of Turks, born in Germany, learned to speak German fluently and adopted much of German culture, they were seldom able to become German citizens, which embittered many. The Turks, too, were not willing to become completely German. They wished to retain Turkish citizenship while adopting German citizenship. In recent years it has become possible for increasing numbers of young Turks to take German citizenship, but a large majority have not been able to do so. Many German politicians, especially those of the Left, have tried to change the laws, with only limited success.

Turks who migrated to other countries have experienced fewer problems. Those who came to the United States and some European countries, such as the Netherlands, were mainly skilled professionals, not manual laborers recruited in villages. They arrived in their new lands with the skills necessary to integrate into European and American society. The culture of the richer and better trained, after all, was essentially European. They spoke European languages, especially English, and had largely been culturally European even before they left Turkey. This gives hope for the future of the Turks in

Germany, as well. If the laws allow political integration, the new generation of Turks raised in Germany will naturally share in German politics and culture. German prejudices against local Turks should subside. An analogy can be drawn to the Irish in America. They too arrived without education or the social skills of their new land. Nevertheless, they were allowed to become part of American political life, which led to their integration into American society. Once strong anti-Irish prejudices in America are now only a memory.

Turkish Landscapes

International Concerns:
Turkey and NATO and the European Union

In 1946, buoyed by its victory in World War II, the Soviet Union demanded concessions from Turkey that would ultimately have made it a satellite of the USSR, like so many other once independent states. The Soviets demanded that Turkey give them part of Northeastern Anatolia, an area that not coincidentally held the best natural defenses for Anatolia. Turkey was also to accept Soviet military forces in bases near Istanbul "to protect the Black Sea." It was obvious that this was only the beginning of the Soviet plan.

Throughout Atatürk's time, Turkey had prized its neutrality. It now could no longer be neutral. Following its traditions of looking to the West, Turkey looked to the leading state of the West, America. The United States guaranteed its support, and Turkey refused the Russian demands. In 1947, President Truman asked Congress for military and economic support for Turkey and other countries threatened by the Soviets. It was the beginning of an alliance that has remained in place.

> **On February 18, 1952, Turkey joined NATO as a full and enthusiastic partner.**

The alliance between Turkey and the United States was to be beneficial to both. Turkey provided its large army, now modernized with American weapons, and a geographic position that would threaten the Soviets if they attacked in Europe. Having Turkey in the Western camp also insured that the Soviets would not easily attack south toward the oil riches of Iraq, Iran, and the Gulf. Turkey gained military and economic assistance. Turkish politicians also began to change their political structure so that it became a democracy like that of its allies. Most important, Turkey retained its independence.

In 1950, Turkey applied for membership in the newly-founded North Atlantic Treaty Organization. Some European members of the alliance found it hard to accept a country that was only then making its tentative steps toward real democracy. There was also more than a bit of prejudice against a Muslim country entering a European club. Turkey's entrance into the Korean War changed any European objections, however. The Turks fought well, sending 25,000 soldiers to Korea, and showed their commitment to the anti-Soviet alliance. On February 18, 1952, Turkey joined NATO as a full and enthusiastic partner.

Turkey became an associate member of the European Economic Community, the predecessor of the European Union (EU), in 1959, with the understanding that Turkey would eventually progress to full membership in the European Community. Turkey's status remained the same for the next four decades. even as other associate members attained full membership. Only in the 1990s was there real change in Turkish relations with the EU. Turkey joined in a customs union with the EU in 1996 and began to integrate its customs duties into the Union's system of tariffs. Then, after three years of refusal to consider Turkey as a candidate, the EU finally decided in 1999 to accept Turkey's candidacy for membership.

While Turkey has become a candidate, it is last in line among 13 candidate states, including many of the ex-Communist states of Eastern Europe. While awaiting accession to the Union, Turkey must adjust its laws and economy to those of the EU, a process of radical change that is to be carried out rapidly. Some members of the EU would be pleased if Turkey went slowly with reforms, and thus delayed the need for a decision on accepting Turkey into the Union, but successive Turkish governments and most political parties have committed themselves to make the changes that will allow rapid accession.

Conforming to the rules of the European Union is a daunting task. There are thousands of pages of EU regulations covering economic, political, and even social life. Particular problems arise over the status of ethnic minorities, the place of the military in government, and the situation in Cyprus. Other points, such as human rights, press freedom, and legal structure, can be addressed. The Turkish parliament has acted to alter Turkish law to EU standards. The issues of the military's place in politics and the Kurdish population are less tractable. Nevertheless, significant progress has been made in altering the Turkish legal and political structure. In 2001, 34 amendments to the Turkish Constitution were passed by Parliament in order to bring Turkish law and practice closer to the EU system. Alterations in courts judicial procedures were made. Although the changes are not all that the EU desires, they are the greatest changes in Turkish law since the days of Atatürk.

> In 2001, 34 amendments to the Turkish Constitution were passed by Parliament in order to bring Turkish law and practice closer to the EU system.

The demands of the European Union have caused resentment, especially among nationalist circles. Turks have a long tradition of retaining their independence in the face of European attempts on their sovereignty. Nevertheless, many of the new laws passed at the behest of the EU have improved civil liberties and the governmental system in Turkey. Freedom of expression, gender equality, equality before the law, and other human rights have been substantially improved in law. Business law, open markets, customs regulations, and consumer protection have improved, as well.

The question is what will happen in the future. Turkey will have greatly changed its political and economic system in order to join the EU. What will be the result if, despite Turkey's efforts, the EU will not accept Turkey? There is good reason to fear this. Some politicians in Europe have openly stated that there is no place for a Muslim country in the EU. Many Europeans fear the mass Turkish migration that they believe will follow the implementation of the Union's "open borders" policy. The counter argument that an improvement in the Turkish economy after joining the EU will keep more Turks at home, as it has done, for example, in Ireland, can fall on deaf ears. Those who wish to block Turkeys entrance will have ammunition, because, in the short time available, Turkey will never be able in to completely adjust itself to Western European governmental and economic practices. If Turkey is spurned by the European Union, will it cause a radical change in the Turkish attitude toward the West? For many decades, Turkey has oriented itself toward the West, both economically and politically, but it could place itself in alliance with Islamist forces, such as Iran, or with a resurgent Russia.

The good news is that many Europeans can see the danger of turning Europe's back on Turkey. Even if Turkey will never be the same as Sweden or Holland, it is still too important geopolitically to abandon. Moreover, it can be readily seen that Turks are indeed Europeans, more so with each passing year. The rational argument for keeping Turkey within Europe may win the day.

Domestic Concerns:
Population Issues

TWENTY-FIVE YEARS AGO, POPULATION GROWTH IN TURKEY SEEMED A CAUSE FOR DESPAIR. WHILE IMPROVED HEALTH SERVICES HAD significantly improved the life-span of Turks, birth rates had remained high. The population was growing at a rate of more than 2% per year. On average, women who lived through their child-bearing years were giving birth to six children. At that rate, the Turkish population would have reached 87 million by 2010. By 2050 there would have been 210 million Turks.

Of course, the population would never have reached 210 million. Long before that date the immense number of people in Turkey would have overwhelmed the ability of the country to provide food, housing, and medicine. Disease, and perhaps starvation and civil conflict, would have reduced the population. That seemed to be the inevitable outcome of a high birth rate.

In the 1980s, the situation began to change. Government had long provided birth control information, but that could not have explained such a sudden change. Birth control methods and information had been widely available for more than twenty years, with only small effect on population growth. Many explanations have been advanced to explain the change,

TURKISH POPULATION GROWTH			
Year	Population (thousands)	Period	Growth Rate
1950	21,122	1950-1960	2.9
1960	28,217	1960-1970	2.4
1970	35,758	1970-1980	2.3
1980	45,121	1980-1990	2.2
1990	56,085	1990-2000	1.6
1991	57,135	2000-2010	1.1
1992	58,179	2010-2020	0.8
1993	59,213	2020-2030	0.6
1994	60,221	2030-2040	0.3
1995	61,189	2040-2050	0.0
1996	62,128		
1997	63,048		
1998	63,946		
1999	64,820		
2000	65,667		

including more effective government programs, better education of women, even the effect of television, which showed different life styles to those who had never before appreciated the benefits of change. Perhaps the most compelling reason for the change was economics. It had previously been beneficial for a family to have more children. On a traditional farm, more children meant more hands to work and more contributors to support one in his or her old age. Mechanization on the farm and migration to the cities to work in shops and factories changed all that. It was no longer economically beneficial to feed children who were not needed on the farm and who might not find work in the city. Rational people adjusted their fertility to match economic reality.

Whatever the reason for the change, almost all agree that greatly lowered birth rates are a good thing. They do not mean, however, that Turkey's population problems are over. The country must still cope with the effects of the high fertility of the past.

The Past Lives On

The first age pyramids[1] show the population of Turkey by age groups in 2000 and 2025. An age pyramid for 1970 would have shown a much greater percentage

---

[1] The age pyramids show the numbers of people by 5-year age groups.

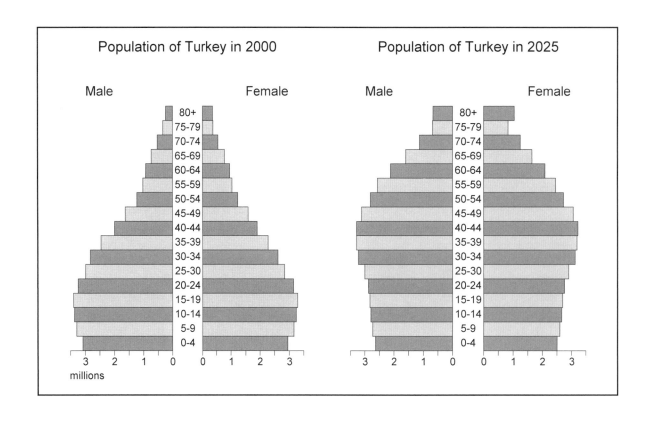

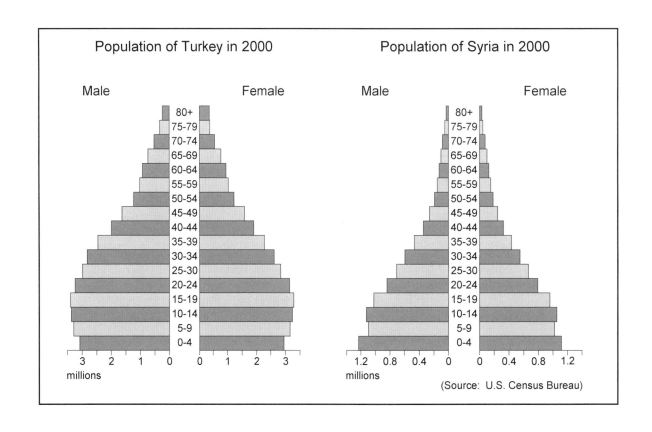

(Source: U.S. Census Bureau)

of the population in the younger age groups. It would have resembled in shape the age pyramid of Syria in the second set of pyramids, which has continued to have a very high birth rate. As the first table shows, the Turkish birth rate began to drop rapidly in the 1980s. This meant that there were fewer to feed in later years, and less need for schools and health care. But the number of children who are born now still put a great strain on Turkey. The many children who were born during the period of high fertility are now having their own children, or soon will do so.

The children now growing up in Turkey, the product of the time of high fertility, need schools. In the year 2000 there were 3.6 million more children age 5 to 19 than in 1980. The result is that Turkey's effort has necessarily been to provide enough schools. Improving the quality of schools has not been neglected, but the main effort has been to provide enough schools and teachers. The numbers in the school age group should drop by almost 20% by 2025. Then it will be more possible to stress quality over quantity.

As mechanization takes increased hold in the countryside, fewer workers will produce more food, and fewer will be needed. The trend began in the 1940s and will undoubtedly continue. The undoubted result will be the migration of people from the villages to the cities, again continuing a long trend. These will strain urban support systems that are already overloaded. Much will depend on the political will to create new urban centers and improve transportation. Based on past experience, however, the economy will sustain the increased population growth. But life would undoubtably be easier and the economy would advance more quickly if there were not so many to share.

The great numbers of children arriving at school age have put a tremendous burden on the Turkish educational system. When the products of the Turkish "baby boom" began to reach school age the state could not keep up with the need for education. Turkey educated a smaller percentage of its populace than most countries with similar levels of economic development. That has begun to change. Between 1980 and 1998, the proportion of Turkish young people who were attending secondary school improved by 66%. The proportion of eligible young people attending post-secondary schools (universities, higher training schools, etc.) rose by more than 400%. Turkey still sends a much smaller percentage of its population to secondary and higher schools than European or North American countries, but the improvement in education has been great.

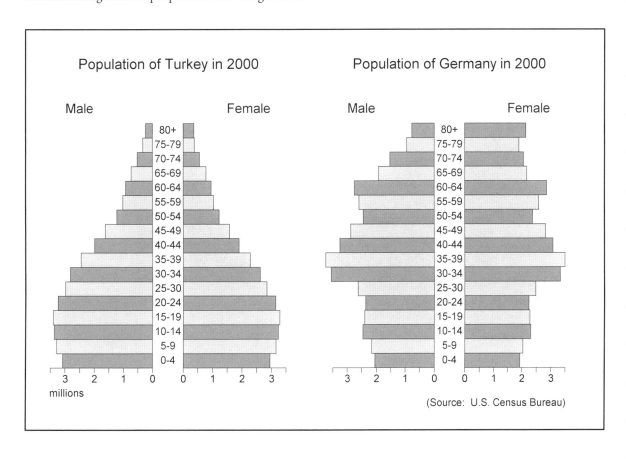

Population of Turkey in 2000 — Population of Germany in 2000

(Source: U.S. Census Bureau)

Turkey's population problem is the opposite of that of Western Europe. In Western Europe, countries such as Germany, shown in the third set of age pyramids, have long experienced low fertility while their populations live much longer. These countries have traditionally depended on the taxes of young workers to support the old, but soon there will not be enough young workers to do so. Taxes will increase and the living standard of the elderly will probably decline.

The American-born population of the United States has a similar problem; fewer children mean fewer to support social security for the old in years to come. In America, however, increased immigration has provided more young workers. While this immigration brings problems of its own, it will provide part of the solution to an aging population. Europe has generally rejected that solution. It would make economic sense for Europe to accept immigration from Turkey and other countries with a surplus of young people. Turkey has too many young people; Europe has too few. Fears of unemployment among native workers and culturally-based prejudices have prevented the Europeans from accepting this immigration. Indeed, the experiences of Turkish migrants in Europe have brought the idea of large-scale migration into serious question.

WORKING AGE POPULATION (15 - 64) AVERAGE ANNUAL INCREASE			
Country	1990-2000	2000-2010	2010-2020
United States	0.9	0.9	0.1
Japan	0.0	-0.5	-0.8
Germany	0.1	-0.5	-0.8
France	0.4	0.4	-0.4
United Kingdom	0.2	0.2	-0.3
Turkey	2.2	2.0	1.1

Opposite Page: Students on the quadrangle at
Boğaziçı Universitesi (Bosphoros University).
Left: At a concert.
Below: Sports fans.

Domestic Concerns:
Ethnic Divisions

It has been estimated that Turkey contains more than 80 ethnic groups, probably an exaggeration, but indicative of the fact that Turkey is made up of Turkish citizens, not of ethnically homogenous Turks. Many of the groups that make up Turkey are the descendents of groups forced out of the Caucasus region and the Balkans by the Russians, Armenians, Serbs, Bulgarians, Greeks, and others during the nineteenth and early twentieth centuries. They have integrated well into Turkish social and political life. Turkey is also the home of Greeks, Armenians, Jews, Nestorians, and other Christian religious groups. Given their religious differences from the majority of their fellow citizens, they are often socially apart from the majority. They are completely integrated, however, in the economic life of the Turkish community. The Turkish Jews, in particular, have a long tradition of friendship with the majority community of Muslims and secularists.

As seen above, Turkey suffered greatly from ethnic divisions and the nationalism of minority groups during World War I and the Turkish War of Independence. Only non-Muslim communities, who were accorded distinct cultural and religious rights, were accepted as minorities in the Lausanne Treaty. Keeping to Ottoman traditions, the concept of minority status did not apply to the Muslim population. The founders of the Republic accepted the principle of unity under an all-encompassing constitutional Turkish citizenship. Thus they did all they could to deny any possible Kurdish separatism. Kurds, like other Turkish citizens, were deemed an integral part of the Turkish nation. The Kurdish language was not accepted for any public function

In many ways, the policy of accepting Kurds only as citizens of the Turkish Republic was a success. Those Kurds who integrated into the national educational

and political system were treated as were other Turkish citizens. Citizens of Kurdish background became politicians (including prime minister and president), generals, judges, and all the other high positions in the state.

None of this successfully ended Kurdish ethnicity, which was rooted in the villages of the East. It can be argued that the real problem of Kurdish villagers was poverty. Southeastern Anatolia had always been poor, and remained so. A mountainous terrain with terrible climate supported neither modern agriculture nor modern industry. In both Ottoman and Republican times the state had been busy elsewhere, fighting life-threatening wars, recovering from those wars, and building a new, Western-oriented system. As long as the Kurds were quiet, the government left them alone. In practice, this meant continued control by tribal and other local leaders, who were generally not friends of modernization. Indeed, until recently, Kurdish opposition to the Republic was mainly inspired by religious dislike of the secular state.

Today, Kurdish-speakers make up approximately 15% of the population of Turkey. Some Kurds have become inspired by Kurdish ethno-nationalism, despite the fact that there are many real linguistic, cultural, religious, and political divisions among the Kurds. Few in Turkey today question that the people of Southeastern Anatolia have special needs and problems. There is less agreement on solutions.

The most radical Kurdish nationalists have called for a separate Kurdish state, carved out of Turkey, Iraq, and Iran. It is impossible to know how widespread is this sentiment. A Marxist guerilla group, the PKK fought and lost a long and bloody revolt against the Turkish government. Backed by European supporters, another group of Kurds have called for what amounts

> **Only non-Muslim communities, who were accorded distinct cultural and religious rights, were accepted as minorities in the Lausanne Treaty.**

to cultural autonomy. Their first priority is the use of Kurdish as the language of instruction in schools in Kurdish regions. The Turkish government, citing the need for one national language understood by all, has refused to consider this. The government has consistently rejected the granting of any sort of autonomy. It has, however, significantly broadened the cultural rights of Turkish citizens: In 2002, the Turkish Parliament passed legislation to allow broadcasts, newspapers, and books in Kurdish. Schools were permitted to offer classes on the Kurdish language, although the language of most instruction would remain Turkish.

The best hope for Turkish citizens in Eastern Anatolia, whatever their ethnic background, is economic. The government and populace of the Republic have recognized this fact. The most significant economic initiative is the GAP (Güneydoğu Anadolu Projesi — Southeastern Anatolia Project), which involves the building of enormous dams on the Tigris and Euphrates to irrigate otherwise unproductive land and eventually double the land under cultivation in Turkey. This and other initiatives are the best chance for real civil peace in the Southeast. Kurds must feel that belonging to the Turkish Republic will bring them real benefits.

One dam of the Southeastern Anatolia Project.

Domestic Concerns:
Urbanization

Turkey has gone from a population that was more than half rural in 1980 to one that was two-thirds urban in 2000. Urban growth has been fueled by the "push and pull" of population pressure and a new economy. High birth rates led to a surplus of workers on farms. This situation was exacerbated by the presence of new agricultural techniques. With the new machinery one farmer might do the work that had been done by 8 or 10 who used only traditional methods. Those who were not needed on the farm naturally looked for work in the towns and cities. But the cities also had an attractive power of their own, just as they have in all other nations. The main attraction is naturally the presence of jobs. Factories and commerce necessarily concentrates in cities and attract workers. Education is also concentrated in cities. Smart village children who rise through the Turkish educational system and go off to university are unlikely to return to their villages with their B.A.s or Ph.D.s. On the darker side of a new economy, those who have been left behind by a new economy find that

the city is a better place to peddle wares on the street or even to beg.

Urbanization is normal, a phenomena seen in all countries as they economically develop. What has been abnormal in Turkey is the speed of urbanization. During another time of rapid economic growth, the years from 1869 to 1900, the population of London doubled, that of Paris did not quite double. In the forty years from 1960 to 2000, Turkey's great period of economic growth, the population of Istanbul increased almost eightfold. Building the roads, schools, hospitals, and sewers for such a population has proved to be a daunting task. Housing was a massive problem. Most of the new immigrants from the villages arrived with little capital. They naturally built the types of houses they could construct cheaply--the types of houses they had made in their villages. These were built on vacant lands surrounding the cities. They became, in essence, villages that surrounded the central cities. Unlike America, however, these suburbs were the poorer parts of the metropolitan area, not the dwellings of the middle class.

Statistics demonstrate the problem in a bloodless form. A more convincing analysis of the problems of urbanization comes from trying to travel from place A to place B in an Istanbul taxi. The traffic, a product of the immigrants to Istanbul driving the cars provided by economic growth, is horrendous, although not quite as bad as the traffic on Los Angeles freeways (another product of urbanization). However, stopped in traffic, and thus with an abundance of time to contemplate the urban landscape, someone who often has visited Turkey over decades cannot help but notice great changes. The people are better dressed than ever before, they are busily going about their various businesses; and they are well fed. Despite the crush of population, the city works. Thirty years before, there were many fewer people, but they were poorer, less educated, and less employed. Goods that are now available in every corner grocery shop were simply nonexistent thirty years ago. Televisions, refrigerators, and washing machines are ubiquitous-- not the situation in the old days, when few had such luxuries.

By no means is urbanization only a set of problems. There are also benefits. When population is compact it is easier to deliver services such as health care and education to them. Urban populations read more newspapers and are more likely to attend school, and to do so for more years. City populations tend to be more politically knowledgeable and active. They are also a greater market for goods and services, which can be delivered to them more easily than to their compatriots in the country. The variety of life is more available in cities or, to put it in another way, there are more things to do in the city, more types of employment and entertainment. These are benefits of the sort seen in Western Europe and North America for generations.

THE POPULATION OF ISTANBUL 1927 TO 2000	
1927	705,000
1955	1,534,000
1960	1,882,000
1965	2,293,000
1970	3,019,000
1975	3,405,000
1980	4,742,000
1985	5,853,000
1990	7,309,000
1995	11,000,000*
2000	14,000,000*

* estimates

Domestic Concerns:
The Environment

IN COMMON WITH OTHER COUNTRIES THAT HAVE EXPERIENCED RAPID ECONOMIC DEVELOPMENT, TURKEY HAS ENVIRONMENTAL PROBLEMS. TO TAKE one indicator as an example, the amount of CO_2 emissions that pollute the air more than doubled from 1980 to 2000. This is to be expected, because energy consumption tripled during the same period, and the number of passenger vehicles was five times higher. Emission controls and other environmental laws are relatively recent. A visitor to Turkish cities cannot help but notice trucks spewing clouds of diesel smoke and the haze of smog in winter.

Some initiatives have had a positive effect on the environment. The use of natural gas has greatly decreased the pollution from coal in cities such as Ankara, whose winter air was once famous for its toxicity. All new electricity-generating furnaces are being fitted with "scrubbers" to reduce emissions. Mass transit systems in Ankara and Istanbul have reduced the need for automobiles and buses, a major source of pollution. Laws on environmental improvement in areas from hazardous waste disposal to water pollution have been passed or are being considered. Much more remains to be done.

Turkey faces one potentially cataclysmic disaster over which it has no control. The Bosphorus Strait, which passes through densely populated sections of Istanbul is an international waterway. Freedom of shipping through the strait is guaranteed by the Montreux Treaty of 1936. Turkey is obliged to allow oil tankers to pass through the Straits, with little control over their cargo or the safety of ships. Small oil spills are frequent, as are collisions and ships running aground. In only two examples, one ship dumped 800 tons of oil into the Bosphorus, another spilled 20,00 tons that burned for five days. The potential for an oil tanker exploding is real. Moreover, the tankers spill oil and refuse daily. The Bosphorus was once a fine ground for fishing, but now 95% of the fish have been killed. The only solution would be to move oil by pipeline, rather than by tanker through dangerous waters, but the world community will not act. Instead, more oil is passing through the Straits than ever before.

To a great extent Turkey shares the same environment vs. development dilemma that faces all countries. Economic growth is needed to keep pace with an increasing population and to improve the lives of the people. Yet this economic growth produces pollution that degrades the very lives that are supposed to be improved. Consumers with new found purchasing power want goods whose manufacture produces pollution. In particular. like the citizens of California, they want personal automobiles. A democratic government has to balance the wishes of the people, the labor sector, and business with the need to protect the environment for future generations. Also, on a world scale, Turkey has comparatively low energy consumption, and thus less pollution than other countries. In 1998, the United States emitted nearly eight times as much carbon per person as did Turkey. Turkish energy consumption

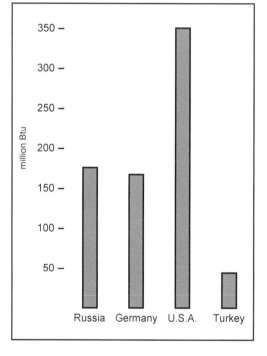

million Btu

is rising, but will not approach that of the major economic powers for many decades. Turkey should reduce energy consumption and emissions, but should not the richer countries do even more?

Bridge over the Bosphoros Straits, and a ship.

Domestic Concerns:
Earthquakes

WHAT MAY BE THE WORST POTENTIAL DISASTER FACING TURKEY IS A FORCE OF NATURE. TWELVE MAJOR EARTHQUAKES, defined as those taking more than 1,000 lives, struck Turkey in the twentieth century. What is most troubling is that the incidence of earthquakes has been moving westwards along the North Anatolian Fault, an earthquake zone similar to the San Andreas Fault in California. Earlier in the twentieth century, earthquakes in less populated regions of eastern Anatolia caused, with one exception, 1-4,000 deaths each. As they begin to occur on the west of the fault line, the earthquakes strike more populated areas. The 1999 quake in the İzmit region caused 17,000 deaths, at least 50,000 injuries, and left hundreds of thousands homeless. Istanbul's millions live only 40 miles from the epicenter of the İzmit quake. It is on the same fault line.

> The 1999 quake in the İzmit region caused 17,000 deaths, at least 50,000 injuries, and left hundreds of thousands homeless.

Like the San Andreas Fault, the fault in Western Turkey is capable of causing great damage. The fault is close to the surface, so the energy from a quake is strongly directed upwards toward populated surface land.

Few Turks build their houses with earthquakes in mind. In villages, houses built of mud brick offer little resistance to the shaking from earthquakes. Town apartment buildings are only somewhat better. The main problem is cost. An increasing population has needed housing and the country has not had the wealth to build more earthquake resistant homes and offices. There is also human nature to contend with. Whether in Japan, California, Mexico, or China, no one truly believes such a natural disaster will happen to them, so steps are not taken to prepare. New building regulations have been passed, but the country cannot afford to tear down old buildings and replace them. Indeed, that would not be possible in California, which is far richer. As in California, the potential for future disaster is high.

Domestic Concerns:
The Economy

BEFORE ECONOMIC REFORMS BEGAN IN THE 1980S, TURKEY'S ECONOMY WAS RELATIVELY BACKWARD. ECONOMIC REFORMS HAD BEGUN in the 1950s, but the still exercised an often heavy-handed control over industry and commerce. A policy of restricting imports, intended to foster domestic industries, had cut Turkey off from the world, frustrated the efforts of Turkish entrepreneurs and making imported consumer goods expensive or unavailable. That changed rapidly. The governments of Turgut Özal and his successors much reduced the government role in the economy and opened Turkish borders to imports and exports, bringing Turkey into the world economy.

Turkey began to look like other market-driven economies. A stock market opened in Istanbul in 1986. By 2000, the Istanbul Stock Exchange was handling more than 400 billion dollars a year in transactions. As in Europe, the privatization of government-owned industries began. Progress was slow, but, by 2000, six billion dollars had been paid for newly-privatized industries. The economy became less reliant on traditional occupations and more on modern employment. Agriculture provided 30% of the Gross Domestic Product (GDP) in 1970, but less than 15% in 2000. In 2000 services provided more than 60% of the GDP in 1999, similar to other modern economies. The machines that dominate modern life, usually imported and rare before the 1980s, became common. For example, very few automobiles were produced in Turkey before 1966, when automobile production began in earnest. By 2000, more than 320,000 cars were produced yearly. In place of unreliable and expensive telephones, an entire new communication industry sprang up, based

MAIN TRADING PARTNERS, 1998 (% OF TOTAL)		
Country	Imports	Exports
Germany	20.2	15.9
United States	8.3	8.8
United Kingdom	6.4	5.8
Italy	6.4	5.8
Russian Federation	5.0	4.7
France	4.8	6.6

on mobile telephones. 3,500 broadcast stations and signal repeaters insured that the entire country received television programs, including cable and satellite. The Turkish construction industry developed into one of the world's major contractors, with 3% of the volume of international (done outside the home country) construction. In short, the Turkish economy bore no resemblance to what it had been.

Even though the trend has been of rapid economic improvement, Turkey has experienced drastic booms and recessions. In much of the 1990s, Turkey's growth was in the top ten in the world. The economy grew in most years at a rate of more than 6%. In the 1994 recession, however, the GDP dropped by 5.5% and in 1999 by 5.6%. Two external factors did damage to the growing Turkish economy, the great earthquakes of 1999 and the Russian financial crisis of 1998-99. The two earthquakes struck in the region of the Sea of Marmara, one of Turkey's most productive areas, and costs of rehabilitation and human services were enormous. The countries that had once been part of the Soviet Union accounted for more than 10% of Turkey's foreign trade, and the Russians and others simply could not pay.

The main long-term problem with the Turkish economy has been financial. Many private banks, decontrolled by the State, proved to be poor custodians of investments and even sources of theft by managers, leading to a financial crisis in 2000-2001.[1] Inflation is endemic in Turkey. Unlike the countries of the European Union and North America, Turkey has long accepted high rates of inflation. This has been institutionalized. Government, business, and the populace have accepted

---

[1]The government, in association with the International Monetary Fund has passed financial reforms in the state sector and banking.

high rates of inflation and adjusted prices and wages accordingly. This, in turn, perpetuates inflation. Inflation has caused fewer economic problems than might be expected. Economic growth has been high, despite inflation. The average Turk is much better off than 40 years ago. High inflation has had its costs, however. It has made planning difficult, harmed those on fixed incomes, such as state employees and pensioners, and hindered foreign investment. Foreign businesses and individuals have not invested significant amounts in Turkey. Government expenditure is one of the main causes of inflation. The deficit in state finances has routinely exceeded 10% of GDP. This deficit has been covered by borrowing internally and from international institutions such as the International Monetary Fund

Such problems are not unusual in rapidly developing countries. Indeed, so-called deficit financing is common in most countries. In a country that wishes to develop rapidly, modern education is needed, as are new machines and skilled teachers and advisers from other countries. All of this is expensive. Newly-educated people, who have a knowledge of lifestyles in more economically developed countries, want the consumer goods that will improve their lives. This, too, is costly. The country borrows to pay for both development and goods. It is expected that a new economy will bring the income needed to pay the debts. The debts, however, always seem to be greater than the ability to pay. The Turkish economy has also been hampered by the need for high military expenditure. For forty years Turkey stood on the front lines against the Soviets. It still remains in what has been called a "rough neighborhood." Guns are expensive.

The economic achievements of the modern Turkish Republic must be viewed in the light of history. The Turkish Republic entered history as a devastated country. After World War I, no other country, not Germany, not Russia, was forced to recover from such mortality and desolation as was Turkey. The East and West of the country were both largely destroyed. One-fourth of the people had died. Added to this were all the normal problems of a developing society--a small industrial base, lack of trained manpower, a low educational level, and a lack of capital. Amazingly, Mustafa Kemal Atatürk managed to hold the country together. Even more incredibly, he bettered the lives of Turkey's people and began their education in the ways of democracy. He radically transformed Turkish society. Secularism and an orientation toward the West became the Turkish Way. Nevertheless, affected by the Great Depression, World War II, and the lingering effects of past disaster, Turkey entered the post-war world as a poor country.

It is surely possible to look at Turkey and say, "What if?" What if the Turks had radically reformed their economy immediately after World War II? What if the government had been more financially astute? What if politics and finance had not been tainted by corruption? Turkey has indeed made mistakes, but the overall Turkish success is more significant that any of the Turkish errors.

Despite problems, the overall economic record of the Turkish Republic has been admirable. Modern Turkey has rapidly industrialized. The value of exports increased more than ten times between 1980 and 2000 (imports increased seven times) and 79% of these exports were industrial goods (versus 39% in 1980). Turkey once imported almost all its motor vehicles, but by 1999 was exporting vehicles to Russia, Germany, Italy, and other countries. Electronics, pharmaceuticals, and chemicals. once also imports, were exported (nearly $4 billion). Turkish-made clothing is seen in stores all over Europe and North America. Turkey's GDP increased nearly threefold between 1980 and 2000. In the 1980s, GDP rose by an average of 5.3% a year, in the 1990s by an average of 3.8% a year. In 1965, the average GDP per person was less than $1,000 a year. By 2000 the GDP has risen to $6,900. Turkey has not become a rich country, but it has become much richer than anyone might have imagined looking at the poor country of the past.

GDP Per Capita in Turkey ($US)	
Year	Income
1950	200
1955	400
1960	500
1965	600
1970	800
1975	1,500
1980	2,300
1985	3,300
1990	4,700
1995	5,600
2000	6,900

[2]Purchasing Power Parity, a figure that adjusts GDP by the cost of living and production.

Domestic Concerns:
Life and Death

THE GREATEST SUCCESS OF THE MODERN TURK-ISH REPUBLIC HAS BEEN IN HEALTH CARE AND HUMAN SURVIVAL. IN THE YEAR 2000 THE average Turk lived ten years longer than in 1980. There were twice as many physicians per person. 10% of babies born in 1980 died before reaching their first birthday. By 2000 two-thirds of the babies who would have better than the poor countries of Asia. Although it is not yet at a level with the rich countries, Turkish health standards are well above those of Africa and almost all of Asia. 70% of Turkish children are immunized (U.S., 95%). 91% of Turks have access to improved sanitation (toilets and sewers, U.S., 100%). Turkish health is now at approximately the standard of Latin America.

IMPROVEMENT IN THE TURKISH LIFE SPAN				
Year	Infant Mortality /1000 births	Life Expectancy at Birth		Population per Physician
		Male	Female	
1980	109	59	59	1,642
1990	52	64	70	1,115
2000	36	67	71	838

died in 1980 lived. Those raw statistics do not adequately express a great national effort to provide better nutrition and health care, especially in rural areas. Some of the measures taken were costly, such as training more doctors. Others were simply intelligent, such as the national campaign to teach mothers how to treat infantile diarrhea. Together, the measures meant significant improvement in the most important area of human development, life and death.

Immediately after World War II, Turkish health standards ranked very low on a world scale, only slightly

The improvements in Turkish health, like those in education, were achieved relatively cheaply. Turkey has spent from 3-5% of its GDP on health. What was accomplished was done through organization and dedication, especially that of the health care community, not through great expenditure. While this is laudable, one cannot help but think that more investment would have produced even greater results. As with education, the problem was money. Turkey had too many calls on its resources, especially the needs of defense. It must be stated, however, that Turkey did remarkably well with what it had.

Literature
and Art

Aesthetics

Literary expression, especially in verse, dominated Turkish creativity in the early centuries. In the beginning was poetry — and it continues to be a compelling force well into our times. Architecture and the plastic arts in general came after the nomadic period, reaching their zenith in the 16th century. Performing arts — mainly music and dance — date from the earliest eras. But it is the literature, as transliterated, that constitutes the most systematic, substantive and reliable body of cultural documentation for the past 15 centuries. It embodies, perhaps better than any other genre, the nation's mythos, pathos and ethos.

The first major written work is a series of inscriptions on stelae which still stand in Mongolia. Erected in the early 8th century, the so-called Orhon Inscriptions furnish vivid accounts, in a well-developed prose style, of the victories and defeats of the Köktürks. In them, we find an explicit national and cultural consciousness — and an idealpolitik whereby the leaders emphasize feeding the hungry, clothing the naked, and helping the poor.

A large body of oral literature developed as well — creation myths, tales of migration and morality, and *The Tales of Dede Korkut*, twelve interrelated tales which came to constitute the national epic. In addition, a vast repertoire of folk tales and popular poetry (often serving as lyrics of songs), came out of the oral tradition, providing entertainment and enlightenment to nomads and settled communities in rural areas through the centuries — as is still true of the Turkish countryside today. A product of the collective imagination as well as the work of individual creative artists, this folk literature has always voiced, in its spontaneous, sincere, and often matter-of-fact fashion, the sensibilities, yearnings and criticisms of the rural people. It exerted little influence on urban culture until the 20th century. Since the turn of the century, however, it has been a dominant force in Turkish aesthetics.

> **Murat IV (d. 1640) once sent a communiqué in verse to his Commander-in-Chief who replied in a poem of his own using the same rhyme scheme.**

Anatolians, since the ancient times, were enamored of dance. So were Central Asian Turks. As a result, Anatolia became and remains a fertile ground for an astounding variety of folk dances. Prof. Metin And, a prominent scholar, has determined that there are about 1,500 types, most of which are distinct with regard to music, steps, rhythms, costumes, themes and accessories.

Turkish folk music — featuring songs and instrumentals — has been remarkable for its continuity. It is an amalgam of Asian, Anatolian, Arabo-Persian and Balkan strains. The distinguished Hungarian composer and musicologist Bela Bartok, after doing research in Turkey in the 1930's, wrote that it is difficult to find a tradition of such duration elsewhere in the world. The melodies range from solemn, slow, soothing to fast, lilting, rousing. Regional variations and flavors are extensive. A variety of string and wind instruments and the drums (with evocations of shamanic rituals) continue to excite audiences at rural weddings and festivities and nowadays at urban festivals and on concert stages.

Ottoman elite culture produced a refined classical literature and music heavily influenced by Islam and by the arts of the Arabs and Persians. No mosque music developed, with the sole exception of the chanting of the "Mevlid" (Ar. "Mawlid"), a long poem of Nativity of Muhammad recited on high holy occasions and to commemorate deceased Muslims.

Music played a focal role in the rituals of the Sufi (Islamic mystic) sects and brotherhoods, especially among the Whirling Dervishes, who perform a ceremony which involves whirling to the accompaniment of instrumental music and chanting of prayers and poems. The ceremony, which the Dervishes do not regard as a dance, is an act of faith whose purpose is to induce ecstasy and inner enlightenment.

In the Ottoman system, whose ideology and creative life evolved under the influence of mainstream Sunni Islam, the mystics provided a heterodox spirituality. Many of them were artists, philosophers and poets who introduced a more liberal, latitudinarian religious faith. Although some were considered heretical and occasionally persecuted, many prominent personalities among them enjoyed an influential status. The ruling establishment, including some Sultans, supported various Sufi sects and sought the advice of their leaders. The collective impact of the Sufis on Ottoman literature, music calligraphy, theology, and spiritual life is immense.

Turkish literature produced its earliest major works from the 1070's onwards with the appearance of *Kutadgu Bilig* (translated into English as *The Glory of Royal Wisdom*), a mirror for princes written by a chancellor named Yusuf Has Hacib in about 6,500 rhymed couplets and *Divan ü Lugat-it Türk* (*Lexicon and Compendium of Turkish*), a study of Turkish dialects and a selection of early poems, compiled by Mahmud of Kashgar. The didactic, mystical and secular literature of the 12th to the 15th century in the Turkish-speaking lands is impressive in size and content. The Seljuk Empire cherished the poetry of two great mystics, Mevlana Celaleddin Rumi, who wrote in Persian (which was like the Latin of medieval Europe) and Yunus Emre, who composed popular hymns and poems in simple Anatolian Turkish. The cultural efflorescence of the period also gave rise to an earthy humor represented by Nasreddin Hoca, an irrepressible wit and story-teller, whose funny pranks and satirical gags have enchanted not only Turks, but also many communities in the Middle East, Asia, North Africa, and the Balkans to this day.

> [The Tanzimat] had far-reaching implications for cultural life. European philosophy and literature became fashionable. New genres — the novel and the short story, and playwriting for the legitimate stage — started along with an extensive translation activity.

The Ottoman establishment was enamored of poetry. Two-thirds of all the Ottoman Sultans wrote verses. Süleyman the Magnificent turned out close to 3,000 accomplished verses. Selim III (d. 1807), also a poet, was a fine composer of songs and instrumental, including Sufi, music. Murat IV (d. 1640) once sent a communiqué in verse to his Commander-in-Chief who replied in a poem of his own using the same rhyme scheme. In the 19th century, some dictionaries (Turkish-French, Turkish-Greek, etc.) and a chemistry textbook were produced in rhymed verse.

The spirit of classical Ottoman poetry was intensely romantic. Love, human and divine, abstract and erotic, held sway, overshadowing most other themes. The prominent 16th century master Fuzuli wrote: "Love is all there is in this world/Science is nothing but idle talk." The couplet was symptomatic of the lack of scientific development, or even the spirit of inquiry, in the Ottoman state until the 19th century when it was finally realized that the Empire, lagging behind in technology, should acquire scientific knowledge from the West.

With thousands of words borrowed from the Arabic and Persian, the Ottoman elite created a hybrid vocabulary which was quite inaccessible to all except the highly educated. The vast majority of the population, being illiterate, relied on the oral traditions of folk poems and tales. The conservative religious officials obstructed the introduction of the printing press until the 1720's, more than 250 years behind its appearance in Europe. Even then, the number of books printed and distributed was rather small until the middle of the 19th century.

Upper and lower classes in cities enjoyed various types of the performing arts — "meddah" (story teller and sit-down comic), orta oyunu (a theater-in-the-round similar to the commedia dell'arte), and the shadow theater. With dozens of colorful figures, manipulated like flat puppets behind a white screen, this type of comic shadow show had the makings of a TV sitcom series. Widely popular among children and adults from the 16th to the 20th century, it provided a cheerful opportunity for the public to poke fun at social mores, human foibles, and public officials.

Classical literature lost its appeal by the early 19th century. Ottoman institutions in general had become outmoded. The still sprawling state was caught in an irreversible decline. Ottoman intellectuals turned to Europe, hoping to save the state by importing technology and culture. A spate of reforms in Ottoman institutions and laws — collectively known as **"Tanzimat"** — was initiated. This had far-reaching implications for cultural life. European philosophy and literature became fashionable. New genres — the novel and the short story, and playwriting for the legitimate stage — started along with an extensive translation activity. European classical music was introduced. Many educational institutions adopted a scientific curriculum from their Western counterparts. In the previous century, there had been a growing interaction between the Ottomans and Europe. In the so-called Tulip Age (1718—1730), the Ottomans had built places and mansions copied from Paris and Vienna. In Europe, there was a brave new fashion which came to be called "Turquerie." Inaugurated in 1839, "Tanzimat" ushered in a program of cultural and scientific modernization patterned after the major European countries.

Since then, the Turkish nation has been modernizing without interruption. The process gained a stunning momentum in the first 15 years of the Republic. Urban elite culture became Europeanized in much of its lifestyle, in its professional life, and in the domain of creative arts. The University of Istanbul, one of the world's oldest (dating from the 1450's), was overhauled and transformed into a European-type institution of higher learning.

In the seven decades of the Republic, aesthetic experience has been as varied as one can imagine in any country. Radio programming is a faithful mirror of this diversity: In the course of a single broadcast day, the audience can hear Ottoman classical music, Argentinian tangos, rock 'n roll, Viennese operetta, jazz, Anato-lian folk music, Italian opera, electronic music, Turkish popular music, rap, French songs, a Mozart symphony, Portuguese fado, rhythm and blues, German lieder, a Broadway musical, African dance music...

The spectrum of literary aesthetics is correspondingly broad. The traditions of Turkish literature are alive and well — folk poetry, neo-classicism, experiments with conventional forms, etc. From the West, virtually all modern movements and ideologies have found their way into Turkish literature: surrealism, symbolism, communism, existentialism, concrete poetry, and others. There is no aesthetic strategy in 20th century Europe and America that has not made its entry into the Turkish creative experience.

A similar phenomenon exists in the plastic arts as well. Particularly modern painting has been enthusiastically responsive to developments in the West while coming to grips in some very imaginative ways with the tradition of Ottoman miniature painting and decorative arts. It is also significant that the Turkish Republic has been the leader in introducing the art of sculpture to the Muslim world where traditionally the religious establishment has discouraged concrete depic-

> Very few cities in the world have a broader range of productions than Istanbul and Ankara. Every season, audiences can see Shakespeare, ancient Greek drama, American and European plays in addition to a wide repertoire by native playwrights...

tions of the human body. Sculpture and statues, contrary to their absence in conservative Islamic countries, are visible everywhere in Turkey.

A remarkable development is in the theatrical activity and dramatic writing. Very few cities in the world have a broader range of productions than Istanbul and Ankara. Every season, audiences can see Shakespeare, ancient Greek drama, American and European plays in addition to a wide repertoire by native playwrights who turn out social realist plays, tragedies in the grand manner, boulevard plays, musical comedies, poetic drama, Brechtian epic theater, black comedy, modern versions of shadow plays, political satire, cabaret, well-made family melodramas, and dramatizations of mythological themes and legends.

TV is a national pastime, perhaps a passion that absorbs the attention of the people from all walks of life. With a score of channels now going full-blast, a vast number of Turks seem to be dividing their time between work and TV. This has had an arresting effect on some types of cultural activity: It is statistically true that, probably because of TV's dominance, newspaper circulation and book sales have not increased at all in two decades although the population has increased about 20 million and literacy has taken strides in the same period. Film production has shifted in the direction of telecasts and the number of movie theaters has decreased due to shrinking audiences. The artistic and technical quality of Turkish films, however, has greatly improved. In recent years, many of them have won awards at major international film festivals.

Opera, ballet, and classical (and modern) music continue to flourish in the major cities. The fact that there are three full-fledged symphony orchestras, two opera companies and two ballet companies as well as a rather impressive number of compositions of music in the Western vein contrasts sharply with the rest of the Third World. This is one of the dramatic proofs of the fact that Turkey is hardly a typical underdeveloped country. In fact, judging by its nine-thousand year heritage of civilizations, its traditional Central Asian and Seljuk, and Ottoman cultures, its modern creativity, and on the strength of the scope, depth and diversity of its cultural life, it is one of the world's most developed, even advanced, nations.

— Talat S. Halman, Ph.D.

General Introduction to Studying and Teaching Turkish Literature in Translation

Students must develop multicultural literacy and cross-cultural competency if they are to become knowledgeable, reflective, and caring citizens in the twenty-first centry

— James A. Banks

AS MULTICULTURAL EDUCATORS, EACH OF US IS ENDLESSLY COMMITTED TO BOTH GIVING ACCURATE REPRESENTATIONS OF CULTURES WE and our students know little about, and to giving our students the tools with which to function as citizens of a diverse nation and world. This commitment gives rise to the philosophy around which the selections in this text were chosen.

Studying Turkish literature and culture in English translation is a challenging task for two primary reasons: the first is the vast cultural divide between American students' experiences, and the experiences of the Turkish authors whose works were composed during the early twentieth century to the present. The second challenge is the limited availability of both a variety of texts in English translation, and a variety of translations of texts themselves.

The first challenge is easier to overcome than the second. For one could argue (convincingly) that the cultural divide between an American teenager's life and that of Chaucer, Shakespeare, Hawthorne, or Stowe's would at times be just as vast a divide as that of a Turkish teenager's from Hikmet, Akın, Karakoç, or Altıok's. The various other challenges to cultural norms, ideas, and characteristics that may be observed due to geography, local customs, language, family life, etc. are accessible to any who are willing to be diligent observers, mindful analysts, and curious participants. The customs of Sunni Islam, which is the dominant faith into which most citizens of Turkey are born and acculturated, as well as the folk traditions of the Anatolian nomadic history, the Persian and Arabic literary and judiciary influences of language and form, and historical and recent contacts with France, Italy, and other countries of the European continent, may each be seen as threads of influence and moments of dialogue that have each in their own ways left impressions upon the texts which are collected here.

Students should be encouraged to not simply look for evidence of influence, but also to look for dialogue. It is encouraged that, rather than reading selections from Turkish literature in English translation in isolation, on a selected "global perspectives" day, they should be read along with literary selections from cultures of other parts of the Middle East, of South America, and of the United States. Students should also be encouraged to identify common themes, and convergent themes: how is love expressed in each of these cultural communities? What is the role of artists and literary intellectuals in conflicts? How is this role different from the role of politicians and policy makers? How is fear and personal struggle expressed in this versus other cultural communities?

> **Poets and authors have very particular reasons for selecting not only the medium for their expression (a poem, a short story, a song, etc.) but for each word... there is a reason for their choice...**

The second challenge is somewhat more difficult to hurdle. Anyone who has fluency, or even a moderate understanding of another language can easily imagine the challenge of representing the emotional and ideological expressions of that culture with differing words. Poets and authors have very particular reasons for selecting not only the medium for their expression (a poem, a short story, a song, etc.) but for each word, and even at times, the font or even case (recall the poet e. e. cummings, songwriter k. d. lang, or cultural critic bell hooks — there is a reason for their choice of lower-case lettering in their names. Also, educators may want to remind students that not all alphabets have upper and lower-case lettering as the Latin alphabet does).

It must be remembered, however, that the authors and works in this collection are representative of the canon of Turkish literary work available in English translation. For this reason, it is important for those studying literatures in translation to talk about the process of translation, the features we look for in a "good" translation, how we decide if something is a "poor" translation, who decides, according to whose framework. For these reasons, any translator who translates literature is faced with a multitude of decisions. One of the most fruitful activities for a classroom that is studying literature and cultures represented in translation is to find alternate translations of the same work, and make comparisons, asking questions like, why did this translator make this choice, and this one another? What is the effect when we read this one versus the other? Who did these translations? For whom? For what purpose? etc.

Although efforts have been made to select the best translations available in English, any selection process is subjective. To balance this subjectivity, I've attempted to include a diversity of translators, while at the same time being mindful of the important, and central themes, motifs, and linguistic choices of the source authors. It is hoped that rather than being a finite collection, the readers will approach this text as a starting point for further investigation and learning into our common human struggles and the diversity of ways in which we express our joys and sorrows.

— Özlem Şensoy
University of Washington

The Book of Dede Korkut

Suggested Time	2-3 classroom periods.
Materials Needed	A class set of readings — **Worksheet 1**

Background Information

The Book of Dede Korkut is an epic of the Oghuz or Turkoman people. It has an adventure-filled plot and is concerned with universal human problems such as honor, jealousy, love, war and hatred. Epics are usually based on old myths and legends of a particular nation or people. The setting of an epic is a distant place at a time long past. An epic includes elements of myth, legend, folktale and history. Though epics contain many myths and exaggerations, they are based on actual people and events. An epic is not the most reliable historical account, but it is an essential key to understanding a people.

The tone of an epic is serious and the language is grand. Epic heroes undertake quests to achieve something of tremendous value to themselves or their people. Therefore epics serve as a rich repository of traditional culture and values. Greek epics include Homer's *Iliad* and *Odyssey*. The great Roman epic is the *Aeneid*. *Beowulf* and *Paradise Lost* are the two major English language epics. *The Song of Roland* and *El Cid* are the French and Spanish language epics. From the ancient Middle East came the Babylonian epic *Gilgamesh*. The best known African epic is the *Sundiata*, named after a thirteenth-century leader who was the founder of the Empire of Mali. In each of these, heroic individuals emerge — individuals who rely on their superior skills and efforts.

The Book of Dede Korkut deviates from the strict definition of an epic in that it is a mixture of poetry and prose; it concerns itself more with the heroism of the Turkomans than any specific individual, and its episodes are connected through style and theme rather than narration. *The Book of Dede Korkut* is one of the most important literary and historical documents of the Middle Ages.

Plot Summary

The story begins in Central Asia between the ninth and thirteenth centuries and reflects the Oghuz contact with Islam during the tenth century.

Each of the twenty-four Oghuz tribes was ruled by a **bey**, or lord, and administered by a superior bey with the advice of a representative council. A joint council, or **divan**, presided over by the **beylerbey**, or bey of beys, who stood immediately beneath the **khan**, or **sultan**, coordinated activities of the whole confederation. Oghuz women, reared in the hardships of nomadic life, had almost equal status with men. In the legends, women are revered as mothers and respected as wives and counselors.

The Book of Dede Korkut is comprised of a prologue and twelve legends told largely in prose and enriched by frequent passages of verse. Each of the twelve episodes concludes with a prayer for the sovereign, or khan, before whom the stories were sometimes recited.

Dede Korkut, or Grandfather Korkut, is a legendary figure who was most likely derived from some historical personage. The main action is largely fictional but must also be seen as documentation of the social and cultural history of the nomadic Oghuz Turks.

Dede Korkut came to represent the traditional bard of Turkish antiquity. The Book of Dede Korkut is a masterpiece of the Turkish oral tradition which is still very much alive today in rural Anatolia. Parts of it are read by Turkish students throughout the Republic.

Notes to the Instructor

Since the reading selection is long, teachers may want to assign it for homework to precede this lesson. Although this selection is a simple and straightforward narrative, its rhythms are unusual. The climax of the story, when Bugach Khan saves the life of his father Dirse Khan, is given less attention than the dedication of the tale to the khan of khans. It is therefore suggested that the students are briefed on the structure of the story before reading it.

The narrative structure of "The Story of Bugach Khan" may be divided into two major sections. In the first section Dirse Khan fathers a son, and in the second section his son Bugach engages in a series of adventures which climax in the saving of his father's life.

The drama of the text is not structured around the plot, however. Instead the drama is structured around the repetition of phrases. Emotions are found in these formal repetitions rather than in any narrative suspense or climax. Therefore, their son meets the lamentations of Bugach Khan's mother and father with a formal, restrained and repetitive response. The modern reader must supply his or her own emotional response in the absence of a familiar emotional structure.

Although the vocabulary in the story is not particularly difficult, certain words should be taught in advance, and the class before reading should practice the names of the principal characters.

One of the strategies suggested for this lesson involves dividing the class into cooperative learning groups of 4-5 students. Each group is given only a portion of the text to review. The task for each group is the same — that is, to identify and list the cultural values and traditions in their part of the selection. Teachers will probably want to model this process by reading the first paragraph with the whole class.

Key Concepts

epic
repetition
symbolism
imagery
dramatic irony

Vocabulary

khan
minstrel
principality
infidel
sterile
vertebrated
dervish

ezan — the Islamic call to prayer chanted five times a day from a minaret by an announcer called a muezzin.

Aim To what degree can an epic help forge national identity?

Major Idea ▷ An understanding of Turkish historical values, traditions and identity can be obtained through a careful study of the Turkish epic, *The Book of Dede Korkut*.

Performance Objectives Students will be able to:
1. Define and identify the following elements of an epic: symbolism and repetition.
2. Identify and discuss cultural values and traditions presented in a work of literature.
3. Compare the customs and values presented in the literature with their own customs and values.
4. Create a plan for a contemporary epic.

Motivation Have students create a chart and label each section with a category of heroism: athletic, spiritual, political, military, science, and so forth. Under each category, have them brainstorm a list of possible heroes. For example:

Athletic	Spiritual	Political	Military	Science
Michael Jordan	Mother Theresa	Kemal Ataturk	Geo. Washington	Jonas Salk

Discuss with the students the qualities common to all the heroes in each category and to all the heroes listed on the chart.

Procedure/ Development ▷ Describe the three tents Bayindir Khan set up for the feast. What did each color mean?
▷ Divide students into small groups. Give each group a portion of the full story and ask the students to identify and list the cultural values and traditions they find in their assigned segments. List the findings on the blackboard.
▷ Why are certain objects, animals, actions and values important to nomadic people? How did the Turkomans meet their survival needs? Contrast with contemporary needs. Do you have the same needs? Do you satisfy your needs in the same way?
▷ How did Bugach Khan prove himself a hero?
▷ Notice the repetition in this story. This story was told for centuries before it was written down. Why do you think repetition is an important element in traditional oral literature?
▷ Review our discussion and your notes from today. We call *The Book of Dede Korkut* an epic. Write a definition of an epic. (Allow students 4-5 minutes to review and to formulate a definition.) Share your definition with a "buddy" and add additional ideas to your original definition. Elicit 2-3 definitions from the full group, encouraging students to continue to add to their own definitions.

Summary   If a young person reads *The Book of Dede Korkut*, what lessons is he/she supposed to learn?

Connecting Reading and Writing   Students should return to their groups to develop a plan for an episode of an epic that will be read in the year 2500 by a class of high school students. Students should dramatize a code of behavior (such as cooperation or balance with nature) that they believe incorporates values important to future survival. Who will be the heroine? Who or what will be the enemy? How will the solution help future generations? Each plan should include:

- Two values which are important to future survival,
- A list of characters and their relationship to each other,
- The setting,
- A plot outline, including the conflict, rising action and climax.

Allow students adequate time to develop plans. When they have completed these episodes, each group may read its plan to the entire class for discussion and analysis.

Making Cultural Connections: Students should select another epic to compare with *Dede Korkut* (some suggestions are listed in the section entitled, **Background Information**).

- Compare and contrast the heroic values in each epic.
- Compare and contrast the ways in which humans and gods interact.
- Compare and contrast the importance of each epic in a national tradition. Do young people still read sections of this epic? Does the epic still have meaning for the culture?

Legend I:
The Story of Bugach Khan, Son of Dirse Khan

ONE DAY BAYINDIR, SON OF GAM KHAN, AROSE AND ORDERED THAT HIS LARGE DAMASCUS TENT BE ERECTED.[1] HIS BROWN PARASOL ROSE high up in the sky. Thousands of silk carpets were spread all around. It was customary for Bayindir Khan, Khan of Khans, to invite all the Oghuz princes to a feast once a year. As usual he gave a feast this year, too, and had many stallions, young male camels, and rams slaughtered for the occasion. He had three tents set up at three different places: one was white, one was red and the third was black. He ordered that whoever was without children be accommodated in the black tent,[2] with a black felt rug under him, and that he be served the stew of the black sheep. He said, "Let him eat if he wants to eat; if he does not, let him go." He then said: "Put the man with a son in the white tent, and the man with a daughter in the red tent. The man without any children is cursed by Allah, and we curse him, too. Let this be clear to all."

The Oghuz princes began to gather one by one. It happened that a prince among them by the name of Dirse Khan had neither a son nor a daughter. He spoke to the men as follows. Let us see, my khan, what he said:

"When the cooling breeze of morning blows,
And the bearded gray lark sings his song,
And the long-bearded Persian chants the ezan;[3]
When the Bedouin horses snicker on seeing their master.
At the time of the twilight,
When the beautiful-breasted mountains
*   are touched by the sun —*
At such a time, the warriors and gallant princes
*   prepare for action."*

At the break of dawn Dirse Khan, accompanied by forty warriors,[4] set out for the feast of Bayindir Khan.

Bayindir Khan's warriors welcomed Dirse Khan and asked him to go into the black tent, the floor of which was covered with a black felt rug. They placed the stew of black sheep before him and said, "My Khan, this is the order of Bayindir Khan."

Dirse Khan asked: "What fault has Bayindir Khan found in me? Is it because of my sword or my table? He has men of lower status accommodated in the white and red tents. What is my fault that I am being put in a black tent?"

They said, "My khan, today Bayindir Khan's order is as follows: 'Whoever is without a son or a daughter is cursed by Allah; we curse him too.'"

Standing up, Dirse Khan said to his men: "Rise and let us be off, my young men. The fault is either in me or in my lady."

Dirse Khan returned home, called his lady and said to her:

"Will you come here, my love, the crown of my home?
Walking along so tall, like a cypress tree,
With long black hair that falls to her feet,
With brows like a tightened bow;
With a mouth too small for two almonds;
Her red cheeks like the apples of autumn.
My melon, my lady, my love!
Do you know what happened to me?

Bayindir Khan had three tents put up: one white, one red, and one black. He had guests with sons put in the white tent; those with daughters in the red tent; and those with neither in the black tent with black felt carpet spread on its floor. He ordered that the stewed

---

[1]Even at this early date Damascus was known for its fine fabrics. Besides being a product of high quality, a Damascus tent may also have been a status symbol.
[2]Black was an unlucky color among the Oghuz and later Turks.
[3]The ezan is the call to prayer chanted five times a day from a minaret by an announcer called the muezzin.
[4]Forty is perhaps the most popular number in Turkish folklore. The world is controlled by Forty Saints, often referred to simply as "The Forty." Princes have forty retainers, and ladies have forty maids. Weddings traditionally last for forty days and forty nights. Many acts of purification involve forty motions or gestures. Later in this legend Bugach's wound is healed by magic remedy in forty days.

meat of the black sheep be served them by saying 'If they eat, let them eat; if they do not, let them go away. Since almighty Allah cursed them, we curse them, too.'" When I reached there they met me and led me to the black tent, laid black felt carpet under me, and served me the stewed meat of the black sheep, saying 'The man without a son or a daughter is cursed by Allah; therefore he is cursed by us, too. Let this be known to you.' "My wife, who of us is sterile, you or I? Why does almighty Allah not give us a healthy son?" Dirse Khan then continued in song.

"O child of khan, shall I now get up
And grasp you by the throat,
And crush you beneath my hard boots?
Shall I draw my sword of black steel
And remove your head from your body,
And show you how sweet life can be?
Shall I spill your red blood on the ground?
O child of a khan, tell the reason to me,
Or I shall inflict something dreadful on you."

The wife of Dirse Khan replied:

"Oh, Dirse Khan, be not cruel to me.
Be not angry and speak so harshly to me.
But come now and have your red tent set up.
Have some stallions, some rams,
*   and some male camels slaughtered.*
Invite then the princes of Inner and Outer Oghuz.
Feed all the hungry, give clothes to the naked,
*   and pay off the debts of the poor.*[5]
Heap up meat like a hill;
Make a lakeful of koumiss, and give a magnificent feast.
Then speak your wish. Maybe Allah
*   will give us a healthy son,*
An answer to prayers of a worthy man."[6]

Following his lady's advice, Dirse Khan gave a large feast and then made his wish. He had stallions, young male camels, and rams slaughtered. He invited all the princes of the Inner and the Outer Oghuz to the feast. He fed the hungry, dressed the naked, and paid off the debts of the debtor; he had meat heaped up like a hill, and a lakeful of koumiss made. The princes raised their hands to the heavens and prayed. Consequently, the wish of Dirse Khan was fulfilled, and his lady became

pregnant. In due time she bore a male child. She had her child brought up in the care of nurses. As the horse is quick of foot, so the minstrel is quick of tongue. As vertebrated and ribbed creatures grow fast, in the same way the son of Dirse Khan was soon fifteen years old.

One day Dirse Khan and his son went to the camp of Bayindir Khan. Bayindir Khan had a bull and a young male camel. The bull could powder harsh stones like flour with the impact of his horns. The bull and the camel were set to fight one another twice a year, once in the summer and once in autumn. Bayindir Khan and the strong Oghuz princes used to enjoy themselves watching these fights.

This bull was let out of the palace one summer day. Three men on each side were holding it with iron chains. The bull was released in the middle of a playing field, where the son of Dirse Khan was playing at knucklebones with three other boys from the camp. When the bull was released the three other boys were told to run away. The other three boys ran away but the son of Dirse Khan stood where he was. The bull ran toward the boy with the intent to kill him. The boy dealt the bull a terrific blow on the forehead, making it stagger backward. Then he pushed the bull to the edge of the playing field with his fist pressing on his forehead. There they struggled to and fro. The bull stood pressing its forelegs against the ground, while the boy kept his fist on its forehead. It was impossible to say which was the winner. The boy thought to himself: The pole holds the tent straight. Why am I supporting this bull?" Saying so, he pulled away his fist and ran to one side, while the bull, unable to stand on its feet, crashed on the ground head downward. Then the boy cut the throat of the bull with his knife.

The Oghuz princes gathered around the boy and said: "Well done, boy! Let Dede Korkut come and name him, then take him to his father and request a principality and a throne for him."

When they called for Dede Korkut, he came. He took the young man to his father and said to him:

"O Dirse Khan!
Give this young man a principality now.
Give him a throne for the sake of his virtue.
Give him also a tall Bedouin horse
He can ride — such a capable man.
Give him ten thousand sheep

---

[5]Such acts as these were regarded by the Oghuz people as being most charitable and virtuous.
[6]The ancient Turks as illustrated in these legends, were in the habit of giving large communal feasts, often clothing as well as feeding the poor, in order to gain the favor of the Deity and thus secure their own wishes. This charitable tradition has continued down to the present.

To make shish kebab for himself; he has virtue.
Give him next a red camel out of your herd.
Let it carry his goods; he has virtue.
Give a large lavish tent with a golden pole
To provide him with shade.
Give a suit to this man
*   and a coat that has birds on its shoulders.*
Let him wear both of these; he has skill.

This young man fought and killed a bull on the playing field of Bayindir Khan, continued Dede Korkut. Therefore, let your son's name be Bugach.[7] I give him his name, and may Allah give him his years of life.

Upon this, Dirse Khan gave his son a principality and a throne.

After the son had sat upon the throne for a while, he began to despise the forty young warriors of his father. As a result of this, they bore him a grudge and plotted among themselves: "Let us turn his father against him, so that he may put the son to death, and thus our esteem with the khan may continue and grow."

Twenty of these warriors went to Dirse Khan and said to him: "Do you know what has happened, Dirse Khan? Your son (may he never prosper) has become a very bad-tempered man. Taking his forty warriors, he attacked the mighty Oghuz people. When he saw a pretty girl, he kidnapped her. He insulted old men with white beards and squeezed the breasts of white-haired old women. The news of these evil deeds of your son will reach the ears of Bayindir Khan — and people will be saying, 'How could the son of Dirse Khan do such terrible things?'" The warriors then continued: "You would rather die than live. Bayindir Khan will call you to his presence and will give you a serious punishment. Such a son is not worthy of you. It is better not to have such a son. Why do you not put him to death?"

"Bring him over here. I shall kill him," said Dirse Khan.

While he was speaking his name, the other twenty treacherous young men came and gave Dirse Khan the following false information. "Your son went hunting in the beautiful mountains where he killed wild animals and birds without your permission. He brought the game to his mother. He drank strong red wine and had a good time in her company and there made up his mind to kill his father. Your son has become an evil person. The news of these deeds will reach Bayindir Khan, Khan of Khans, over Ala Mountain and people

will begin to say, 'How could Dirse Khan's son do such terrible things?' They will call you before Bayindir Khan and punish you there. Such a son is not worthy of you. Why do you not kill him?"

"Bring him over here. I shall kill him. I do not want a son like him," said Dirse Khan.

His warriors said: "How can we bring your son here? He will not listen to us. Get up; take your warriors with you, call on your son and ask him to go hunting with you. Then kill him with an arrow during the hunt. If you cannot kill him in this way, you will never be able to kill him."

When the cooling breeze of morn blows,
And the bearded gray lark sings his song,
When Bedouin horses snicker on seeing their master,
And the long-bearded Persian chants the ezan,
At the time of the twilight when girls
And brides of the mighty Oghuz
*   wear their gorgeous gowns,*
When the beautiful-breasted mountains
*   are touched by the sun —*
At such a time, the warriors and gallant princes
*   prepare for action.*

At the break of dawn, Dirse Khan arose and set out for the hunt, taking his son and forty warriors with him. They hunted wild animals and birds for a while. Then some of the treacherous warriors approached Dirse Khan's son and said to him: "Your father said, 'I want see how my son rides, and how he uses his sword and shoots his arrow. This will make me happy and proud and will give me confidence.'"

Not knowing his father's real intention, Bugach chased the deer and drove them toward his father and killed them before him. While doing this Bugach said to himself, "Let my father see me ride and be proud; let him see me shoot my arrow and have confidence; let him see how I use my sword and rejoice."

The forty treacherous warriors then said to Dirse Khan: "Dirse Khan, do you see how he is driving the deer toward you? He means to shoot his arrow at you and kill you. Kill him before he kills you."

After the young men had driven the deer past his father several times, Dirse took out his strong bow strung with the tendon of a wolf. Standing in his stirrups, he pulled his bowstring hard and let his arrow go. He shot his son between the shoulder blades. When the

---

[7]The name Bugach was given the young man because he had killed a bull, buga in Turkish.

arrow pierced his chest, red blood poured out, filling his shirt. He clasped his horse's neck and slipped to earth. Dirse Khan wanted to fall upon the body of his son, but his men did not let allow him to do so. He then turned the head of his horse in the opposite direction and rode to his camp.

Dirse Khan's lady had decided to celebrate her son's first hunt by giving a feast to the mighty Oghuz princes, and for this purpose she had stallions, young male camels and rams killed. She now arose and taking with her the forty narrow-waisted girls of her household went to welcome Dirse Khan. Lifting her head, she looked first at Dirse Khan, and then gazed around, but nowhere could she see her dear son. She was shocked, and her heart began to beat fast. Her black eyes were filled with tears. Let us hear what she said to her husband.

"Come to me here,
The crown of my head, the throne of my house,
My khan father's son-in-law,
My lady mother's favorite,
You, who were given me by my parents,
You whom I saw when I opened my eyes,
The one whom I loved at first sight.
O Dirse Khan, you arose from your place;
You mounted the back of your stallion strong,
And hunted the mountain with beautiful breasts.
You rode off as two, but return now alone.
Where is my son whom I found in the dark of the night?
My searching eye — may it be confounded
*   — twitches badly,*[8] *Dirse Khan*
My child-nursing breast — may it go quite dry — is sore.
My white skin is swollen,
*   though bitten by no yellow snake.*
My one son is lost! My poor heart is burning!
Water I poured into beds of dry rivers.[9]
Alms I have given to black-suited dervishes.[10]
The hungry I saw I have fed.
I had meat heaped up like a hill;
I had lakefuls of koumiss fermented,
And I managed with great travail, to bear a son.
Tell me, Dirse Khan, what befell my only son!
Say if you let our son fall down Ala Mountain out there.

Say if you let our son be carried down
*   the fast-flowing river.*
Say if you let our son be eaten by lions and tigers.
Say if you let black-dressed infidels,
*   they of a savage faith,*
Capture our son.
Let me go to my father, the khan,
*   and take money and soldiers,*
To strike at the infidels, they with the savage religion.
Let me never return from the search of my son
Before I am wounded, fall off my strong horse,
Wiping away my red blood with my sleeve,
And sprawl on the road with broken limbs.
Tell me, O Dirse Khan, what befell my only son.
Let my luckless head be a sacrifice for you this day."

So speaking, she wept and gave voice to her sorrow. But Dirse Khan did not answer her.

Meanwhile, those forty treacherous men came along. They said to her: "Your son is safe and well. He has been hunting. He will be back today or tomorrow. Do not worry about him. He cannot speak now, because he is a bit drunk."

Dirse Khan's lady turned back, but she could not rest. With her forty slim girls, she mounted and rode in search of her son. She climbed Kazilik Mountain from which snow and ice never melt all the year round. She spurred her horse and rode in that direction.

This was the place where the young man had collapsed. When the crows had seen blood, they wanted to come down upon him, but his two dogs kept the crows from his body. When the young man had fallen there, the gray-horsed Hizir had appeared to him and, stroking his wounds three times, had said: "Do not be afraid of these wounds. You will not die of them. Mountain flowers mixed with your mother's milk will be balm to them." Having said this, he disappeared.

Then the young man's mother came upon him. Seeing her son lying there covered with blood, she addressed him with the following song. Let us see, my khan, what she said.

"Your black eyes now taken by sleep — let them open.
Your strong healthy bones have been broken,

---

[8]Twitching of the eye, like a ringing of the ears, is an omen of coming difficulty or disaster. The belief is still common in Turkey.

[9]A figurative expression to suggest the utmost effort to be charitable.

[10]In Islamic countries, men belonging to various religious sects once wandered in groups to visit cities, towns, villages, and tribal communities. There they read from the Koran, sang hymns, and in turn, received alms from the people. It was believed that largesse to such wandering dervishes would win the favor of Allah. These beliefs derived from the ancient religious concepts of the Turks as well as from the traditions of Islam, which the Turks later accepted.

Your soul has all but flown from your frame.
If your body retains any life, let me know.
Let my poor luckless head be a sacrifice to you.
Kazilik Mountain, your waters still flow;
Let them, I pray, cease their flowing
Kazilik Mountain, your grasses still grow;
Let them, I pray, cease their growing.
Kazilik Mountain, you deer still run fast;
Let them cease running and turn into stone.
How can I know, my son, if it was lion
Or tiger? How can I know, my son?
How did this accident happen to you?
If your life is still in your body, my son, let me know.
Let my poor luckless head be a sacrifice to you.
Speak a few words to me now."

As she said these things, her words entered his mind. He lifted his head, opened his eyes, and looked at his mother's face. He spoke to her. Let us see, my khan, what he said.

"Come closer, my mother,
Whose milk I once drank,
White-haired, beloved, and honorable mother.
Curse not running streams;
Kazilik Mountain has done no wrong.
Curse not its growing grass;
Kazilik Mountain has no sins.
Curse not its swift-running deer;
Kazilik Mountain has no fault.
Curse not the lions and tigers;
Kazilik Mountain has no guilt.
The evil and guilt all belong to my father.

The young man then went on, "Do not cry, Mother. Do not worry. This wound will not kill me. The gray-horsed Hizir came to me and stroked my wound three times, saying, 'You will not die of this wound. Mountain flowers mixed with your mother's milk will be your balm.'"

As the horse is quick of foot, so the poet is quick of tongue. My khan, the young man's wounds were healed in forty days and he recovered completely. He was once again able to ride and wear his sword, to hunt and shoot birds. Dirse Khan knew nothing of all this. He thought that his son was dead.

But his forty treacherous men soon heard of this and discussed among themselves what they should do. They said: "If Dirse Khan sees his son, he will kill us all. Let us catch Dirse Khan, tie his white hands at his back, put a rope around his white neck, and take him to the

land of the infidels." They did as they had decided. They tied his white hands behind him, and they put a rope around his white neck. Then they beat him until blood oozed from his white flesh. Dirse Khan was made to walk while they accompanied him on horseback. They led him to the land of the bloody infidels. While Dirse Khan was thus a captive, the Oghuz boys knew nothing of his plight.

Dirse Khan's lady, however, learned of this. She went to her son and spoke to him. Let us see, my khan, what she said.

"Do you know what has happened my son? Not only the steep rocks but the very earth should have shaken, for although there were no enemies in our lands, your father was attacked. Those forty treacherous companions of his captured him, tied his white hands behind him, put a rope around his neck, and forced him to walk while they rode on horseback. They took him toward infidel territory. Come now, my son. Take your warriors with you and save your father from those faithless men. Go now and spare your father, even if he did not spare you."

The young man followed his mother's advice. He arose, strapped on his big steel sword, took his tight bow in one hand, and held his golden spear under his other arm. Then, as his strong horse was held, he mounted and, accompanied by his forty young men, went in pursuit of his father.

The treacherous retainers of Dirse Khan had stopped along the way and were drinking strong red wine. As Bugach Khan rode along, the forty treacherous men saw him approaching. They said, "Let us go and capture that young man and take both him and Dirse Khan to the infidels."

Dirse Khan said: "Oh, my forty companions, there is no doubt about the oneness of Allah. Untie my hands, give me a lute, and I shall persuade that young man to go back. Let me loose or kill me." They untied his hands and gave him his lute.

Dirse Khan did not know that the young man was his own son. He went to him and sang.

"If the stallions have gone, let me count them my loss.
Tell me if any of yours were among them,
So that I may restore them without any fight. Turn back!
If a thousand sheep have gone from the fold,
    let me count them my loss.
Tell me if any of yours were among them,
So that I may restore them without any fight. Turn back!
If red camels have gone from the herd,
    let me count them my loss.

Tell me if any of yours are among them,
So that I may restore them without any fight. Turn back!
If some golden-topped tents have gone,
    let me count them my loss.
Tell me if any of yours are among them,
So that I may restore them without any fight. Turn back!
If brides with brown eyes and white faces have gone,
    let me count them my loss.
And if your betrothed was among them, tell me,
So that I may restore her without any fight. Turn back!
If white-bearded elders have gone,
    let me count them my loss.
If your white bearded father was among them, tell me,
So that I may restore him without any fight. Turn back!
If you came after me, I have killed my own son.
Young man, it is not any sin that it is yours. Turn back!"

The young man replied to the song of his father.
Let us see, my khan, what he said.

"Tall stallions may count as your loss,
But one of the lost ones is mine;
I shall not give him up to the forty base men.
From the herds the red camels may count as your loss,
But some of those camels are mine;
I shall not give them up to the forty base men.
Thousands of sheep may be counted your loss,
But among them are some that are mine;
I shall not give them up to the forty base men.
The brides with brown eyes and white faces
    may count as your loss,
But among them is my betrothed;
I shall not give them up to the forty base men.
If the golden-topped tents may be counted your loss,
Mine too is among them;
I shall not give them up to the forty base men.
If white-bearded elders are counted your loss,
My foolish old father is also among them;
I shall not give them up to the forty base men."

He waved a handkerchief to his own forty young men, and they came and gathered around him. With their aid, he fought with the enemy. Some of these he killed and some he captured. When he had saved his father in this manner, he returned home.

Dirse Khan thus discovered that his son was alive. Bayindir Khan, Khan of Khans gave the young man a principality and a throne. Dede Korkut sang songs on the occasion and composed this legend of the Oghuz. Following this, he sang:

"Even they passed away from this world.
They stayed for a while and then moved along,
Just as the caravan does.
Even they were removed by death
While this world remained behind,
The world where men come and go,
The world which is rounded off by death."

Then he said: "When black Death comes, may Allah keep you safe. May He let you rule in good health. May Almighty Allah whom I praise be your friend and keeper."

This I pray, my khan. May your tall, stately mountains never fall. May your big shade tree never be cut down, and may your clear running waters never run dry. May your wings never be broken. May your gray horse never slip while running. May your big steel sword never be notched and may your spear never be broken in battle. May your white-haired mother's and white-bearded father's place be paradise. May Allah keep your household fire burning. May our merciful Allah never abandon you to the guile of the treacherous.

From *The Book of Dede Korkut: A Turkish Epic.* Translated into English and Edited by Faruk Sumer, Ahmet E. Uysal, and Warren S. Walker, University of Texas Press, Austin & London.

Nasreddin Hoca Stories

Suggested Time	3-4 classroom periods.
Materials Needed	A class set of **Worksheet 1**
Background Information	Oral literature has been an abiding Turkish tradition, and Turkey still remains strongly rooted in oral tradition. The Book of Dede Korkut and the poems of Yunus Emre are both from the oral tradition. In many of the villages in rural Turkey, much of the lore governing the activities of daily life is transmitted from generation to generation by the spoken word. Each region has distinctive folk dances and songs, and villages boast folk poets who compose songs of love and adventure that are sung at weddings and other public occasions. Teams of storytellers participate in competitions. In one competition storytellers are accompanied by a stringed instrument called a **saz** as they compose poems spontaneously according to rhymes suggested by the audience. Each minstrel must recite his poem with a needle between his lips and must avoid the pronunciation of the consonants B, M, and P, all of which cause the needle to pierce the lips.
	In this unit we will first read anecdotes about Nasreddin Hoca, one of the most beloved and celebrated personalities of the Middle East. He lived in the 1200's. He was very cunning, clever and humorous and seemed to have an answer for everything. The name "Nasreddin" means "Helper of the Faith," and the word "**Hoca**" denotes a learned man.
Key Concepts	folktale anecdote character theme
Aim	To analyze the extent to which the Hoca stories reveal Turkish culture.
Major Idea	▷ The narrative tradition of folktales and anecdotes are an important component of Turkish aesthetic life. Folktales about archetypal folk characters reflect Turkish values and identity.
Performance Objectives	Students will be able to: 1. Define folktales and anecdotes. 2. List elements of culture presented in folktales. 3. Compare their own traditions with those found in folktales.

Motivation　Ask students: How might a culture show that it values wisdom? Have students create a list of images that they associate with each of the following: a wise person, a somewhat wise person, and a fool. Discuss these images. After they finish reading the Hoca story, have them compare their images with the ones used in the story.

Development　Myths and **folktales** tell about the beginnings of things. They are the stories of a culture which are repeated from one generation to the next. Folktales record forms of work, customs, dress, traditional greetings, power relationships and festivals. They may often convey the theme that a struggle against severe difficulties in life is unavoidable and that if one confronts life's hardships head on one can master obstacles and emerge victorious.

An **anecdote** is a short tale, set in the real world. The Nasreddin Hoca anecdotes that we will read are based on humorous situations and reveal the insight of the peasant mind. They moralize, satirize and illustrate social truths.

▷　Distribute **Worksheet 1** to students. Since the stories are short, students can easily read the three anecdotes and complete the questions in 10 minutes. Ask for a volunteer to read each anecdote aloud to class and review questions. Teacher will write the following guiding questions on the chalkboard.
  ♦　Describe Nasreddin Hoca.
  ♦　How does he allow us to stumble upon the truth?
  ♦　Although some may call Hoca a fool, is there a "method to his madness"?
  ♦　Describe the moral or spiritual lessons of the stories.
▷　Have students silently read the supplementary anecdotes, select a favorite and practice reading this anecdote aloud to the other students in the class. Call on volunteers to "perform" their anecdotes.

Homework　Assign Cengidilaver (**Worksheet 2**) for homework. Ask students to find two examples of customs in the story.

Backward on the Donkey

ONE FRIDAY AS NASREDDIN HOCA WAS GET-
TING READY TO GO TO THE MOSQUE TO READ
THE LESSON FROM THE KORAN TO THE
congregation, he heard a Tak! Tak! Tak! at his door. As
he opened the door he found all the boys from school
standing in the courtyard. "What is this!" he exclaimed.

"Well, Hoca Effendi, we decided to go with you to
the service today," said one. And the others agreed that
this was so.

"I'll be happy to have you attend the service," said
the Hoca, "but I'm not quite ready yet to leave. Just wait
out there, and I'll be along in a minute or so."

The Hoca shut the door and quickly put on his
long coat and his ample turban. Then he hurried to the
door, opened it, slipped into shoes beside the doorstep,
and rushed across the courtyard to mount his donkey.
But in his haste, he mounted his donkey backward!

The boys began to grin and nudge one another,
wondering what the Hoca would find to say about his
ridiculous mistake. As for the Hoca, he was wondering,
too, but he kept a firm grasp on his wits as he glanced
from one boy to another.

"I suppose you are all wondering," he said "why
I have seated myself backward on my donkey, but I
have my reasons. If I were to seat myself forward on
my donkey and ride ahead of you, I could not keep an
eye on you.

On the other hand, if I were to sit forward on the
donkey and ride behind you so that I could watch you,
that would be improper, for I am your master. Therefore, I am riding ahead of you and keeping my eye on
you!"

▷ Tak! Tak! Tak! is best translated as:
  A. hello, B. goodbye, C. knock, knock.
▷ The real reason Nasreddin Hoca mounted the donkey backwards was because he:
  A. wanted to make the boys laugh, B. was in a hurry, C. wanted to keep his eye on the boys.
▷ Hoca tried to recover his dignity by appealing to the boys':
  A. sense of shame, B. respect for elders, C. love of fun.
▷ Have you ever tried to "cover up" an embarrassing situation in the same way? Did your excuse
  convince others?

Nasreddin Hoca as Preacher

ONCE NASREDDIN HOCA WAS ASSIGNED AS RELIGIOUS LEADER IN A VILLAGE. TAKING OVER THE DUTIES OF THE FORMER PREACHER, Nasreddin Hoca appeared at the mosque for the Friday noon service. But he had just moved to that village, and had not had time to prepare a sermon. From the mimber, he addressed the congregation in the mosque: "O people, do you know what I shall talk to you about today?"

Hesitating for only a moment, the congregation answered, "No, we don't."

"Well neither do I," said the Hoca, and he climbed back down the steps of the mimber and went along home.

On the next Friday, Nasreddin Hoca went to the mosque again and having ascended the mimber, he asked the congregation the same question: "O people, do you know what I shall talk to you about today?"

"Yes we do," was their reply.

"In that case," said the Hoca, "it will be unnecessary for me to repeat it."

And he climbed down the steps of the mimber and went along home.

On the third Friday, the people gathered ahead of time in order to decide what to say when the Hoca asked them his difficult question. They decided that half of them would say that they knew what he was going to talk about and the other half would say they did not know.

When Nasreddin Hoca arrived at the mosque and had mounted the mimber, he addressed the congregation: "O my good people, do you know what I going to talk to you about today?"

Some said "Yes, we do."

"Others said "No, we don't."

Upon hearing this, the Hoca replied, "If that is the way it is, then let those who know tell those who don't know." And descending the steps of the mimber, he went along home.

On the following week, the people again gathered before the Friday noon service. One of them said, "This new man is so quick at repartee that no matter what we might say, he would find a reason for not preaching a sermon. Therefore, this week let us not give any answer at all to whatever question he may ask us." Everyone agreed with that suggestion.

Shortly the Hoca entered the mosque, ascended the mimber, and asked, "O people, do you know what I shall talk to you about today?"

No one answered a single word. He asked the same question a second time and then a third time. Still no one uttered a sound.

"Ah!" said Nasreddin Hoca. "It seems that no one has come to the mosque today to hear my sermon!" With that, the Hoca walked down the steps of the mimber and went along home without having delivered a sermon.

> A **mimber** is a:
> A. bell, B. place where the sermon is delivered, C. prayer.
> Each time the Hoca comes to the mosque he:
> A. tricks the congregation, B. delivers a sermon, C. says nothing.
> One can conclude from the story that on Fridays people traditionally:
> A. clean house, B. attend political meetings, C. go to the mosque.

The Hoca and the Drought

ONE DAY, NASREDDIN HOCA HAPPENED TO BE VISITING IN A SMALL VILLAGE WHICH HAD NO RAIN FOR MANY WEEKS. THE VILLAGERS, despite great care in the use of their water, had at last found themselves reduced to just a cupful for each family.

"Oh, Hoca," begged one of the men, "please do something. If this drought continues, we shall all die."

Do something about rain? Rain was in the hands of Allah. No one could be certain when it would rain...Suddenly the Hoca smiled. "Bring me a bucket of water," he said, "and, Allah willing, the rain will come."

The villagers hurried to bring their small hoards of water, a cup here, a cup there. With all their supplies, they could fill no more than a pail.

To their astonishment, the Hoca removed his shirt and began to wash in the precious water. "Aman, Hoca!" said one of the men. "How can you do that? We have been saving that water to preserve the very lives of our children!"

But the Hoca made no response at all, either to this protest or to the increased grumblings that followed. He scrubbed earnestly at his shirt until it had been thoroughly washed. Then, wringing it out carefully, he hung it on a bush to dry.

No sooner had the shirt been safely draped over the bush when the skies opened and a veritable cloudburst came. Drenched by the welcome rain, the villagers gathered around the Hoca and asked him how he managed such a miracle. "Well, you see," said the Hoca, "I never yet have hung my clean shirt out to dry but what the heavens have sent a regular deluge!"

▷ A **deluge** is a:
  A. drought, B. cloud, C. rainfall
▷ The people were shocked when Hoca washed his shirt because:
  A. he was always dirty, B. he used their whole supply of water, C. only women washed clothes.
▷ It finally rained because:
  A. it always rained when Hoca left clothes out to dry, B. Hoca prayed to God, C. it had been raining for forty days.

Supplementary Anecdotes

On being asked his age , Nasreddin Hoca said, "Forty."

"But, Hoca, that's what you said last year!"

"That's right. I'm a man of my word. I always stick to what I say."

~

Nasreddin Hoca, with his son, was going to visit a friend in a village. He put the boy on the donkey and he walked alongside.

"Look at these young men of today," some people who saw them said. " What a shame! making his old father walk while he rides the donkey in comfort!"

"Father, it is not my fault," said the boy to his father. "You said that I should ride the donkey."

So saying, the boy dismounted and Hoca mounted the animal. But no sooner had they gone a short distance than several passing people called out, "Oh, look at that hard-hearted brute! Isn't it a shame to make the poor lad run like that and bake in the sun while he himself rides the animal comfortably!"

Hoca thereupon pulled the boy up, and put him behind him on the donkey. But they had not gone far before others saw them and said, "What cruelty! Two people riding on a poor donkey!"

At last Nasreddin Hoca lost his temper. They both got down and drove the donkey before them.

It wasn't long before still others came along, and seeing them, cried "Look at those stupid people! Letting their donkey go free and easy while they trudge in the heat. What idiots there are in this world!"

Hearing this, Nasreddin Hoca said to himself, "How true it is! No one can please everyone."

~

One day the neighborhood boys arranged to play a trick on Nasreddin Hoca: they would make him climb a tree, and while he was up there , they would steal his shoes. Standing at the foot of the tree, they began to discuss the question in great excitement. "No one can climb this tree," they cried.

Nasreddin Hoca passed by, and hearing what the children had said, went up to them and said, "I can climb that tree." And tucking up his skirts he proceeded to squeeze his shoes into his pocket.

"Why do you put your shoes in your pocket?" they asked. "You won't need them up the tree."

"How do you know I shall not?" Nasreddin Hoca said. "Let me keep them handy in case I find a road up there."

~

A poor man found a crust of dry bread and was thinking how he could find something to give it a relish when he passed by a sidewalk cooking stand. There was a saucepan of meat sizzling and boiling on the fire. It gave out delicious aromas.

He broke the bread into little bits and pieces and held them in the steam until they became quite soft. Then he ate them. The cook, however, caught hold of this poor man and demanded payment.

The man refused to pay, saying that he had not taken any of his food. Besides he had no money. The cook took him to the court. It so happened that the kadi, the judge, was none other than our friend Nasreddin Hoca.

After listening to both men, Judge Nasreddin Hoca, took a few coins from his pocket and, shaking them in his palm, asked the cook if he heard the coins rattling. "Yes, your Honor," he answered.

"Well, the sound of these coins will be your payment," Nasreddin Hoca said. "Take it and leave."

"What kind of judgement is this, your Honor?" the man protested angrily.

"It is a perfect settlement of your claim," Judge Nasreddin explained. "Anyone who is so mean to ask money for the steam from his meat deserves the sound of these coins."

~

While carrying a load of glassware home, Nasreddin Hoca dropped it in the street. People gathered around him and all the smashed glassware.

"What's the matter with you people?" asked Nasreddin Hoca. "Haven't you ever seen a fool before?"

~

On a frigid and snowy winter day Nasreddin Hoca was having a chat with some of his friends in the local coffee house. He said that cold weather did not bother him, and in fact he could stay, if necessary, all night without any heat.

"We will take you up on that, Hoca," they said. "If you stand by all night in the village square without warming yourself by any external means, each of us will treat you to a sumptuous meal. But if you fail to do so, you will treat us all to dinner."

"All right, it's a bet," Hoca said.

That very night, Nasreddin Hoca stood in the village square till morning despite the bitter cold. In the morning he ran triumphantly to his friends and told them they should be ready to fulfill their promise.

"But as a matter of fact you lost the bet, Hoca," said one of them. "At about midnight just before I went to sleep, I saw a candle burning in a window about three hundred yards away from where you were standing. That certainly means that you warmed yourself by it."

That's ridiculous," Nasreddin Hoca argued. "How can a candle behind a window warm a person from three hundred yards?"

All his protestations were to no avail, and it was decided that Hoca had lost the bet. Nasreddin Hoca accepted their verdict and invited all of them to a dinner at his home.

They all arrived on time, laughing and joking, anticipating the delicious meal Hoca was going to serve them. But dinner was not ready . Hoca told them that it would be ready in a short time and left the room to "prepare" the meal. A long time passed, and still no dinner was served. Finally, getting impatient and very hungry, they went into the kitchen to see if there was any food cooking at all. What they saw, they could not believe. Nasreddin Hoca was standing by a huge cauldron, suspended from the ceiling. There was a lighted candle under the cauldron.

"Be patient, my friends," Nasreddin Hoca told them. "Dinner will be ready soon. You see it is cooking."

"Are you out of your mind, Hoca?" they shouted. "How could such a tiny flame boil such a large pot?"

"Your ignorance of such matters amuses me," Nasreddin Hoca said. "If the flame of a candle behind a window three hundred yards away can warm a person, surely the flame will boil this pot which is only three inches away from it!"

~

One winter Nasreddin Hoca was very hard up. He cut down his family's expenses to make ends meet, but still was having a very tough time. He decided to cut down his donkey's oats as well.

So every time he fed the animal, he gave him a little less than before, and the donkey remained as lively as ever. Later on, when he had reduced the feed by one handful, the donkey did not seem to mind.

Nasreddin Hoca went on his way until he had reduced the ration by one half. Although the donkey had become very quiet, he still looked very fit.

Two months passed and he had reduced the donkey's ration to less than a half. But now the poor brute was not only quiet but looked miserable. He could scarcely stand. He now rarely touched his straw. His ration of oats was just a handful.

One morning Nasreddin Hoca entered the stable and found the animal dead. "Ah! My poor donkey," he said to himself, "just when he was getting accustomed to living on nothing, he died!"

~

Nasreddin Hoca went to the bazaar and bought his household's weekly vegetables and other groceries. He put them in a sack over his shoulder, mounted his donkey and headed home.

On the way he met a friend who wondered why Hoca was carrying the sack on his shoulder rather than tying it onto the animal.

Nasreddin Hoca answered, "My poor donkey has a big enough load carrying me, and he doesn't need any extra weight, so I carry the sack myself."

~

Nasreddin Hoca was invited to a feast, and he went there in his everyday clothes. He was seated at the far end of the room where no one paid further attention to him. The guests who were all finely dressed were casting scornful glances at his modest attire, and the food servers acted as if Hoca was not in the room. Realizing that it would be a long time before he was served, he got up ran home, put on a fine fur coat, and returned to the festive hall where he was now received with great deference and was seated at the head of the table with the important people of the town. When the soup was brought, Nasreddin Hoca took a spoonful of it, and spilled it drop by drop onto the collar of his fur coat saying in a clearly audible voice, "Eat, my fur coat, eat! All this honor is not for me but for you alone! It is not I, but you who were invited here!"

~

Although he was an imam, the religious leader of his community, Nasreddin Hoca did not mind speaking about death humorously. One day just before a funeral, one of the mourners asked him on which side of the coffin he should walk in the procession.

"It doesn't matter on which side of the coffin you are," Nasreddin Hoca answered, so long as you are not inside it."

~

One rainy day Nasreddin Hoca was sitting indoors, and as he looked down the street he saw one of his neighbors pass by in a great hurry for fear of getting wet. Nasreddin Hoca opened the window and cried out, "Aren't you ashamed of yourself running away from God's gift?"

By a strange coincidence the same man was looking out of his window one rainy day and saw Nasreddin Hoca run past although only a few drops had fallen.

"Hoca," he cried, "why are you running from rain? Rain is God's gift?"

Nasreddin Hoca paused for a moment and said, "I'm running because I don't want to tread God's gift under my feet."

From: *The Wit and Wisdom of Nasreddin Hoca*, by Nejat Muallimoğlu.

Folktales: Cengidilaver

Major Idea ▷ The narrative tradition of folktales and anecdotes are an important component of Turkish aesthetic life. Folktales about archetypal folk characters reflect Turkish values and identity.

Performance Objectives

Students will be able to:
1. Define the concept of a heroic figure.
2. To assess the cultural values in *Cengidilaver*
3. Create a modern fairy tale.

Materials A class set of **Worksheet 1**

Procedure/ Development

▷ Ask students to list one person, they consider heroic. Allow three to five minutes for students to briefly write out their reasons for this selection. After students finish, call on volunteers to share their writings.

♦ On the chalkboard develop a set of criteria used by the students in their selection.

▷ Divide the class into groups of three or four. Based on the story they read for homework (**Worksheet 1**) ask each group to review the content of the story by answering the following questions:

♦ Compile a list of the "tests" or trials that the brother must endure.

♦ What does *Cengidilaver* represent?

♦ How does the boy's success change the world around him?

♦ Look back at the story. Note the sections or paragraphs that are repeated two or more times. Have one student in each group read the repetition aloud. What is the storyteller's purpose in using this technique? Can you think of other literary examples which employ repetition for artistic effect?

▷ When students have finished, call on one or two groups to share findings with class.

▷ Review the set of criteria that is on the chalkboard. According to these standards, would you consider the brother to be a hero? Explain.

▷ Refer to the list of customs and values that students wrote down for homework. What do these customs and values tell us about society?

Summary A folktale is an oral speech act whose narrative structure includes the development of plot and character and whose theme interprets, reinforces and perpetuates community values.

To what extent do 21st century societies use folktales to convey concepts of right and wrong? Be prepared to give concrete examples of the use of folktales drawn from your own experiences.

Writing Assignment   *Cengidilaver* has many of the traditional elements of other folktales and fairytales. There is an evil witch-like character; babies taken from their real homes/mothers and floated down a river; poor but honest and kind rescuers; three wishes available to the protagonists; and stylistic repetition. Select one or more of these traditional ingredients and create a modern day fairytale.

Cengidilaver

ONCE THERE WAS AND ONCE THERE WASN'T, WHEN THE FLEA WAS A PORTER AND THE CAMEL A BARBER, WHEN I WAS ROCKING MY father's cradle tingir mingir — well, in those times, there was a powerful sultan. The sultan had all the good things of this earth. But above them all, he prized his wife, a woman as patient and good as she was beautiful. If only, they could have a child!

Now, at this time in the palace there was a clever woman, beautiful but mean and envious, who wished above all else to bring ruin to the lovely sultana and to marry the sultan herself. Learning that the sultana would soon bear a child, this evil woman arranged to be a midwife. In a little while, not one, but two children were born, a boy and a girl, as like as two halves of the same apple, and beautiful, besides. As soon as the mother had fallen asleep, the midwife wrapped the two babies in a blanket and hid them in her own room. In the mother's bed, she put two puppies in place of the babies. Then she sent word to the sultan that he might come in to see his children.

Eagerly, the sultan bent to look at the babies. But what was this? Puppies in the bed? He turned to question the midwife.

"Sire, these are the babes your wife bore. But, alas, they are not what you expected. How strange that a woman should bear puppies." And she was pleased as the sultan's horror and anger grew.

"This woman!" he exclaimed at last. "Aman, aman! My wife is a monstrous, unnatural mother. But what to do about it?"

"Sire," suggested the woman, "surely such an unnatural woman should be exposed to shame. Perhaps she could be buried alive."

"But that is not enough," said the sultan. "I shall have her buried in earth up to her neck, and require all to pass by to spit upon her face."

Roughly awakening his wife, the sultan had her carried away and buried up to her neck in place just outside the palace gate. And to make certain she would live to endure her shame, he ordered that food be pro-vided to her four times a day. As for the puppies, they were given into the care of the midwife.

Meanwhile, the evil-minded woman had put the two babies into a basket and sent them adrift on the river which flowed past the palace. Time came, time went, and the river carried them at last to a mill.

The next morning the miller was puzzled to find that his mill wheel was still. "Perhaps some branch has caught in the stream," he thought, and he hurried out to look. To his surprise, he found a basket washed up. He pulled out the basket and looked inside, and "Allah be praised!" he exclaimed. "Here are two babies for my very own!" Carefully he took the basket to his little hut behind the mill. Since he had no wife anymore, he tended the children himself, and no woman could have cared for them better than he. His two goats were milked to feed the babies, and they grew strong on the simple fare.

Sixteen years passed, with the children happy and contented in the only home they knew. Then one day the miller called the boy and girl to his bedside. "I am old and ill," he said, "and it is the will of Allah that I shall soon die. My death I regret not for myself but for you, my children. Who will look after you when I am gone? I have nothing but the mill to leave you — ah, the mill and these three magic feathers." And he took from beneath his pillow three silver-gray feathers, each more beautiful than the others. Handing them to the boy, he said "When you are in danger or distress, burn one of these feathers. Allah willing, you will receive aid. But do not burn a single feather until you have need of it. And now, may Allah preserve you both." With these words, the miller stretched out a hand to each child. Sighing deeply, he breathed his last breath and was gone.

After the miller's death and a proper burial , the boy and the girl agreed between themselves to leave the mill and seek shelter in the town at the far edge of the forest. "Come, my sister," said the boy. "If we walk quickly, Allah willing, we can have a roof over our

heads before nightfall." And the two began walking along the worn path through the forest, with the girl weeping as they went.

Suddenly through her tears she saw a stone sparkling at the edge of the path. "Ah, look, my brother, at this diamond," said the girl, and she bent to pick it up.

"Diamond!" the boy scoffed. "It is only a stone, my sister. Come along. We must hurry , for it will soon be dark."

But as the girl picked up the stone, she saw others even more beautiful, and she turned aside and gathered them into her sash. "Come, my brother. You have room in your sash, too. Who knows? Perhaps these stones will buy bread for our mouths. And she and the boy gathered all the shining stones they saw. Then they went on their way again, and came at last to the town.

Hungry from their long walk, the children went first to a bakery. "Sire," the boy said, holding out one of his stones to the baker, "Is this stone of any worth? If it is, we should like to buy some bread with it."

Shaking his head from side to side, the baker said, "I don't know, my boy. I think Hasan Bey the jeweler is still in his shop. Go next door and ask him. He will know."

The children hurried to the jeweler's shop. "Sire," said the boy, laying one of the stones on the counter, "is this stone of any worth? We would like to trade it for a bit of bread and a night's shelter."

The jeweler stared at the stone, amazed. Then he looked curiously at the children. "Tell me where you found this precious stone. And tell me, too, why you are in need of bread and shelter. Where are your mother and father?"

From the first to last, the boy told the jeweler their story, beginning with the miller's finding them and ending with their arrival at the jeweler's shop.

"And you have no parents?" the jeweler asked.

"None, sire, that we know of," answered the girl.

"Then you shall be my children," decided the jeweler. And he took them home to his little house. "My wife died many years ago," he said, "but you will be comfortable here."

And little by little, the stones were exchanged for money, and the jeweler and his children began to live even more comfortably in a house as fine as a palace. But such news does not take long to travel, and soon the evil woman, now the sultan's wife learned that there were two children, as like as two halves of the same apple, living in the fine house. Curious to learn more about them, she went patur kitur to the house while the jeweler and the boy were away. Tak! Tak! Tak! She knocked at the door.

The girl answered the door, and, as was the custom, she invited the woman in. "Welcome," she said as she led the woman inside.

"I feel welcome, my dear neighbor," the woman replied, looking about in amazement at the fine furnishings. "Now, tell me about yourself, child." As she sat listening and sipping the cup of good Turkish coffee that the girl had prepared, the woman realized that this girl was none other than the sultan's own daughter. Fearing that the sultan would someday discover the truth, she determined to destroy the children.

Slyly she said, "My dear, you have a lovely home. If I were living here, I would yearn for only one more thing." She paused.

"Yes? And what is that?" asked the girl eagerly.

"Ah," sighed the woman, "if you had but one rosebush from the garden of Cengidilaver, your garden would be complete. Such beautiful roses! Such a wonderful scent!" And she looked about her as if suddenly the house had lost its charm because it lacked the rosebush.

"A rosebush from the garden of Cengidilaver," murmured the girl. "Yes, perhaps you are right. I shall ask my brother about it when he comes home this evening."

Soon after that, the visitor left, and the girl began to look here and there about her. Soon, wanting the rosebush had become needing the rosebush, and the girl began to weep. By the time of her brother's return, the girl could think of nothing else. "We must have a rosebush from the garden of Cengidilaver or I shall die of grief." And it seemed as if she might.

"Hush,sister; hush, sister," the boy said at last. "If your heart is set upon the rosebush, then I must try to get it for you." And carefully removing from his sash one of the three magic feathers, he went out into the garden to burn it.

No sooner had the smoke begun to curl from the feather than there came a gash of lightning and a crash of thunder sufficient to shake the boy to the soles of his sandals. Suddenly there stood before him an enormous jinn, with his toes touching the earth and his turban scraping the sky.

"Ask whatever you will. Your wish I must fulfill," said the jinn, his eyes fixed upon the boy.

For all his fright, the boy somehow found his tongue. "Sire," he began, "my sister longs for a rosebush from the garden of Cengidilaver."

"No!" roared the jinn. "It is impossible. Cengidilaver is a monster. He would tear you apart piece by piece."

The boy was resolute. "Whatever Cengidilaver may do to me, I must try to get the rosebush. Tell me what I must do."

"If you must, then you will," grumbled the jinn. "But listen carefully to me, and do exactly as I say. Tomorrow at the first silver streak of dawn, you will find a white horse standing in front of your door. That horse will take you with the speed of the wind to the garden of Cengidilaver, but you must at no time look behind you. When you come to the garden gate, you will find a wolf and a sheep. Before the wolf lies some grass; before the sheep there lies a piece of meat. Give the meat to the wolf and the grass to the sheep. You can then pass through the gate. Inside the garden you will find two doors, one closed and the other open. Open the closed door. Beyond the doors, at the center of the garden, Cengidilaver will be seated at the foot of a great tree. If his eyes are closed, he is awake. If his eyes are open, he is asleep. If his eyes are open, run and pull up a rosebush, thorns and all, and then leave the garden as fast as you can. Remember, you must never look behind you, no matter what happens. Once you pass through the garden gate again, you will be safe."

Just as the jinn had said, the next morning in the silver dawn there was a white horse standing before the house. The boy rode the horse — Prrt! — and in the wink of an eye he came to the gate of Cengidilaver's garden. As the jinn had directed him, he gave the meat to the wolf and the grass to the sheep, and so he was able to pass through the gate into the garden. As the jinn had directed him, he opened the closed door and closed the open door, and then he found himself at the center of the garden. There sat Cengidilaver, horrid monster that he was, with his eyes wide open. "Ah, praise be to Allah, Cengidilaver is asleep," thought the boy, and he went straight to a rosebush and tugged and tugged until he had pulled it up, thorns and all.

At the moment the roots left the earth, all the other rosebushes began to cry, "Awake, awake, Cengidilaver! Cengidilaver, awake! Your rosebush has been stolen."

Instantly, Cengidilaver blinked his eyes and was awake. Seeing the boy run toward the doors, he shouted, "Closed door, closed door! Catch the thief who took my rosebush."

But the closed door answered, "I will not help you. You have kept me closed for forty years, but today the boy opened me. I will not catch him."

Then, "Open door, open door!" shouted Cengidilaver. "Catch the thief who took my rosebush."

The open door called, "I will not help you Cengidilaver. You have left me open for forty years, and today the boy was kind enough to close me. I will not catch him at all."

Seeing that the boy had safely passed through the doors, Cengidilaver called out, "Wolf catch him! He has taken my rosebush."

"Indeed, I will not," answered the wolf. "For forty years you have give me nothing but grass to eat. Today the boy came along and gave me meat. I will not catch him."

"Then, sheep, you catch him!" shouted the Cengidilaver.

But the sheep said, "I will not catch him, either. For forty years you have given me nothing but meat to eat. Today the boy came along and gave me grass. I will not catch him."

The boy ran safely through the gate, leapt on the white horse, and with the speed of wind came home to his own house. He and his sister planted Cengidilaver's rosebush in their garden, and the wonderful scent of the roses reached every corner of the house.

Not many days after that, the evil woman happened to pass that way, and she smelled the roses in the jeweler's garden. Tak! Tak! Tak! She knocked at the door, and the girl came at once to answer it.

"Welcome," said the girl, and led the woman inside.

"I feel welcome, my dear neighbor," answered the woman. "I see that you have one of the rosebushes from Cengidilaver's garden. How happy you must be!"

"Ah, yes," said the girl. "I had no idea how much our garden needed a rosebush like that." And she prepared a cup of fine Turkish coffee for her visitor.

"My dear," said the woman slyly, "it is true that your house is very lovely. But I miss the song of a nightingale. If I lived here, I could not bear to be without a nightingale from Cengidilaver's garden. But then, I suppose you scarcely miss it."

"A nightingale?" the girl asked. "I never thought of a nightingale. Yes, a nightingale would please me very much."

Not long afterward, the woman left, and the girl began thinking about a nightingale. Thinking led to yearning, and soon she was weeping. Her brother was troubled to see her in tears, and it was not long before she told him, "Oh, my brother, I cannot live without one of the nightingales from Cengidilaver's garden."

"My sister, do not weep about a nightingale ," he said. "After all, one bird is as good as another. Our garden is full of birds already."

"But there are no nightingales," she sobbed. "How I long for just one nightingale from the garden of Cengidilaver!" And she cried and would not be comforted.

At last her brother removed from his sash the second magic feather and went into the garden to burn it. No sooner had the smoke begun to curl from the feather than there came a gash of lightning and a crash of thunder that shook the boy to the soles of his sandals. Suddenly that enormous jinn appeared with his toes touching the earth and his turban scraping the sky.

"Ask whatever you will. Your wish I must fulfill," rumbled the jinn, gazing straight at the boy.

Frightened as he was, somehow the boy found his tongue. "Sire," he said, "my sister longs for a nightingale from the garden of Cengidilaver."

"No! It is impossible!" roared the jinn, "Cengidilaver is a monster. He would tear you apart piece by piece."

But the boy was resolute. "I do not care what Cengidilaver may do to me. I must have a nightingale for my sister, for she is most unhappy without it."

"If you must, then you will," grumbled the jinn. "But listen carefully, and do exactly as I say. In that, you may still escape from Cengidilaver." And the jinn told the boy, as he had done before, to ride the white horse as far as the garden gate, to place the meat before the wolf and the grass before the sheep, to open the closed door and close the open door, and to beware above all, of looking behind him. As for the nightingale, he warned, ""Be sure that Cengidilaver's eyes are open before you try to take the nightingale. Take only one, and then run as fast as you can. If you can pass through the garden gate, you will be safe."

Just as the jinn had said, the next morning in the silver dawn there stood the white horse. The boy rode — Prrt! — and in the winking of an eye he came to the gate of Cengidilaver's garden. He did exactly as he had been told, placing the meat before the wolf and the grass before the sheep, and thus he was able to enter the gate safely. Coming to the doors, he opened the closed door and closed the open one. Finding himself at the center of the garden he stood quietly and watched Cengidilaver. The monster's glowing eyes were open, so the boy tiptoed to the corner of the garden where the nightingales perched. Gently he picked up the nearest one and turned to leave the garden. But the moment the bird's feet left the branch, all the other nightingales began to sing, "Awake , awake, Cengidilaver! Cengidilaver, awake! Your nightingale has been stolen."

Instantly, Cengidilaver blinked his eyes and was awake. Seeing the boy running towards the doors, he called, "Closed door, closed door! Catch the thief who stole my nightingale!"

Again the door replied, "Indeed, I will not catch him."

And the open door also refused to catch the boy, so he ran and ran toward the gate.

Angrily, Cengidilaver called, "Wolf, wolf! Catch the thief who stole my nightingale."

Again, the wolf replied, "No, indeed, I will not catch him, for today he gave me meat."

As the sheep also refused to catch the boy, he ran out safely through the gate. Leaping upon the white horse, with the speed of the wind the boy came home to his own house. He and his sister found a fine palace for the nightingale in a corner of the garden, and its songs brought new joys to their lives.

One evening not many days after that, the evil woman happened to pass that way and she heard the glorious song of the nightingale in the garden. The next morning — Tak! Tak! Tak! — she knocked at the door, just after the boy had gone to the shop with the jeweler.

Answering the door the girl cried, "Welcome," and she led the visitor at once to their garden. "See," she said, "over in that corner we have the nightingale. How right you were! We needed that lovely song in our garden."

Biting her lip, the woman tried to think of some way in which she might truly be rid of the two children. At last she had arrived at a plan. "My dear," she said slyly, "you have a beautiful garden, but it would be even lovelier if you have Cengidilaver himself as your gardener. Those roses need pruning, and the walks should be trimmed and weeded. No one in all the world is as fine a gardener as Cengidilaver."

After a cup of good Turkish coffee and talk of this and that, the woman left, and the girl went back to look more closely at the garden. Yes, the visitor was right. Near the fountain, there were spots of mildew. The rhododendron looked straggly, and the whole garden had an untidy air about it. The longer she looked, the more dissatisfied and disappointed she became, until she fell to weeping. By the time her brother came home for dinner, she was truly miserable.

The boy, surprised to find his sister weeping again, asked her what could be troubling her now that she had the lovely rosebush and the sweet-voiced nightingale.

Alas, my brother," she cried, "what good are rosebushes and nightingales in an untidy garden? I want a good gardener to care for our garden. I want Cengidilaver himself to come be our gardener." And from yearning for that gardener, the girl wept afresh.

"Cengidilaver!" the boy exclaimed, his heart suddenly chilled. "my sister, you do not know what you are asking."

But the girl cried and cried, and would not be comforted. At last the boy sighed and carefully took from his sash the last of the magic feathers. Putting one foot before the other, he went to the garden to burn the feather. No sooner had the smoke begun to curl upward than there came a gash of lightning and a crash of thunder that shook the boy to the soles of his sandals.

Suddenly the enormous jinn appeared, with his toes touching the earth and his turban scraping the sky.

"Ask whatever you will. Your wish I must fulfill," rumbled the jinn, staring straight at the boy.

Though the boy trembled with fright, he somehow found his tongue. "Sire," said he, "my sister wishes to have Cengidilaver as her gardener."

"No, no, no!" shouted the jinn, and every leaf in the garden quivered with the force of his voice. "You know well that Cengidilaver is a monster. Allah alone has spared you, or Cengidilaver would have torn you apart, piece by piece."

Pale but determined, the boy said, "No matter what happens to me, I must seek Cengidilaver himself."

"If you must then you will," groaned the jinn. "But listen very carefully, and do exactly as I say. In that way you may escape with your life. And certainly your courage will stand you in good stead." And the jinn told the boy, as he had done before, to ride the white horse as far as the garden gate, to place the meat before the wolf and the grass before the sheep, to open the closed door and close the open door, and above all, to beware of looking a single time behind him. "As for Cengidilaver himself," continued the jinn, "there is something very strange about him. I have heard it said that Cengidilaver has been placed under a spell, and remains a monster as long as he stays in the garden. But if someone is brave enough to lift him and strong enough to carry him beyond the garden gate, he will become harmless. He will lose his monster form and will be no more dangerous than any other man — indeed, he will become a man himself. The danger lies within the garden. Go, my boy, and may your way be open."

Just as the jinn had said, in the silver dawn the white horse stood again before the house. Murmuring, "Bismallah!" the boy mounted the horse, and — Prrrt! — in the winking of an eye he came to the gate of Cengidilaver's garden. Once again he placed the meat before the wolf and the grass before the sheep. Once again he opened the closed door and closed the open door, and came to the center of the garden.

There sat Cengidilaver beneath the tree, his glowing eyes wide open and his great arms folded across his chest in sleep. Tense and watchful, the boy stood for a moment, gathering all his strength for what he must do. The striding forward, he grasped the monster firmly and flung him over his shoulder. As fast as he could, he hurried toward the garden gate. This way and that, Cengidilaver struggled, and the two were locked together in deadly combat. But the boy's determination gave him greater strength, and at last he was able to carry the monster beyond the gate.

At that very moment, Cengidilaver lost his monster shape and became a gentle, grave man. "You have great courage, my boy. Again you have finished what you set out to do. As for me, the spell that made me a monster and put me in that garden is now broken, and in gratitude I shall serve you all my life. Take me where you will." The boy and Cengidilaver mounted the white horse and in scarcely more than a thought's worth of time they arrived at the boy's home.

That evening in the garden Cengidilaver drew the boy aside and gave him a small gold ring. "This ring," he said "belongs to your mother. Your mother was once the wife of your father the sultan, but through the deceit of an evil woman she was buried up to her neck. She still lives, Allah be praised! But your father does not know that you are his children, for at your birth that evil woman stole you and your sister out of your mother's bed and put two puppies there instead. She set

you adrift in a basket, and you were saved by the miller, who brought you up as his own children."

The boy was surprised indeed to learn these things about himself and his family, and he grieved for the injustice done to his mother. "If I could save her...," he said.

"This is what you can do," said Cengidilaver. "Invite the sultan here for dinner. Among the other foods, serve pilav, and in the pilav you serve to the sultan, hide the gold ring I gave you. When the sultan sees the ring, he will recognize it, and then you can tell him what I have told you."

After a few days, the boy sent a messenger to the palace to invite the sultan to honor their home by coming to dinner. Now, the sultan had noticed the jeweler's house, as beautiful as a palace, and he was curious to see who lived inside it. So he came at the boy's invitation. For dinner, many fine dishes were served, among them an elegant platter of pilav. As the sultan was eating his portion of pilav, he bit down on something hard, and, surprised, he removed a small object from his mouth. He stared at it, and then he exclaimed, "This is my first wife's ring! Where did you get it?"

"It is the ring which belonged to my mother," cried the girl, running to put her arms around the sultan's neck.

"We are your children," said the boy. And he told the sultan what had happened at their birth, and how they had fared since the evil woman had set them adrift on the river.

"Ah!" exclaimed the sultan. "There is only one woman who could have done that evil thing, and she is now my wife. Tomorrow she will pay with her life for the harm that she has done to you and to your mother."

That very evening, the sultan and his children went to the palace together. At once the sultan ordered his first wife removed from the earth and bathed and dressed and brought to them. In almost the same breath, he sent his men to take the life of the evil woman.

The sultan and his beautiful wife were married all over again, with a celebration lasting forty days and forty nights, and the two dwelt with their children in happiness all the rest of their lives.

From: *The Art of the Turkish Tale: Volume 1*, Barbara K. Walker, Texas Tech University, 1990.

Twentieth Century Poetry: Nazim Hikmet
Human Landscapes, An epic novel in verse

Suggested Time 3-4 classroom periods

Materials A class set of readings (**Worksheet 1**)

Objectives
1. To respond to a contemporary verse form that explores Anatolian influences.
2. To analyze the use of figurative language to convey meaning

Background Nazım Hikmet is arguably one of the most influential poets of contemporary Turkish literature. His influence comes despite the controversies that surrounded his life and his politics. Born into an affluent Ottoman family in 1902, Hikmet led a content childhood in Istanbul. In his late teens, he went to Moscow to write poetry, study politics, and experience the work of Mayakovsky, the leading poet of Russian Revolution.

In 1928, Hikmet returned to Istanbul in what was now the Republic of Turkey and began working in various capacities in local magazines. His literary style which featured a uniquely new verse form, as well as his political leanings towards the far left, quickly gained attention. He criticized the works of popular poets such as Namık Kemal and Abdülhak Hamid for their weak ideas and predictable verse, labeling them as poets of the bourgeoisie. He was repeatedly arrested for his political beliefs, and in 1938, he was sentenced to twenty-eight years in prison for allegations that he incited the army to revolt. He served twelve years, and was given amnesty in 1950, followed by an International Peace Prize in November of that year.

His charming personality, his love of the land, and its people, his love of pleasures of drink and women are all among the most visible of images and influences in his work. The selections here are chosen for their reflection of the formative impulses in Turkish literature that were to later influence generations of poets after him.

Narrative Summary *Human Landscapes* was composed during the poet's imprisonment in Bursa from 1940-1950. The period he spent in prison is often cited as the time when Hikmet, came to know the Anatolian population of Turkey. The verse-novel reveals influences of folk-life, nature, war, technology, and song in its pages as it tells the stories of a cross-section of characters all tied together along an Anatolian train-route. One of the main themes in the work is the way in which all citizens, throughout Turkey and the world are tied to one another. The static sounds of the radio and the soft humming of Spanish melodies, the view of the world from both above the ground (by the stork) and below the waters (by Jevdet Bey), the juxtaposition of colors, of flight in air and motion thorough water, the story of thousands told through the story of one or two characters — all of these are important elements of the work and demand special attention.

Notes to the Instructor *Human Landscapes* is described as an "epic novel in verse". It would be interesting to have students read this as a modern counterpart to *The Book of Dede Korkut* (see

Lesson 1). You might want to have the students review the "background notes" in the earlier lesson in order to discuss the poet's rationale for calling this an "epic novel in verse".

This selection from the poem can be divided into five sections (editor's device-not in the original). The first section deals with the friendship between Kerim and Halil and the appearance of the storks. Subsequent sections reveal the stories of a cross-section of characters all tied together along an Anatolian train-route. One of the main themes in the work is the way in which all citizens, throughout Turkey and the world are tied to one another (see **Narrative Summary** above.)

Key Concepts
epic
repetition
symbolism
imagery
dramatic irony

Development
▷ The teacher should read the first section of this poem to the class. After the reading, ask students to begin to fill in the outline below. (As they continue the reading of this poem, they should continue to develop this outline.)

OUTLINE FOR *HUMAN LANDSCAPES*				
Characters	**Description**	**Setting**	**Historical Events**	**Geographic Locations**
Kerim		prison		Bursa, Turkey
Halil				
Jevdet Bey				
Hans Mueller				
Anna				

▷ This poem relies heavily on **symbolism**. (Review meaning of symbolism if necessary). In the first section, some of the most obvious symbols are the stork and the radio.
▷ Brainstorm student associations with the stork and list on chalkboard. Then have students read the following information about storks in folklore.

STORKS IN OTHER TRADITIONS

Storks play a very important role in many cultures. In Ukrainian folklore, the stork is a symbol of life, of prosperity and of hope for the future. In Lithuanian customs people believed that the stork would bring fortune to the homestead where its nest had been made. Children used to believe and some still believe that the stork can bring a baby brother or sister from a pond or a river. Greeks, Romans, Indians, Hebrews, and Egyptians all wrote about storks. These birds' lives were associated with close bonds in their relationships. The mothers are best known for having a strong responsibility to their young, and pull out their own feathers in order to keep them warm. This self-sacrifice shows the mothers put their children's needs above their own comfort. This motherly aid will be repaid to the parents when they get older, and their youth will take care of their parents. This bird has an extremely long lifetime for bird standards, and modern day research has shown that they live up to seventy years. A large factor that causes these long life spans is this cooperative care-giving pattern.

The Chinese were another nationality that referred to the stork in their ancient folklore. These superstitions came down from the Wei and Jin Dynasties (220-420), and were also influenced from Taoist and Buddhist beliefs much earlier. They believed the stork had the ability to bring people up to the heavens. In their ancient legends they believed, "A young flute-player and wandering minstrel who carries a basket laden with fruit. His soul-searching songs caused a stork to snatch him away to the heavens." In this instance the stork has the power to bring this man to heaven for his enjoyable songs. Like other cultures, the Chinese interweaved these myths with their culture. China is a country with a history of wars, and this country received a drastic decline in their population during the turmoil. It was often believed that the souls of these heroic Chinese warriors were taken up to heaven with the stork's aid. The stork once again is associated with having a godly status, and this time is believed to transport the souls of soldiers to heaven. The Chinese depiction of the stork went along with other views and proclaimed the bird as a messenger of God.

▷ Continue to read the poem, stopping after each section so that students can continue chart and clarify meanings. The next section (Part II) deals with "radiomania." What does the symbol of the radio represent? Why did the poet choose to use a radio? If the poet were writing today, what other forms of technology might he select as a symbol?

▷ Have students record the geographic locations that are present in this section of the poem? What do they represent? (**Teacher's Note:** The mountains, sky, city, harbor, the Mediterranean, seabed, Berlin, London, Spain, Moscow are all mentioned, and there are other geographical markers. These are mostly to spotlight how temporary geography can be. It can be an imagined place, as Jevdet Bey imagines himself at the bottom of the sea; or a constructed place, like a city; or a natural place, such as a mountain or plain. Students may have other ideas).

▷ Part III deals with an imagined place. Jeydet Bey imagines himself under the sea and has an encounter with Hans Mueller and then Harry Thompson. Have students recount each of their stories. Why does the poet include these people? What point is the poet making about war?

- ▷ Part IV continues Jeydet Bey's own story. What new details of his life are revealed?
- ▷ PART V is a grimly, realistic account of the German attempt to capture Moscow. (**Teacher's Note:** You will probably have to quickly explain why the Germans were trying to capture Moscow. The story of Zoe/Tanya is an illustration of how one person's suffering can impact anyone anywhere, despite what they may or may not know of her. Not only do we know of the girl, but we are made to feel responsible for her as her story is made personal, "I've got a daughter your age." Also, the account forms a stark contrast to the way the stork is treated by Jevdet Bey (look for the parallels in the way the stork and the girl are described for evidence). The repeated use of label terms, "partisan", "human," "German," "the hangman" all creates an even stronger image of Tanya.)
- ▷ Contrast the life of the soldiers with that of the citizens of Moscow.
- ▷ What does the story of Zoe (Tanya) add to our understanding of the work?
- ▷ Ask students to select particularly vivid lines and phrases and discuss what makes these so effective.

How does this information about the role of storks in folklore enrich your understanding of the poem? Do you think the poet chose to use storks in his poem because of all these associations? What does this tell us about the language of poetry?

Select some of the phrases that you thought were particularly effective in describing either Hans Mueller or Harry Thompson. Once again, what does these phrases reveal about the craft of poetry?

In the lesson on *Dede Korkut*, a traditional epic was described as a work that, "…includes elements of myth, legend, folktale and history. Though epics contain many myths and exaggerations, they are based on actual people and events. An epic is not the most reliable historical account, but it is an essential key to understanding a people." To what extent can *Human Landscapes* be classified as an "epic novel in verse"?

Based on your reading of *Dede Korkut*, *Human Landscapes* and other epics you may have read, describe the relationship between epic literature and history.

Human Landscapes:
An Epic Novel in Verse
Nazim Hikmet (1902-1963)

(excerpts from part 4, translated from the Turkish by Randy Blasing & Mutlu Konuk)

I

It was Sunday.
The thirteen year old worker Kerim
    — the heart of my heart! —
        headed for the prison
        to visit Halil.
They had become fast friends.
And after Halil's return from the hospital,
    he and Kerim had arithmetic lessons
and discussed world affairs.

It was Sunday.
His arithmetic notebook in his hand
    and his pockets stuffed with roast chickpeas,
Kerim strode past the armory in the induction center yard,
directly across from Halil's barred windows.
Suddenly he stopped
and raised his eyes
    toward the racket in the sky:
there were storks,
    storks spiraling
        higher and higher in the air.
They were migrating.
They came in flocks-
    spreading out, pulling in,
        and spiraling higher and higher in cloudless space.
Then they formed a single line.
They must have numbered over five hundred.
The wisest one took the lead.
The city lay below
    at the edge of the steppe:
        the hospital, prison, and city hall,
        the thirteen year old worker Kerim,
            looking up from the induction center yard
        plus a variety of chimneys...
But the city was quickly lost
    like a fallen nestling.
Heavy wings barely moving,

beaks pointed straight ahead, necks taut,
and needle-thin legs sticking out behind,
                    the storks continued south,
more swimming in the air than flying.
That evening they crossed into the province of Ankara
and spent the night in the fields outside Chandir,
beaks thrust under wings
                    and up on one leg...
And at dawn they flew off.
The journey south took days.
Soon they were out of Ankara
and into the endless province of Konya:
flat sky above,
        flat earth below.

Mountains appeared at last,
not hills
but real mountains with snow and forests.
They flew over a lake and a river.

Then they entered the province of X,
the air warming up by the hour.
And finally, one Wednesday afternoon,
the Mediterranean-
        way down in the distance,
                    fused with the sky,
spotless, and serene,
        like a long drawn flash.
The storks gleefully clacked their beaks.
And they stopped over in the harvested rice fields.
The next day they spread out
            in flocks and pairs.
Only the leader flew alone
            into the city center.
Fields passed below
        and turned to groves:
            lemons, oranges, and tangerines
                    (still green).
The sea sped closer, growing bigger and wider.
And now the stork was over the city:
Tree-lined boulevards, roofs, and chimneys.
The city stood on a bluff overlooking the water.
Far out in the harbor, a single ship lay anchored.
The air was salty and hot
        and smelled of bananas.
The stork circled over the city,
then veered left,

flexed its wings,
let go,
    and glided down.
Up on a chimney its old nest
    swayed closer.
The stork swerved to the right adjacent roof
    to miss the wires on the
        (they were radio antennas,
                over twenty of them),
but it couldn't clear its left wing:
it spun around, thrashing, and collapsed on the roof,
    tangled in broken wires
    just twenty meters from its nest...

II

Suddenly the voice of America
    was silenced by a strange static.
Jevdet Bey did not get excited
He put on his glasses
to check it out:
no sound on any station.
He went over to the second set,
    a 1940 RCA:
nothing there, either.
He tried the third set,
    a six-tube Telefunken
nothing.
The fourth set: the same.
Strange.
Jevdet Bey sucked his long white mustache
He stepped back
and sat down in the only chair, at the exact center of the room.
He studied the sets:
radios first came on the world market
going back to when
(from those with earphones to those with gramophones),
the most famous models of every make
stood lined. up by year and number of tubes.
Jevdet Bey slapped his bald head,
and his white mustache popped out of his mouth
as he cried: "Eureka!"

He rushed out of the room-
hallway, steps, attic, roof, antennas.
He repaired the antennas.
And rushing back-

roof, attic, steps, hallway-

Jevdet Bey returned to the radio room, carrying a huge stork.

The bird had a broken leg.

He bandaged it.

Then he clipped the wings

   so the bird wouldn't try to fly

   (it wasn't easy — bird and man both fought).

Then he took some meat from the refrigerator

   and offered it to the bird.

The bird ate

   and limped off to a corner.

And from there it stared at Jevdet Bey in amazement

"I hope you enjoyed the meal, Haji Baba," said Jevdet Bey.

"We'll be bosom friends from this day forward.

I'll reserve the adjoining room for you.

   just make yourself at home in there.

Of course, my whole house is yours.

Except you're not allowed in here without me:

   God forbid, you might break my toys.

You can go out in the yard during the day.

After all, you're a stork:

    you'd get bored hanging around radios all day.

They're all I had in the world,

      but now I have you.

And now I'm all you have-

   plus my radios.

Just as there are

  heroin freaks,

    cocaine freaks,

      nicotine freaks,

        ego freaks, and so on,

I'm a fifty-five year old radio freak.

I mean,

  I suffer from radiomania.

I listen to the voices of people

calling me from the four corners of the world.

We have a distant relationship:

I could care less what they do,

I'm just curious how they tell about it.

And I must admit I like their songs, too-

all the world's songs,

   in any language or style.

But have you noticed?

These days they sing

  at the same time they're at each other's throat.

And when they tell how they fight,

you'd think they were singing love songs.

Now, with your permission,
       we'll listen to Berlin.
You don't know German, do you?
I'll translate.
It won't do you much good,
but I can practice translating out loud."
Jevdet Bey had always known French and Arabic,
but he'd taught himself German, English, Russian, and Italian
after he caught radiomania.

Jevdet Bey tuned in Berlin
       and translated:
"The Ukraine capital of Kiev has been taken.
665,000 prisoners
Tanks, artillery
Okay.
Cut.
I already heard this last night.
So there's nothing new from Berlin yet.
Let's try London.
The number killed in last month's air raids.
I've heard this, too.
Still in London, let's find you a jazz band
                     Just a few frequencies away.
Here you are..."

Jazz filled the room and scared the stork.
The bird flapped its clipped wings
and tried to run away somewhere,
but couldn't with its injured leg.
Jevdet Bey laughed:
"So jazz does nothing for you, Haji Baba?
Then let's go to Spain, to Barcelona.
Barcelona, Spain...
How? Why
       did Dolores Ibarruri La Pasionaria fall silent?
The woman's voice was like, the sun.
I still search the Spanish stations for a voice like hers-
              thick
                     luminous
                            and warm...
I don't know Spanish,
       but she could be cussing you out and you'd love listening..."

And Jevdet Bey turned hopelessly to Barcelona.

III

"I'm lying at the bottom of the Atlantic, effendi,
                leaning on my elbow
                                at the bottom of the Atlantic.
I look up:
high overhead I see
a submarine
cruising at a depth of fifty meters
like a fish, effendi,
sealed off and secretive
        inside its armor and the water.
The light is bottle green up there.
There, effendi,
it's all stars
sparkling like a million candles
all blazing bright green.
And there, my iron propelled soul,
are couplings without thrashing around, birth without screams
the first moving flesh of our world-
there, effendi,
        the sensual intimacy of a steaming bath
and the red hair of the first woman I had.
Rainbow-colored grasses, rootless trees,
        and wiggly sea creatures,
life, salt, and iodine:
there, Haji Baba,
            there is our beginning,
and there-steely, treacherous, and cunning-
                is a submarine.

Light seeps down about four hundred meters
Then, the deepest
                            darkness.
Sometimes strange fish
        crack the darkness,
                    scattering light.
Then they're gone, too.
Now just layers and layers of thick water
            all the way down, final and absolute,
                and at the very bottom, me.
I'm lying, Haji Baba, at the very bottom
                            of the Atlantic,
                        leaning on my elbow
                        and looking up.
America and Europe are separated just on the surface,
                            not at the bottom of the Atlantic.

Tankers pass overhead.
I see their backbones,
                              their keels.
Their propellers spin happily,
and the rudders look so funny underwater
I feel like reaching up to turn them myself.
Sharks glide underneath,
mouths
        on their bellies.
Suddenly panic seizes the ships.
Surely it can't be the sharks.
No, effendi, it's a torpedo-
                the submarine has fired a torpedo!
Rudders frantic
                with fear,
keels scanning the water for help,
the tankers protect their soft underbellies
                like men fending off knives.
The submarine becomes three, then six, seven, eight.
And the tankers go down,
shooting at the enemy
                and spilling cargo and men into the sea.
Diesel oil, kerosene, gasoline-
the sea surface bursts into flame.
Now it's a river of fire up there, effendi,
a fiery river
                slick with oil.
Blood-red, sky blue, pitch-black
a scene from the chaos before the Creation.
The water is boiling at the surface,
the foam choked with wreckage.
See that tanker, effendi, sinking
like a sleepwalker,
                a lunatic?

Its struggle is over,
it has entered the sea's heaven
and keeps falling,
lost in the liquid dark.
Soon, now, it will explode from the pressure.
And a mast or a smokestack
        may land next to me.
The sea teems with men up there, effendi,
and they'll all settle to the bottom
                              like sediment.
Feet first or headfirst,
arms and legs reaching out in vain

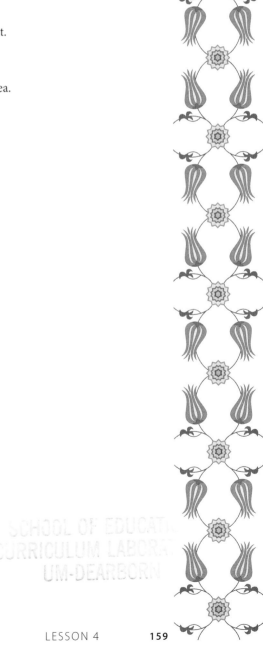

for something to hold on to,
            they'll sink to the bottom, too.

Suddenly a submarine lands next to me.
The hatch on the bridge snaps open like a coffin lid,
and out steps Hans Mueller from Munich.

Before becoming a submariner in the spring of '39,
        Hans Mueller from Munich
was the third soldier from the right in the fourth squadron
        of the first company of the sixth battalion
                of Hitler's storm troopers.
Hans Mueller
        had three loves:
1) A foaming golden brew.
2) Anna, fleshy and white like an East Prussian potato.
3) Red cabbage.

Hans Mueller
        had three duties:
1) To salute his superior officer
        like lightning.
2) To take an oath on a gun.
3) To round up a minimum of three Jews a day
        and damn the sly ones who got away.

In his head and heart and on his tongue,
        Hans Mueller had three fears:
1) Der Fuehrer.
2) Der Fuehrer.
3) Der Fuehrer.
Hans Mueller
with his loves, duties, and fears
        lived
                happily
        until the spring of '39.
Except he was surprised
        to hear Anna
— magnificent as a C major in a Wagnerian opera,
fleshy and white like an East Prussian potato-
complain so
        about the shortages of eggs and butter.
He'd say to her:
'Just think, Anna,
I'll have a brand-new gun belt
and bright and shiny boots.
You'll have a long white dress and wear

wax flowers in your hair.
We'll walk under crossed swords.
And we'll have a dozen kids
all boys, of course.
Anna, think:
if we don't make guns and cannons today
just so we can have eggs and butter, how will our twelve sons fight tomorrow?'

Mueller's twelve sons never got to fight,
because they never got born
because, effendi, before the nuptials could be consummated
      Hans Mueller himself went to war.
And now in late autumn
    of 1941,
        he stands before me on the ocean floor.
His fine blond hair is wet,
his pointed red nose shows regret,
and his thin lips are pinched with sadness.
Though he's right beside me,
he looks at me from far away,
as the dead do.
I know he'll never see Anna again
Or drink a brew
      or eat red cabbage.
All this, effendi, I know,
but he does not.
There are tears in his eyes,
which he doesn't dry.
He has money in his pocket,
which will never get
        any more or less.
But the strangest thing is,
he can't ever kill anyone.
Soon now he'll swell up and rise to the top.
He'll be rocking on the waves,
fish nibbling his pointed nose...

I was staring at Hans Mueller,
Haji Baba, and thinking all this when suddenly there appeared next to us
Harry Thompson of Liverpool.
He was a quartermaster on one of the tankers.
His eyebrows and lashes were burnt,
his eyes shut tight.
He was clean-shaven and overweight.
Thompson had a wife:
a broomstick of a woman, effendi,
tall and skinny, tidy, fastidious,

and, like a broomstick, slightly ridiculous.
And Thompson had a son,
Haji Baba, a six year old boy
all peaches and cream, cuddly, plump, and blond.
I took Thompson's hand.
He didn't open his eyes.
I said: 'You died.'
'Yes" he said, 'for freedom and the British Empire-
for the freedom to curse Churchill if I want, even in wartime,
and the freedom to go hungry, even if I don't want.
But this last freedom will change:
We won't go hungry and jobless after the war.
One of our lords has devised a solution:
justice without revolution. —
Churchill said: "I'm not here to break up the British Empire.'
And I'm not here to make a revolution:
the Archbishop of Canterbury, —
    the president of our union,
                and my wife
would never approve.
I beg your pardon.
That's all —
    period, the end.'

Thompson was silent.
And he didn't open his mouth again.
The English don't like to talk a lot,
    especially those with a sense of humor.
And Thompson was quite droll.
I laid Thompson and Mueller side by side.
They swelled up together,
and together they rose to the top.
The fish ate Thompson with pleasure,
but they wouldn't touch the other_
scared, I guess, that Hans's flesh was poison.
Don't say they're just animals, Haji Baba;
you're an animal, too,
    but a smart one..."

And Jevdet Bey looked at the stork fondly.

IV

The night air was heavy with the fragrance of Seville oranges.
Jevdet Bey and the stork sat in the garden.
They'd taken a radio outside:
London reported on the Atlantic war.

Jevdet Bey was slowly getting drunk,
having a good time
  imagining himself at the bottom of the Atlantic.
Wings clipped,
the stork rested its straight red beak
          on its white chest
and napped up on one leg.
Below in the harbor, the Mediterranean was like a young mother
        with generous bare breasts
         And smiling eyes.
And up above, the Sweet Williams craned their long thin necks
        and listened to the air.
The orange trees were bursting with stars.
Now the memory of a woman he'd never forget
  filled Jevdet Bey's garden, glass, and heart.
Not the dead
  at the bottom of the Atlantic now:
the distant dead give way
  to those who have died at our side.
Five years ago Jevdet Bey's wife, Leyla Hanum, had died
    in his arms
        at her appointed hour
   (not for Hitler
or for the British Empire and the freedom to curse Churchill
or even from something like pneumonia or cancer,
    but just because her time had come).

"Are they in Moscow yet, Jevdet Bey?"
"Jevdet Bey, won't you tell us the good news?"
"Jevdet Bey, what's the word from London?"
 "Are they in Moscow yet, Jevdet Bey?"
Jevdet Bey came back to himself
and shivered as if suddenly chilly.
He turned to the voices:
Koyunzade, Mustafa Shen and Jemil Bey from Crete
  — three of the five biggest effendis of the province —
stood at the garden gate.
They were returning from the club,
half lit,
and life was sweet
  on this warm, happy Mediterranean night
    under the acacias.

"Jevdet Bey, what's the word from London?"
"Are they in Moscow yet, Jevdet Bey?"

Jevdet Bey lay back on the chaise lounge

and gazed up at the oranges and the stars.
The oranges were close, the stars far away.
And Jevdet Bey wanted to reach beyond
                                   the oranges to the stars.
Without sitting up, he put on his glasses
and, still flat on his back,
        found Moscow on the radio
        without looking.

World and country,
house and tree,
man, wolf, and jackal,
all rivers
(Ganges, Amazon, Volga, Nile, Meander),
all actions; and all words:
the sound came closer and louder,
        and a grand music filled the Mediterranean garden.
Jevdet Bey closed his eyes,
and as if surrendering himself to the sea
he abandoned his old heart to the symphony.

The radio in the garden of Seville oranges
was an eight-tube, 1939 model.
The dial glittered with the station names
like the magic kingdom of the faeries.

V

The radio at the prison was a four-tube, 1929 model.
It had been sent over from the Civic Center fifteen days ago
and set up in the corridor…

…It was the sixteenth of November in the year 1941.
Fifty divisions, thirteen armored,
3000 pieces of artillery,
and 700 planes
would attack Moscow once more.
The plan:
to seal off the Soviet capital on two sides,
penetrate deep in the north and south,
isolate the units defending the city,
                and wipe them out.
Hitler was in a better position with respect to the number of tanks.
Tanks
        are important, without a doubt.
But with them, tanks drove the men —
        not men the tanks.

The men tanks drove
            had started marching one summer morning.
Their hair was combed, their uniforms looked sharp.
And they marched,
                            bleeding, the length of two seasons.
Then, one winter night, paradise lay before them.
But now their hair wasn't combed,
            and their uniforms didn't look so sharp.
They walked waist-deep in snow,
heads buried in their shoulders.
They hadn't shaved for weeks,
and the skin on their foreheads cracked in patches.
The army that had come to conquer Moscow
            was wounded, hungry, and cold.
They'd taken anything warm they could find:
women's skirts covered their shoulders,
            and they used children's socks for gloves.
And before them lay paradise.
But first,
        that endless pack
        of white-clad red devils.
A boundless white plain stretched out around them.
But before them lay paradise:
before them lay Moscow,
the end of bleeding, hunger, and cold-
Moscow
        was so close.
Moscow was a stove,
a larder,
a feather pillow.
Hot water from the faucets
and stores full of furs.
just break the lock with your bayonet
and throw the softest, warmest skin on your bed
Wherever you turn, caviar;
sausages wherever you turn,
and mountains of butter.
Plus pillows, beds,
and sleep
        on a full stomach.
No more raids, fronts, or partisans.
Sleep
wake up
get warm
eat.
Sleep

wake up
get warm.
Until not a lump of coal remained to burn
or a shot of vodka to drink.
Then the war could end.
And they could return,
heroes.

The army that had come to conquer Moscow
was wounded, hungry, and cold.
But with the instinct of an animal
    — an animal left out in the snow,
      wounded, hungry, and cold —
        with the instinct of an animal —
        furious, head down, tail taut —
        it fought
            For food and warmth.
Hairs all on end, it fought,
and Moscow was still in danger...

Moscow was calm and confident.
It fired its anti-aircraft guns
    and carried in its pocket
      a dog-eared poetry book.
It attended the theater, movies, and concerts,
    listening to Strauss and Tchaikovsky
      between bursts of artillery,
and played chess behind the black-draped windows.
Its young workers were sent ahead to the front,
its new machine tools shipped back to the interior.
The old workers retooled old machine shops
        and made them run like clocks.
Moscow dug tank traps and built barricades.
And Pushkin,
his cast bronze shoulders under snow,
stood by as if in a daze,
maybe writing, a new Eugene Onegin.

The enemy reached Yakroma to the north of Moscow
          and the city of Tula to the south.
And in late November
and early December
they threw in their reserves
      all along the front.
In the first days of December
the situation was critical.

And in the first days of December,
near the city of Vereja in Petrishchevo,
the Germans hanged an eighteen year old girl
against a snow blue sky.
An eighteen year old girl should be getting engaged,
    not hanged.

She was from Moscow.
She was young and a partisan.
She was full of passion:
  she understood, believed, and took action.
The child hanging from the rope by her slender neck
  was, in all her glory, human.

A young girl's hands felt around in snowy darkness
as if turning the pages of War and Peace.
In Petrishchevo, telephone wires were cut.
Then a barn burned, with seventeen German army horses.
And the next day that partisan got caught.

They caught the partisan at the site of her new target —
  suddenly, from behind and red-handed.
The sky was filled with stars,
her heart with speed,
her pulse with her heartbeat,
and the bottle with gasoline.
She had only to strike the match.
But she couldn't.
She reached for her gun.
They fell on her.
They took her away.
They brought her in.
The partisan stood up straight in the middle of the room-
her bag on her shoulder,
fur hat on her head, sheepskin coat on her back,
and cotton pants and felt boots on her legs.
The officers looked closer at the partisan:
inside the fur, felt, and cotton was a slender young girl
like a fresh almond inside its green shell.

The samovar simmered on the table:
five gun belts, a gun,
and a green bottle of cognac on the checked cloth.
And a dish with pork sausage and bread crumbs.

The owners of the house had been sent into the kitchen.
The lamp had burned out.

The fire in the hearth painted the kitchen dark red.
And it smelled like crushed beetles.
The owners of the house — a woman, a child, and an old man —
huddled close together,
far from the world,
all alone on a deserted mountain, fair game for wolves.

Voices come from the next room.
They ask:
"I don't know," she says.
They ask:
"No," she says.
They ask: ,
"I won't tell you," she says. They ask:
I don't know," she says. "No" she says. "I won't tell you," she says.
        And the voice that's forgotten everything but these words
is clear as the skin of a healthy child
and direct as the shortest distance between two points.

A leather strap cracks in the next room:
the partisan is quiet.
Bare human flesh answers.
One after another, straps crack.
The snakes hiss as they leap toward the sun and fall back.
A young German officer walks into the kitchen
and sinks down in a chair.
He covers his ears with his hands,
shuts his eyes tight,
and stays like this through the interrogation.
Straps crack in the next room.
The owners of the house count:
                           200...
The partisan is hauled outside.
No fur hat on her head.. .
sheepskin coat on her back,
or cotton pants and felt boots on her legs,
she's in her underwear.
Her lips are swollen from biting them,
and her forehead, neck, and legs are bleeding. Barefoot in the snow,
arms tied behind her back with rope,
and flanked by bayonets,
the partisan walks.

The partisan
knows she'll be killed.
In the red glare of her rage
she sees no difference

between dying and being killed.
She's too young and healthy to fear death
           or feel regret.
She looks at her feet:
they're swollen,'
cracked, and frozen scarlet.
But pain
        can't touch her partisan:
her rage and faith
        protect her like a second skin...

Her name was Zoe;
she told them it was Tanya.

        Tanya,
        I have your picture here in front of me in Bursa Prison
        Bursa Prison.
        You probably never heard of "Bursa."
        My Bursa is soft and green.
        I have your picture here in front of me in Bursa Prison
        It's no longer 1941 —
                the year is 1945.
        Your side isn't fighting at the gates of Moscow
                but at the gates of Berlin.

        Tanya,
        I loved my country
                as much as you loved yours.

        They hanged you for loving your country.

        I'm alive,
        and you are dead.
        You left us long ago,
        and you were here just eighteen years.
        You didn't get your share of the sun's warmth.

        You're the hanged partisan,
        Tanya,
        and I'm the poet in prison.

        I called in my friends to look at your picture:
        "Tanya,
        I've got a daughter your age."
        "Tanya,
        my sister's your age."
        "Tanya,

she's your age, the girl I love.
We live in a warm country:
     girls become women overnight."
"Tanya,
I have friends your age in schools, factories, and fields."
"Tanya,
you died —
so many good people have been and are being killed.
But I –
I'm ashamed to say it-
    I,
who never once put my life on the line
                in seven years of war,
    even in prison I have a sweet life.]

In the morning they put Tanya's clothes back on,
all except her hat, coat, and boots:
                those they kept.
 They brought out her bag
 with the bottles of gasoline, matches, sugar, salt, and bullets.
They strung the bottles around her neck,
threw the bag on her back,
and wrote across her chest:
     "PARTISAN."

In the village square they set up the gallows.
The cavalry had drawn swords,
and the infantry formed a circle.
They forced the villagers to come and watch.

Two wood crates sat stacked on top of each other,
two spaghetti crates.
Above the crates
    dangled
      the greased noose.

The partisan was lifted onto her throne.
Arms tied behind her back,
the partisan
stood up straight under the rope.

They slipped the noose around her long slender neck.

One of the officers liked photography.
The officer took out his camera, a Kodak.
The officer wanted a snapshot.

The noose around her neck, Tanya called out to the farmers
  "Brothers, don't lose heart. Now is the time for courage.
Don't let the Fascists breathe —
smash, burn, kill..."

A German slapped the partisan across the mouth,
and blood flowed down the girl's swollen white chin
But the partisan turned to the soldiers and went on:
"We are two hundred million strong.
Can you hang two hundred million?
I may go,
but more of us will come.
Surrender while you can..."

The farmers cried.
The hangman pulled the rope.
The slender necked swan started to choke
But the partisan stood on tiptoes.
And the HUMAN called out to life:
"Brothers,
    so long!
Brothers,
    the fight is to the end!
I hear the hoof beats — our people are coming!"

The hangman kicked the spaghetti crates.
The crates rolled away.
And Tanya swung from the end of the rope.

Top: Mehmet Siyah Kalem, 15th century.
Topkapı Sarayı Museum. 26 x 37 cm.
Middle: Istanbul skyline at sunset.
Bottom: Stairway to the Sokollu Mehmet Paşa Mosque.

Poetry: Painting Pictures with Words

Objectives
1. To respond to poems that deal with feelings about nature andordinary objects.
2. To analyze mood and imagery in a poem.

Background Information

The period between the formation of the Republic and the death of Atatürk (1923-1938) was a time of transition in many ways in Turkish life, and this period of transitions, and spirit of newness and innovation can be seen reflected in the literature of the period as well. The poets of what is termed the Garip (or Strange) period (1941-1950), were in their own way, influenced by Nazim Hikmet, and along with him, would influence the literary culture for many years to come. Oktay Rifat and Orhan Veli were childhood friends, and classmates in Ankara. Joined in high school by Melih Cevdet, the three shared a friendship bonded by a common love of poetry and theatre. Despite a brief period of time apart, at university, and out of the country, they manage to compose poetry and publish in journals, often together. The 1941 publication of Garip is a milestone event in Turkish literature. It is a collection of the works of all three of these poets, organized in alphabetical order Melih Cevdet (Anday) first with 16 poems, followed by Oktay Rifat (Horozcu) second with 20 poems, and Orhan Veli (Kanık) third with 24 poems.

The work is an illustration of the main philosophy that shaped the poetry of these poets: the belief that artists must find a place for the real, lived experiences of the public in their art. The criticism was hailed at the Divan poetic tradition (of the Ottoman Period) that for so long avoided the public and representing their experiences in art, in favor of courtly motifs, and what was considered overused allusions to divine love. Their experimental poems were the first attempts, after the language reforms of the Republic of Turkey, to create a uniquely different poetic voice than the heavily canonized Divan poetic tradition. The poems were simple, short free verse poems, influenced by surrealism and haiku, and aimed to show that any thing and any object had a poem concealed within it.

Motivation

Have students think about their favorite natural setting. Ask them to record specific imagery-sights, sounds, smells, tastes, and sensations-that they associate with this setting.

Procedure

▷ Teacher will read *I Am Listening to Istanbul* aloud to class (**Worksheet 2**). How does the speaker in *I Am Listening to Istanbul* feel about Istanbul? Give examples from the poem to explain your answer.

▷ Imagine that you know someone who is thinking of visiting Istanbul. Based on this poem, do you think his experiences might be romantic, depressing, adventurous, peaceful, exotic, spiritual or something else? Explain your answer.

▷ Think about the images in this poem and their effect on you. Work with a partner and select 5 images from the poem. Then for each image, tell the senses to which the images appeal, the feelings that they arouse in you and the mood that they help to create. Write your notes in the chart below (**Worksheet 1**).

▷ Have students read the short poems on **Worksheet 3** and answer the summary question.

Summary   Traditional Japanese haiku poems reflect the essential themes of change and permanence, and they include references to the seasons. The three line, seventeen-syllable haiku offers readers a single clear image and then forces the readers to complete the poems by associating their own experiences, emotions and images. How are these Turkish poems influenced by the style of haiku poetry?

Imagery in *I Am Listening to Istanbul*

Image	Senses	Feelings	Mood

I am Listening to Istanbul
Orhan Veli[1]

I am listening to Istanbul, intent, my eyes closed;
At first there blows a gentle breeze
And the leaves on the trees
Softly flutter or sway;
Out there, far away,
The bells of water carriers incessantly ring;
I am listening to Istanbul, intent, my eyes closed.

I am listening to Istanbul, intent, my eyes closed;
Then suddenly birds fly by,
Flocks of birds, high up, in a hue and cry
While nets are drawn in the fishing grounds
And a woman's feet begin to dabble in the water.
I am listening to Istanbul, intent, my eyes closed.

I am listening to Istanbul, intent, my eyes closed.
The Grand Bazaar is serene and cool,
A hubbub at the hub of the market,
Mosque yards are brimful of pigeons,
At the docks while hammers bang and clang
Spring winds bear the smell of sweat;
I am listening to Istanbul, intent, my eyes closed.

I am listening to Istanbul, intent, my eyes closed;
Still giddy since bygone bacchanals,
A seaside mansion with dingy boathouses is fast asleep,
Amid the din and drone of southern winds, reposed,
I am listening to Istanbul, intent, my eyes closed.

I am listening to Istanbul, intent, my eyes closed.
Now a dainty girl walks by on the sidewalk:
Cusswords, tunes and songs, malapert remarks;
Something falls on the ground out of her hand,
It's a rose I guess.
I am listening to Istanbul, intent, my eyes closed.

---

[1](1914-1950) Orhan Veli Kanık and the Garip movement succeeded in crystallizing the free verse structure, so effortlessly used by Nazım Hikmet. Veli's work, impacted by his personal interest in Japanese haiku, is a simple and stark illustration of his belief that anything could be the object of poetic verse.

I am listening to Istanbul, intent, my eyes closed;
A bird flutters round your skirt;
I know your brow is moist with sweat
And your lips are wet.
A silver moon rises beyond the pine trees:
I can sense it all in your heart's throbbing.
I am listening to Istanbul, intent, my eyes closed.

Turkish title: "İstanbul'u Dinliyörüm"
Translated by Talat Sait Halman

Istanbul Views:

Previous Page: Some of the city's many kinds of trees, from cypress and redbud, to linden and others, frame views of the Bosphorus from both sides of the water.

Top: One of Istanbul's many mosques, from Imperial constructions to small neighborhood ones. The big mosques have large courtyards, and like Trafalgar Square in London or the big cities in America, they have resident flocks of pidgeons. Istanbul is also home to many other species of birds, from seagulls to nightingales.

Bottom: An Ottoman mansion, or yalı, on the water, like the one mentioned in Veli's poem.

Istanbul Views:

Top: The Kapalı Çarşa, or Grand Bazaar mentioned in the poem.
Right: A city street.

Poetry of Orhan Veli, Melih Cevdet, Oktay Rifat

Poetry of Orhan Veli

?

Why is it that when I say harbour
I recall a mast
And sails when I say the open sea?

And cats when I say March,
Workers when I say rights
And why does the old miller
Believe in God, without thought?

And why does the rain fall crooked
In windy weather?

—Turkish title, "?".
Translated by Özlem Şensöy

My Shadow

I am through
Dragging it
All these years
At the tip of my feet.
About time
We live a little,
My shadow
At someplace,
I
Someplace else.

—Turkish Title: "Gölgem"
Translated by Murat Nemet-Nejat

Poetry of Melih Cevdet[2]

The Guest

Oh, to be a guest
To have a clean bed set out for me
To forget everything, even my name
To sleep...

—Turkish title: "Bir Misafirlige"
Translated by Özlem Şensöy

Puzzling Encounter

"I remember having had this experience before,"
You say in utter amazement.

The house you've stepped in for the first time and the stairs
And that sudden shaft of sunlight striking the panes

And the train's whistle at its appointed time.
This was how, one evening
Long before you'd come into this world
The colors and patterns were blended.

"Can it be that living is but recollection?"
I doubt it. We may well have once been
A mere sound for someone else
In this puzzling encounter.

—Turkish title: "Şaşırtıcı Karşılaşma"
Translated by Ender Gürol

---

[2](1915-) Born Melih Cevdet Anday, Cevdet was born in Istanbul, and attended a military college in Ankara. After, he spent two years in Belgium, and upon his return to Istanbul worked as a teacher, translator, and journalist. His poems are known for their unexpected turn of plot, and attention to real life situations.

Poetry of Oktay Rifat[3]

Bread and the Stars

The bread is on my knee
The stars are far, far away
I am eating the bread, watching the stars
But so distracted am I
that there are times, instead of the bread
I eat a star.

> —Turkish title: "Ekmek ve Yildizlar"
> Translated by Özlem Şensoy

Waiting

The woman looks out of the window
the man returns home
the child plays in the street
the clock ticks on the wall.
Evening is waiting at the door
a yellow evening, a good evening.

> —Turkish title, "Bekleyen"
> Translated by Richard McKane

---

[3](1914-1988) Oktay Rifat Horozcu, was born in the city Trabzon, along the Northern, Black Sea, coast of Turkey. He was the son of Republican period poet Samih Rifat. Completing law school in Ankara, he studied for a graduate degree in Paris, but due to conditions of the Second World War, he was unable to complete doctorate and returned to Turkey in 1940. He is the only one of the Garip poets to be considered a formative figure in both the Garip movement, and the Second New movement. For this reason, it may be informative to look closely at his work, and its development, in relation to other Second New poets.

*C*alligraphy

Turks, like Muslims, adapted the basic calligraphy of the religion, and stressed Arabic script as the noblest of the art forms. Primarily, the art of beautiful writing, was held in the highest esteem because it was used to transcribe The Word of God, or the Koran, the holy book of the Muslims. In addition, since Islam discouraged representational (or figural) art, the written word was seen as a symbol/representation in the most abstract form, farthest removed from the thing or concept it represents.

Turks used the Arabic script until they adopted the Latin alphabet in 1928. Until then, the Ottoman religious and political emblems were developed making use of the Arabic script, in addition to several representational motifs (such as the crescent, double-pronged sword, the cypress tree, etc.). The most significant calligraphic emblem to be used by the Ottomans was the tughra. The **tughra** was a sultan's monogram or the imperial cypher which spelled out his given titles, names and the name of his father. The titles remained the same but, understandably, the names changed with the names of the rulers. A tughra is an ornamental arrangement; the outlines of the cypher is shaped like a hand with the thumb extended, but the origins of the shape cannot be adequately explained. The Turks, even before converting to Islam, had a variety of emblematic "seals" or "signs"

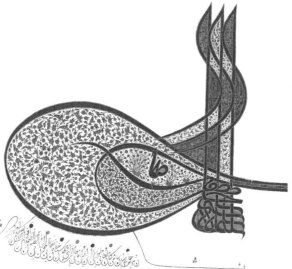

used by various tribes and families. It is thought that the tughra is a carry-over from the ancestors of the Ottomans. Such signs are called **damga** or imprint, similar to those branded on cattle belonging to a specific ranch in the American West. The tughra constituted the Great Seal of the Ottoman Empire, and as such, it was fixed by the court calligraphers on the most important documents issued from the court.

Arabic script has its roots in antiquity, before Islam, but it was developed gradually to an art form after Islam. The Turks have produced the best calligraphers in the Muslim world. The Arabic script has at least twelve different styles of writing from the highly ornate "geometric" style best suited to architecture to barely legible cursive style used by the Ottoman scribes on highly sensitive court documents. In all of its forms, the script has stringent rules as to its epigraphy. Within these rules and limitations (e.g., it has to be legible), the Turkish calligraphers penned extraordinary samples of epigraphy from religious texts to romantic poetry, which appears on official buildings as well as on love letters. The pages are decorated with floral and geometric patterns, and with ornamental designs known as "illumination." These illuminated Koran pages are among the best that Turkish art offers.

— Ülkü Bates Ph.D.

Suggested Time	Three classroom periods.
Materials Needed	Drawing paper, pencils, rulers, colored markers, gold and silver markers, Reproductions of calligraphy designs (two illustrations at end of lesson).
Objective	Students will gain an appreciation of the calligraphic style of Sultan Süleyman the Magnificent from the aesthetic and spiritual perspective.
Background Information	See the essay which precedes this lesson.
Notes to the Instructor	In preparation for this lesson, students may be asked to consider the importance of calligraphy in other cultures (it has also been considered the highest art form by the Chinese, for example, and produced masterpieces like the *Book of Kells* in Irish art). Students may find examples of calligraphic and ornamental designs in magazines or other publications. Other possible preparatory activities may include asking students to find examples of "illuminated" manuscripts. The essay on the preceding page may be used as an introduction or for follow-up enrichment activities.
Key Concepts/ Vocabulary	**calligraphy** – the art of beautiful handwriting; derived from the Greek *kallos* = beauty and *graphien* = to write **logo** – a symbol or group of letters used to describe something **geometric** – characterized by straight lines, triangles, circles, squares or other similar geometric forms **floral** – to look like flowers **curvilinear** – consisting of a curved line or lines **tughra** – seal of Sultan's name **Sultan Süleyman the Magnificent** – one of the greatest art patron of the Ottoman Empire **Koran** – holy book of Islam
Aim **Major Ideas**	Why was calligraphy considered among the noblest of art forms? ▷ An understanding of calligraphy as a form of self-expression and self-advertisement. ▷ An understanding of why calligraphy flourished under the Ottomans in Turkey.
Performance Objectives	Students will be able to: 1. Design their name in elaborate calligraphy. 2. Explain several reasons for the purpose of calligraphy. 3. Evaluate their design.
Materials	Drawing paper, pencils, rulers, colored markers, gold and silver markers, examples of calligraphy.
Procedure/ Development	▷ Display examples of ornamental type and decorations from magazines and newspapers. (Theses may be collected as a homework assignment or may be part of teacher's collection.) If students wish, they may create an ornamental design of their own name. Share examples. Teacher will lead class to develop criteria for evaluation (style, originality, self-expression). ▷ Display reproductions of calligraphy. Ask students to note shapes of lines, e.g. curved, geometric or floral.

▷ How is calligraphy a form of self-expression?

▷ Review calligraphy illustrations. Ask students to draw their own name in one of the three styles (curvilinear, geometric or floral).

Summary   It is very fashionable today for people who are planning formal weddings or other elaborate events to have invitations written by a calligrapher. Why do you think people still choose to use calligraphy, which is time consuming, when they could print the same invitations on a computer? (In fact, there are calligraphy computer programs.)

From what you know of Ottoman beliefs, why did calligraphy flourish in Ottoman Turkey?

Students will evaluate design for:

- style
- originality
- self-expression

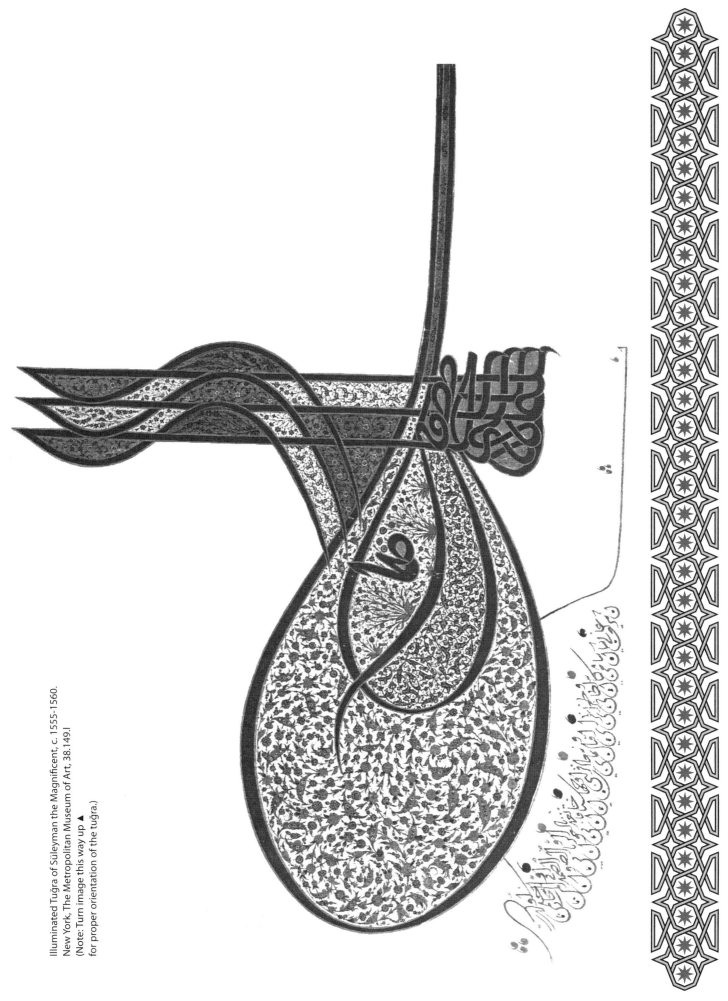

Illuminated Tuğra of Süleyman the Magnificent, c. 1555–1560.
New York, The Metropolitan Museum of Art, 38.149.I
(Note: Turn image this way up ▲
for proper orientation of the tuğra.)

Tiled wall from the Green Mosque in Bursa

Tiled wall from the Green Mosque in Bursa

Plate with galleon, late-16th century.
Copenhagen, The David Collection, 24/1975.

Plate with rumi scroll, late 16th century.
New York, Metropolitan Museum of Art, 66.4.13.

Turkish Ceramics

A WORLD MAP POINTS TO THE "BRIDGE-LIKE" CHARACTER OF THE ANATOLIAN PENINSULA WHICH STRETCHES BETWEEN ASIA AND Europe. This characteristic of the land has been compounded with the flow of people throughout history from East to West (Persians who invaded Anatolia and threatened Greece in the 5th Century B.C.E., or the Turks who migrated from Central Asia to Anatolia beginning around the 11th century C.E., or the Mongols of the 13th century), has yielded to a conglomeration of cultures in Anatolia. Turks of Anatolia have channeled the artistic traditions from East to West, and less so, from West to East. As the Ottoman Empire broadened its borders as far west as Vienna, Turkish words, customs, cooking, musical instruments and rhythms spread to Europe. However, some of the cooking, music and words had been adapted by the Turks from other people living to the east of Anatolia, such as Persians.

Plate with saz spray, mid-16th century.
Private collection

The visual arts played a prominent role among the cultural traits that Turks transmitted from the East to Europe. The most remarkable transmission occurred when the so-called "Turquerie" of the 18th century became the "high style". It appeared in the decorative programs of the European palaces. It was a contrived style, based on what Turkish art might look like rather than the actual Turkish art. The aim of the decoration was opulence, prettiness and sensuality, in sum, what Europeans associated with Turkish culture. The "Turquerie" style was an interpretation of the Turkish cultural world. The ambassadorial visit of the Ottoman dignitaries to Paris in 1718 created such a stir that it became fashionable among the French upper classes to dress in the "Turkish" style. It is important to note that the various artistic styles which had their origins in Western Europe, such as the Baroque style, were being incorporated into the Turkish art just about this time.

The Iznik Wares

The art of the Turkish ceramics, especially of those known as the "Iznik" pottery, is the most outstanding example of Turkish art that made an impact in the West. Iznik, the ancient Nicaea, not very far from Istanbul, became the center for ceramic production, especially in the 15th, 16th and early 17th centuries. The products of the Iznik kilns were much prized in Europe. Some of the best examples of the Iznik ware are found today in public and private collections in Europe and the United States. It seems that alongside with the Turkish carpets and kilims (flatwoven rugs), the Iznik ceramics were exported to Europe in large numbers in the early 15th century. The motifs and patterns found on pottery and on textiles (including Turkish silks and velvets which were imitated in Venice), made their indelible imprint on the decorative arts of Europe.

The Iznik wares had a complicated history of their own. They were inspired by the blue-and-white Ming Dynasty porcelain from China. Thus, Turks were responsible for transmitting Far Eastern aesthetics in ceramics to the West. The Topkapı Palace in Istanbul, the

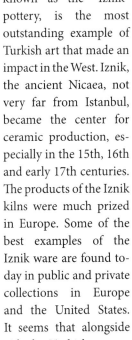

former seat of the Ottoman court and today a world-renowned museum, is one of the largest repositories of Chinese ceramics in the world, outside of China. The collection was built up gradually by the Ottoman sultans through the centuries as they bought the much celebrated Chinese celadons, stoneware and porcelain. The banquet tables of the Ottoman sultans were enriched not so much with objects in precious metals, but with the aesthetically more pleasing Chinese ceramics. Since the imported fragile ceramics were too costly for everyone to own, or even for everyday use at court, the local kilns, especially those of Iznik began to produce imitations of the Chinese ceramics. The Iznik ware was made of a white composite paste, slip painted under the glaze, and was fired at a high temperature, but was not porcelainous. (Kaolin, the main ingredient of porcelain was not available in Turkey, therefore, true porcelain could not be produced until the 19th century.)

Although 15th and early 16th century Iznik ceramics followed the Chinese models closely, both in color (blue-and-white) and in decorative motifs, the Ottoman potter enriched the decorative vocabulary around 1550 by adding naturalistic renderings of native flowers, such as tulips, carnations, hyacinths, bluebells and so on, and broadening the color palette. We find bright tomato reds, deep blackish purples, several shades of blue and green, in addition to a less often used yellow. The broadening of the decorative motifs and color scheme pointed to the "flowering" of the Turkish taste and competence in decorative arts around 1550, which was the beginning of the classical period which lasted until about 1700. From 1700 to about 1900 is the period during which Western (European) artistic traditions influenced Turkish arts.

If we were to summarize the general characteristics of the principles of ornamentation on Iznik ware (including tiles which were extensively used as revetments for the interiors of buildings): (a) the most popular motifs were floral ones; (b) the second favored were geometric patterns, especially staggered, repeated, multi-pointed, enclosed or open-ended stars; (c) representation of human figures, and of living things were rarely attempted (those remained mostly at the "folk art" level); (d) the combination of floral and geometric patterns were quite frequently employed to very pleasing effects (when floral motifs were used, the objective was not to produce a realistic rendering, but to effect a naturalistic and sometimes quite stylized presentation); and, finally, (e) the arrangement of the compositions was often symmetrical, even when asymmetry was favored, it was still a balanced composition.

It seems that the earliest blue-and-white "Oriental" pottery that was imported to Europe was not Chinese but the Turkish Iznik pottery. The kilns in the Netherlands, and later in England, produced a blue-and-white pottery in imitation of Iznik ware. Only later, in late 16th and 17th centuries, Europe began to import directly from China. In the 19th century, following the stylish "Turquerie" mode in the European court circles, potters in Italy, England and the United States produced quite remarkable imitations of Iznik ware. The Tiffany workshops incorporated some of the "Turkish" themes in the form of sensuous and curvilinear flora, into their vocabulary of ornamental motifs.

The history of the Iznik ware truly attests to the "bridge-like" character of Turkey: Chinese ceramics, which were the earliest pottery to be elevated to an art form in the world, were appreciated for their very fine quality by the Ottoman Turks who amassed a treasure in Istanbul. The Ottoman potters were inspired by the high quality of Chinese ceramics and produced their own versions. Europeans, in turn, avidly collected Iznik ware, and the kilns in the West made their own version, producing similar effects. This may have been the earliest global effort in the production of similar art objects which would surpass the political and geographic boundaries and unite peoples of different cultures in the pursuit of an aesthetic satisfaction.

— Ülkü Bates Ph.D.

Art Project 1	Iznik Plate Design.
Art Project 2	Turkish Tile Design.
Suggested Time	Two to three classroom periods for each project.

Materials Needed
1. drawing paper, compass, pencils, brushes, tempera paint OR gray clay, underglaze, overglaze (see notes to the instructor).
2. graph paper, drawing paper, pencils rulers, compasses, colored markers.

Objective Students will gain an understanding of Iznik ceramic designs which clearly demonstrate the "bridge-like" character of Turkey.

Background Information For more information, please see background essay on preceding page. This essay may be assigned as homework before the lesson.

Notes to the Instructor This lesson contains suggestions for two art projects. Teachers may select one or both depending on interest, materials, and time available. Both projects demonstrate the transmission of Chinese aesthetics via Turkey to Europe.

Art Project 1 can be painted onto drawing paper or clay. Most ceramics are in shades of blue with white, green or red.

Key Concepts/ Vocabulary
arabesque - abstract designs based on forked leaves, interlaced vines and scrolls
interlaced - to cross one another as if woven together
motif - the smallest unit of a pattern
peripheral - located away from the center, the outer edge
geometric - characterized by straight lines, triangles, circles, squares or other similar geometric forms
two-dimensional - length and width of a shape

Aim 1 Students will gain an understanding of Iznik ceramic wares by designing a floral plate.

Major Idea
▷ An understanding of cultural diffusion can be obtained through a careful study of ceramic plate designs from China to Turkey to the Netherlands.

Performance Objectives Students will be able to:
1. Contrast and compare Iznik ceramic plates with Chinese and Dutch plates.
2. Paint a floral and curvilinear design on a plate.

Materials Compass, pencil, tempera paint, brushes OR gray clay, underglaze, overglaze.

Visual Aids
▷ Photographs or illustrations of flowers.
▷ Examples of Iznik, Chinese, and Dutch ceramic plates.
▷ Illustrations in background information and at end of lesson.

Discussion Topics
▷ Compare Iznik ceramic plates with ceramic plates from China and the Netherlands. Make special note of color, motif, and composition.

▷ Istanbul has the largest selection of Chinese porcelain outside of China. Using what you have learned in your other classes and the following facts, create a hypothesis to explain this great collection of pottery in Istanbul. (If students read essay for homework, they should include this information).

- Ottoman Empire controlled eastern trade routes
- Both Chinese Emperors and Ottoman Sultans were patrons of the arts and highly appreciated nature and flowers.

Activity   Today we are going to begin to design our own ceramic plates.

▷ Students will draw several thumbnail sketches of flowers

▷ Students will draw a floral and curvilinear design on drawing paper in a circular form.

▷ Students will paint their design with tempera paints
OR

▷ Students will paint their design with underglaze on a gray clay plate.

Summary   Students will display completed artwork for class critique.
Students will evaluate design for

- use of curvilinear, arabesque or floral motifs
- choice of color

Tiled walls in Sultan Ahmet Mosque (also known, by tourists, as the Blue Mosque, for the color of its tiles).

Aim 2   Students will gain an understanding of Iznik ceramic wares by designing a Turkish tile.

Major Ideas   ▷   An understanding of cultural diffusion can be obtained through a careful study of ceramic plate designs from China to Turkey to the Netherlands.

Performance Objectives   Students will be able to:
1. Differentiate between asymmetrical and symmetrical designs.
2. Design their own symmetrical geometric pattern using color.
3. Identify and explain the basic elements of Islamic art.

Materials   Graph paper, drawing paper, pencils, rulers, compasses, colored markers.

Visual Aids   Examples of Islamic Art demonstrating geometric patterns — See illustrations in front of and following the lesson and in the background information.

Procedure/ Development   ▷   Teacher will ask students to identify:
   ♦   Objects which are symmetrical in the classroom.
   ♦   Objects which are asymmetrical in the classroom.

   ▷   Teacher will display reproductions of geometric patterns found in Islamic art. Have students identify each of the following patterns.

ISLAMIC GEOMETRIC PATTERNS		
square	triangle	circle
hexagon	octagon	6-pointed star
8-pointed star	10-pointed star	diamond

   ▷   Students should copy each geometric pattern into notebooks and label.
   ▷   Students will practice drawing geometric patterns with compass and ruler.
   ▷   Students will draw their own symmetrical geometric pattern with compass and ruler on graph paper   (Note: design should be five or six inch squares to appear as a tile design).
   ▷   Students will transfer their design to white drawing paper.
   ▷   Students will color their design with markers. Turkish tile designs are usually shades of blue, with accents in white, green and red.

Summary   What are some basic elements of Islamic art?
   ♦   two-dimensional design
   ♦   symmetrical
   ♦   geometric pattern
   ♦   repetitive pattern which radiates from a central point

The completed artwork will be displayed for a class critique.
Students will evaluate tile designs for:
   ♦   symmetry
   ♦   use of repeating patterns
   ♦   use of geometric patterns and color

Plate with diaper pattern, second quarter of 16th century.
New York, Metropolitan Museum of Art, 14.40.727

Plate with 3 bunches of grapes, second quarter of 16th century.
New York, The Metropolitan Museum of Art, 66.4.10.

Plate with peacock, mid-16th century. Paris, Musée du Louvre, 3449.

Piyale Paşa Mosque.

Turkish Art:

A 13th century manuscript page by Muhlis bin Abdullah el-Hindî, for Mevlâna's Mesnevî. Konya, Turkey, the Mevlâna Museum. Mevlâna is also known as Rumi. He wrote the Mesnevî and founded the Sufi sect of Islam that bears his name. They are famous in the West as the whirling dervishes.

Turkish Art:

Right: A modern example of Turkish gilded work and calligraphy, which is still taught and produced today.

Bottom right: İznik ceramic ware from the collections of the Topkapı Sarayı Museum (top plate, 15th century) and British Museum (bottom plate, 16th century).

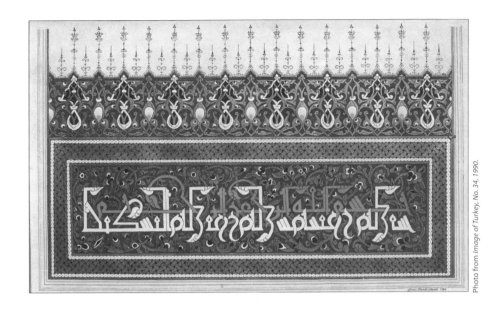

Photo from *Image of Turkey, No. 34*, 1990.

Photo from *Masterpieces of Turkey*.

Photo from *Masterpieces of Turkey*.

Bottom left: An Ottoman dancer, from an 18th century album in the Topkapı Sarayı Museum, page 18a, 15½ x 8½ cm.

Photo from *Masterpieces of Turkey.*

Turkish Architecture:

Left: The Mevlâna Türbe, or mausoleum, inside the Mevlevî Convent, in Konya. The original construction of the convent dates to the 13th century. It was later expanded and restored. This striking, sixteen-lobed structure is commonly called "the Green Dome" in Turkish, because of the color of its tile decoration.

Bottom: The Şehzade Mosque in Istanbul, foreground, with Süleymaniye Mosque behind it.

Opposite Page:

Top: Domes and decorations of the Selimiye Mosque in Edirne, Turkey. The classic Turkish imperial mosque has a central space beneath a dome that rests on half-domes, in the manner of Hagia Sophia. Ottoman mosque architecture developed a more unified central space than its predecessor, and filled it with a different kind of decoration. This better fit the requirements of Islam, which does not need a nave and aisles for a processional liturgy (unlike Western Christianity and the early Byzantines). Like some Protestant groups which object to statues and icons in church, Islam does not put this kind of imagery in mosques. Calligraphy and non-figural ornament are used instead.

Bottom left: A Bergama prayer carpet of the palace style, 17th century, Topkapı Sarayı Museum. It is one of the five pillars of Islam that the faithful should pray five times a day. Prayer carpets typically have a stylized version of a mosque mihrab woven into their design.

Bottom right: The interior of Bayrampaşa Mosque, showing the minber (the pulpit, a carved wooden structure with stairs) and mihrab niche, which is placed to indicate the direction of Mecca and thereby orient Muslims for prayer.

Photo from *Masterpieces of Turkey.*

Turkish Architecture and Related Arts:

Top: Ceramic wall tiles, colored glass windows, and decorated ceiling of a room in the Harem of the Topkapı Palace.

Right: The dining area in the country house of Emirhoca-zâde Ahmet Bey in the town of Safranbolu in Zonguldak province.

**Top Left and
Bottom Right:** Houses in the town of Safranbolu, where the old structure of the city, with its homes, streets and fountains, has been preserved. The houses date from the 15th to the 19th centuries.

Top Right: Tile facade of part of a medical center in Sivas that included a hospital, medical school, and türbe (mausoleum). Built in the 13th century by the Selçuk Sultan İzzettin Keykavus.

Photo from *Masterpieces of Turkey*.

20th century ebru (marbling) with flowers, by Mustufa Düzgünman.

Photo from *Masterpieces of Turkey*.

Karagöz puppets from the traditional shadow theatre, made of camel leather for transparency, Yapı ve Kredi Bankası collection.

Photo from *Masterpieces of Turkey*.

Photo courtesy of the Turkish Foreign Ministry.

Top left: Caftan of Mehmet the Conqueror, 15th century, gold and silver thread on velvet, Topkapı Sarayı Museum.
Bottom left: A modern example of the traditional art of ebru, or marbling.
Bottom right: A 16th century helmet made of iron and decorated with gold and precious gems, Topkapı Sarayı Museum.

Photo from *Masterpieces of Turkey*.

Representational Art

URKISH ART AT ITS HIGHEST LEVEL IS AB-
STRACT AND CONCEPTUAL. TURKS, WHO ARE
MUSLIMS, DEVELOPED ART FORMS THAT WERE
abstracted from the
descriptive and rep-
resentational art. The
Turkish artist did not
attempt to make "re-
alistic" representa-
tion of nature or
living things until the
mid-19th century,
when Turkish paint-
ers went to Europe to
learn painting in
Western styles.
Therefore, "linear" or
"scientific" perspec-
tive was not em-
ployed. Painting on
canvas and three-di-
mensional sculpture
(representational art)
were introduced to
Turkey only 150
years ago.

Turks have expressed themselves through a system
of very complex abstractions, in the form of symbols
and signs, stylization and reduction to geometric
patterns. As mentioned before, the Arabic script was
primarily used by the Turkish artist to express the religious, social and political aspirations of the Ottoman
Empire. The most readily recognizable symbol of the
Turks was the cres-
cent which symbol-
ized their religious
as well as political
affiliation.

Representa-
tional or figural art
was not completely
banned by Islam but
relegated mainly to
manuscripts to illus-
trate a text, themati-
cally or formally.
Miniature illustra-
tions in books were
for the upper or elite
classes of the society.
The production of a
manuscript with il-
lumination and min-
iature painting was
very costly and time
consuming; only
persons of wealth could own such a treasure. Therefore,
figural art remained as a rarity for the general Turkish
Muslim population.

— Ülkü Bates Ph.D.

Aim	Students will design and execute miniatures in the style of Ottoman Turkish art.
Major Ideas	▷ An understanding of contour overlapping, and linear design can be obtained through a careful study of Turkish miniature paintings. ▷ An understanding of the concept that Turkish miniature paintings illustrated a story.
Performance Objectives	Students will be able to: 1. Observe and discuss some characteristics of Turkish miniature paintings. 2. Draw and paint their miniature in the style of Turkish Miniature paintings. 3. Decorate a border for their painting with a repetitive pattern. 4. Design a frame to enhance their painting.
Materials	Pencils, rulers, drawing paper, brushes, tempera paint, oaktag, colored markers, silver and gold markers, construction paper.
Procedure/ Development	▷ Teacher will display three examples of paintings — one from Renaissance Europe, one Turkish miniature and one Chinese landscape. ▷ Teacher will ask class to compare and contrast the three artworks. (sample organizer below).

How can we compare Turkish Miniature paintings with European and Chinese artwork?

COMPARISON OF PAINTING TRADITIONS		
European	**Turkish**	**Chinese**
religious	secular	secular
themes of religion or mythology	themes of war, hunting or love scenes	landscapes
man dominates nature	man dominates nature	nature dominates man
painterly quality, use of shading for three-dimensional effects	flat, linear design, contour and overlapping for three-dimensional effects	flat, linear design, contour and overlapping for three-dimensional effects

▷ Students will compare and discuss the examples of the paintings.
▷ Students will list the characteristics of Turkish Miniature paintings.
▷ Students will draw a sketch for their painting.
▷ Students will transfer their drawing onto oaktag.
▷ Students will decorate a border with a repetitive pattern.
▷ Students will design a frame for their painting using construction paper.
▷ Students will decorate the frame with an elaborate geometric pattern using colored, gold and silver markers.

Summary	In a class critique the completed paintings will be displayed. Students will evaluate artwork in terms of: ♦ composition of the painting, border and frame ♦ Middle Eastern characteristics

battle march

Army marching with Sultan Süleyman's coffin, from *Tarih-i Sultan Süleyman* of Lokman transcribed in 1579/1580.
Dublin, The Chester Beatty Library, MS. 413, fols. 113b-114a.

Sultan Selim I praying outside Belgrade from *Tarih-i Sultan Süleyman* of Lokman transcribed in 1579/1580.
Dublin, The Chester Beatty Library, MS. 413, fols. 116b-117a.

circumcision celebration

Polo game (left) and entertainment of a prince (right) from the *Divan-ı Jami*, c. 1520
İstanbul, Topkapı Sarayı Müzesi, H987, fols.1b-2a

Turkish Carpets

Carpets, whether knotted or flat woven (kilim) are among the best known art forms produced by the Turks from time immemorial. There are environmental, sociological, economic and religious reasons for the wide spread art of carpet weaving among the Turkish people from Central Asia to Turkey.

The geographical regions where Turks have lived throughout the centuries lie in the temperate zone. Temperature fluctuations between day and night, summer and winter may vary greatly. Turks — nomadic or pastoral, agrarian or town-dwellers, living in tents or in sumptuous houses in large cities — have protected themselves from the extremes of the cold weather by covering the floors, and sometimes walls and doorways with carpets. The carpets, are always hand made of wool or sometimes cotton, with occasional additions of silk. These carpets are natural barriers against the cold. The flat woven kilims which are frequently embroidered, are used as blankets, curtains and covers over sofas, or as cushion covers.

In general, Turks take their shoes off upon entering a house. Thus, the dust and dirt of the outdoors are not tracked inside. The floor coverings remain clean, and the inhabitants of the house, if need be, can comfortably rest on the floor. In the traditional households, women and girls take up carpet and kilim weaving as a hobby as well as a means of earning money. Even technological advances which promoted factory-made carpets could not hamper the production of rug weaving at cottage-industry level. Although synthetic dyes have been in use for the last 150 years, hand-made carpets are still considered far superior to industrial carpeting.

Turkish carpets are among the most sought after household items all over the world. Their rich colors, warm tones, and extraordinary patterns with traditional motifs have contributed to the status that Turkish carpets have maintained since the 13th century. Marco Polo, who traveled through Anatolia in the late 13th century, commented on the beauty and artistry of the carpets. A number of carpets from this period, known as the Seljuk carpets, were discovered in several mosques in central Anatolia. These were under many layers of subsequently placed carpets. The Seljuk carpets are today in the museums in Konya and Istanbul.

It is very exciting to imagine that we may be looking at the very same carpets that Marco Polo praised in the year 1272.

Turkish carpets in the 15th and 16th centuries are best known through European paintings. For example, in the works of Lotto (15th century Italian painter) and Holbein (16th century German painter), Turkish carpets are seen under the feet of the Virgin Mary, or in secular paintings, on tables. In the 17th century, when the Netherlands became a powerful mercantile country, Turkish carpets graced many Dutch homes. The Dutch painter, Vermeer, represented Turkish carpets predominantly to indicate the high economic and social status of the persons in his paintings. "Turkey carpets," as they were known, were too valuable to be put on floors, except under the feet of the Holy Mother and royalty.

Anyone who enters a mosque has to take off his/her shoes. The mosque is the common house of a Muslim community, therefore, shoes are cast off before the door. Moreover, the ritual of prayer requires the faithful to kneel and touch the ground with one's forehead in humility before God. There are no chairs or benches in a mosque, only carpets. A Turkish mosque is often covered "from wall to wall" with several layers of carpets. To deed a carpet to a mosque is an act of piety and many Muslims do so. Prayer carpets that are small enough to be carried easily accompany many Muslim travelers. The Muslim, wherever he or she is, upon determining the direction of the Ka'aba in Mecca, lays down the prayer carpet and through the ritual of prayers communicates directly with God.

The Turkish carpets have exuberant colors, motifs and patterns. No two carpets are the same; each one is a creation from anew. Because traditionally women have woven the carpets, this is one art form that is rarely appreciated as being the work of a known or a specific artist. Nevertheless, the Turkish women silently continue to create some of the most stunning examples of works of art to be distributed all over Turkey and the world.

— Ülkü Bates Ph.D.

Art Project	Turkish Rug Design.
Suggested Time	Two to three classroom periods.
Materials Needed	graph paper, rulers, pencils, colored markers, cray-pas, 18" x 24" white drawing paper, Turkish rug motifs, compass, illustrations at end of lesson.
Objective	1. Students will begin to understand the place of carpets and kılıms in Turkish culture. 2. Students will gain an aesthetic appreciation for Turkish carpets and see why they have been valued and imported for centuries into Europe and America.
Notes to the Instructor	Teacher should assign essay on Turkish carpets for student reading in preparation for class. Students should work on projects in groups of four.
Key Concepts/ Vocabulary	**weave** — an interlocking of yarn to make a cloth or rug **warp** — lengthwise threads on a loom for weaving **weft** — the yarns that go over and under on the loom **loom** — a frame for interlacing at right angles two or more sets of yarn to weave the rug **Turkish knot** — a symmetrical knot woven under and over the warp yarn **Persian knot** — an asymmetrical knot woven under and over the warp yarn **motif** — the smallest unit in a design **pattern** — a design made from repeated colors, lines or shapes
Aim	How can we design a Turkish rug?
Major Ideas	▷ An understanding of the importance of rugs can be obtained through a careful study of the family life, the role of women in rug weaving and the influence of Islam in Turkey. ▷ An appreciation of the aesthetic beauty of Turkish rugs can be obtained through a careful study of creating their own rug design.
Performance Objectives	Students will be able to: 1. Recognize and distinguish some of the symbols on Turkish rugs. 2. Explain the process of rug weaving. 3. List some of the reasons the art of rug weaving flourishes in Turkey. 4. Create their own rug design.
Materials	graph paper, rulers, pencils, compass, colored markers, cray-pas, 18" x 24" white drawing paper, illustrations of Turkish design motifs and rugs.
Procedure/ Development	▷ Show illustrations of Turkish rugs (found at end of lesson). ▷ From what you have learned in the other sections of this chapter about daily life among the Turks, list some reasons why rug weaving flourished and excelled in Turkey: ◆ Large extended families; rural women rarely work outside the home and the rug weaving process is almost exclusively performed by women.

- Islamic custom — it is disrespectful to walk in mosques without removing your shoes. If you are a woman, you should also cover your hair with a scarf. (Until the mid-1960s in America, women also covered their heads in most churches by wearing hats or special coverings. By Jewish custom, it is the men who wear a special cover for their heads. These are all customs to show respect in a holy place.)
- Turks are immaculate housekeepers, and they also remove shoes at the entrance of their homes, in order to keep their houses clean of outside dirt and dust. It is polite for visitors to do the same. The Japanese are also known for this custom.
- Turks were nomadic tribes from central Asia, woven rugs kept their tents warm.

Activity Students will:
  ▷ Observe and discuss the process of rug weaving.
  ▷ Observe various Turkish rugs and differentiate among the designs.
  ▷ Choose motif designs for their rug design.
  ▷ In groups of four, draw their rug design on graph paper.
  ▷ Transfer their design onto white drawing paper.
  ▷ Color their designs.

Summary In a class critique the completed rug designs will be displayed.

Students will evaluate rug designs for:
- visual impact
- arrangement of various motifs and choice of color
- understanding of the rug weaving process

Kuş or Bird Motif

This motif has carried many meanings over the centuries. To the ancient Romans, whose empire included Anatolia, birds were used to represent the souls of the dead. Birds have also been interpreted as both good and bad luck, happiness, joy and love, women, longing, an expectation of news, power and strength.

◄ Göz or Eye Motif

This is a stylized eye. It is believed that the best way to prevent the harm caused by the evil eye is to ward it off with another eye.

This motif shows the importance of water in the life of mankind.

Water has always had a place of special import in Middle Eastern conceptions of paradise, which is represented in both ancient tales and in Islamic art as a garden with fountains of water.

Su Yolu Running Water Motif
▼

Milas wool prayer rug

Maden wool rug "Seccade""

Kars wool carpet "Karyola"

Yıldız or Star Motif.

This motif is an old symbol, originally expressing happiness and fertility. It dates back to pre-Islamic use as a symbol for the womb of the mother goddess. It is based on the six-pointed star, generally known as the Solomon's Seal. Star motifs with eight or more points are used in Anatolian weaves.

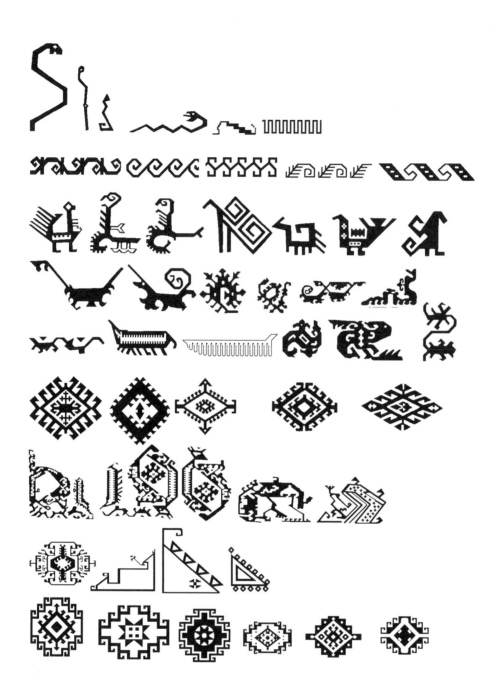

Yılan or Snake Motif.

This motif also has ancient roots, dating back to the earliest recorded history of mankind. It was originally thought to have protective properties. Black snakes were symbols of hapiness and fertility in the ancient world.

There is also an ancient mythological theme of a winged creature, with the feet of a lion and the tail of a snake, believed to be the master of air and water, the cause of lunar eclipse, the guard of treasures and of secret objects as well as of the tree of life.

A related theme is the fight of the Dragon and the Phoenix, which was believed to produce fertile rains of spring. The Dragon was represented by a cloud.

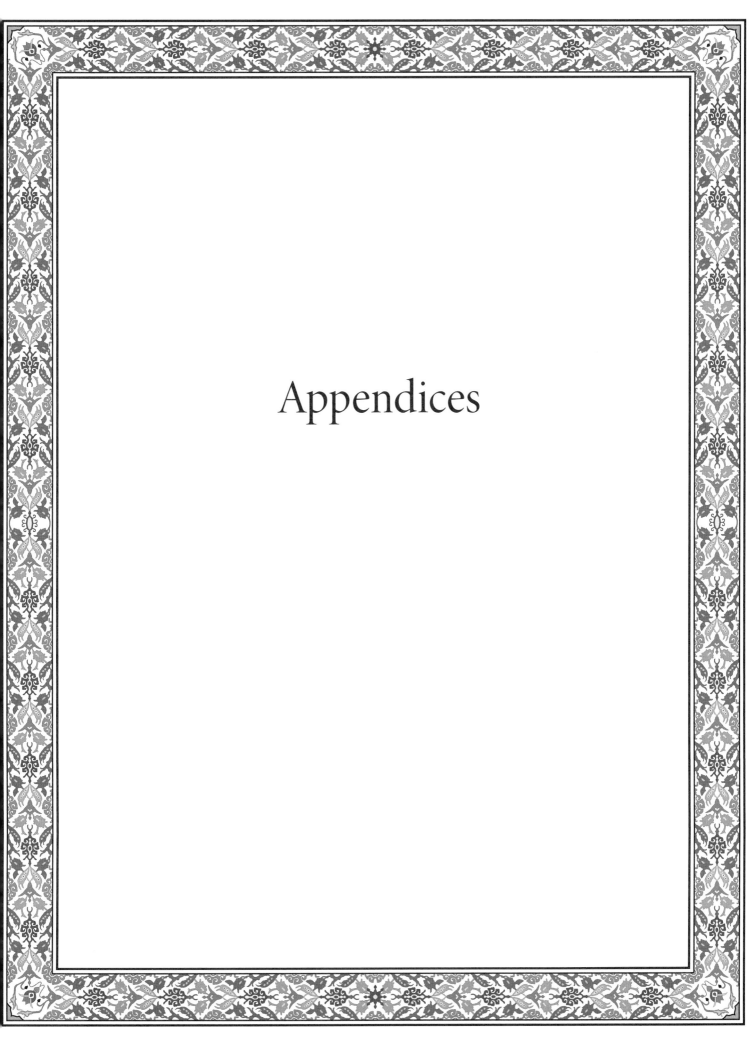

Appendices

Ottoman Sultans

Osman I	1281-1324		İbrahim	1640-1648
Orhan	1324-1362		Mehmet IV	1648-1687
Murat I	1362-1389		Süleyman II	1687-1691
Bayezit I	1389-1401		Ahmed II	1691-1695
Mehmet I	1413-1421		Mustafa II	1695-1703
Murat II	1421-1444		Ahmed III	1703-1730
Mehmet II	1444-1446		Mahmud I	1730-1754
Murat II	1446-1451		Osman III	1754-1757
Mehmet II	1451-1481		Mustafa III	1757-1774
Bayezit II	1481-1512		Abdülhamit I	1774-1789
Selim I	1512-1520		Selim III	1789-1807
Süleyman I	1520-1566		Mustafa IV	1807-1808
Selim II	1566-1574		Mahmud II	1808-1839
Murat III	1574-1595		Abdülmecid I	1839-1861
Mehmet III	1595-1603		Abdülaziz	1861-1876
Ahmed I	1603-1617		Abdülhamit II	1876-1909
Mustafa I	1617-1618		Mehmet V	1909-1918
Osman II	1618-1622		Mehmet VI	1918-1922
Mustafa I	1622-1623		Abdülmecid II*	1922-1924
Murat IV	1623-1640			

*caliph only

Presidents of the Turkish Republic

Mustafa Kemal Atatürk	1923-1938	Fahri Korutürk	1973-1980
İsmet İnönü	1938-1950	Kenan Evren	1982-1989
Celâl Bayar	1950-1960	Turgut Özal	1989-1993
Cemal Gürsel	1961-1966	Süleyman Demirel	1993-2000
Cevdet Sunay	1966-1973	Ahmet Necdet Sezer	2000-

Governments and Prime Ministers of the Turkish Republic

Prime Minister	Dates of Government
İsmet İnönü	30 October 1923-6 March 1924
" "	6 March 1924-22 November 1924
Ali Fethi Okyar	22 November 1924-3 March 1925
İsmet İnönü	3 March 1925-1 November 1927
" "	1 November 1927-27 September 1930
" "	27 September 1930-4 May 1931
" "	4 May 1931-1 March 1935
" "	1 March 1935-1 November 1937
Celâl Bayar	1 November 1937-11 November 1938
" "	11 November 1938-25 January 1939
Refik Saydam	25 January 1939-3 April 1939
" "	3 April 1939-9 July 1942
Şükrü Saraçoğlu	9 July 1942-9 March 1943
" "	9 March 1943-7 August 1946
Recep Peker	7 August 1946-10 September 1947
Hasan Hüsnü Saka	10 September 1947-10 June 1948
" "	10 June 1948-16 January 1949
Şemsettin Günaltay	16 January 1949-22 May 1950
Adnan Menderes	22 May 1950-9 March 1951
" "	9 March 1951-17 May 1954
" "	17 May 1954-9 December 1955
" "	9 December 1955-25 November 1957
" "	25 November 1957-27 May 1960
Cemal Gürsel*	30 May 1960-5 January 1961
" "	5 January 1961-20 November 1961

*president of National Unity Committee

Prime Minister	Dates of Government
İsmet İnönü	20 November 1961-25 June 1962
" "	25 June 1962-25 December 1963
" "	25 December 1963-20 February 1965
Suat Hayri Ürgüplü	20 February 1965-27 October 1965
Süleyman Demirel	27 October 1965-3 November 1969
" "	3 November 1969-6 March 1970
" "	6 March 1970-26 March 1971
Nihat Erim	26 March 1971-11 December 1971
" "	11 December 1971-22 May 1972
Ferit Melen	22 May 1972-15 April 1973
Naim Talu	15 April 1973-26 January 1974
Bülent Ecevit	26 January 1974-17 November 1974
Sadi Irmak	17 November 1974-31 March 1975
Süleyman Demirel	31 March 1975-21 June 1977
Bülent Ecevit	21 June 1977-21 July 1977
Süleyman Demirel	21 July 1977-5 January 1978
Bülent Ecevit	5 January 1978-12 November 1979
Süleyman Demirel	12 November 1979-12 September 1980
Bülent Ulusu	20 September 1980-13 December 1983
Turgut Özal	13 December 1983-21 December 1987
" "	21 December 1987-9 November 1989
Yıldırım Akbulut	9 November 1989-23 June 1991
Mesut Yılmaz	23 June 1991-20 November 1991
Süleyman Demirel	20 November 1991-25 June 1993
Tansu Çiller	25 June 1993-15 October 1995
" "	15 October 1995-5 November 1995
" "	5 November 1995-12 March 1996
Mesut Yılmaz	12 March 1996-8 July 1996
Necmettin Erbakan	8 July 1996-30 June 1997
Mesut Yılmaz	30 June 1997-11 January 1999
Bülent Ecevit	11 January 1999-28 May 1999
" "	28 May 1999-18 November 2002
Abdullah Gül	18 November 2002-14 March 2003
Tayyip Erdoğan	14 March 2003-

Food

Turkish cooks are the inheritors of one of the world's great cuisines. The best chefs in the Ottoman Empire vied to create special dishes to please the Sultan and the court. Many of these delicacies filtered down, over time, to ordinary people, elevating the quality of everyone's diet. The Turks brought traditions with them out of Central Asia, and they also found new foods and new ways to prepare them, in Asia Minor. Later, like the rest of the world, they were happy to add New World foods like tomatoes, potatoes, corn, and peppers to their diet. As with the geography and some other aspects of the culture, East meets West in the food of the country.

Americans, used to supermarket food that often looks good but suffers from a lack of flavor, find markets in Turkey are stocked with some of the best fruits and vegetables they have ever tasted. This is due both to the great location and climate for growing foods that Turkey is fortunate to have, and to the fact that food is still more seasonal there, where it is picked, prepared, and served at its peak.

Breakfast   A typical Turkish breakfast consists of freshly baked white bread or toast and jam (usually sour cherry or strawberry) or honey, a mild white cheese called **beyaz peynir**, that comes in an enormous variety of forms, black olives, and strong tea. Turks like to drink their tea with sugar, from elegant, handleless glass cups on glass, metal, or porcelain saucers. Some years ago, a Turkish newspaper proudly reported that Turks drank more tea than the English.

Bread   Turks have been making bread from wheat flour since they lived in Central Asia. They make several kinds. This is one of the foods both Turks (and former residents of Turkey) miss most when they are away from home. There is a kind of flat bread that is served with meals. There are the rings of white bread encrusted with sesame seeds, called **simits**, that you can buy in bakeries or from street sellers who hawk their wares from a kind of tray with legs that can be carried easily and piled high with these soft treats. There are the ubiquitous loaves of bread baked fresh every day, crusty golden on the outside, and soft and white inside. They can be bought warm from the baker's, for breakfast, or anytime. Turks also make bread topped with cheese and meat — a kind of cousin to pizza, but with a distinctive and delicious Eastern Mediterranean twist. In the Ottoman Empire, the bakers of Istanbul believed that Adam, the first man in the Bible and the Koran, was a baker and their patron saint.

Drinks   Besides tea and coffee, Turks make and consume a variety of other beverages, some familiar to us, and some more exotic. Turkey produces many different kinds of fruits, so some are made into fruit juices such as apple, orange and cherry. The cherry drink is made from a variety of sour cherry different from those generally grown in America, and it makes an appetizing change from the flavor we know.

Another drink that is unfamiliar to many Americans is called **ayran**. It is made by mixing mild, unflavored yogurt with water. Yogurt is said to be one of the foods that the Turks brought with them from Central Asia. And, yogurt was known in the Middle East from ancient times. Certainly, Turks are great consumers of different varieties of yogurt, to which they attribute the sort of health-giving properties Americans are more likely to attribute to chicken soup. Except that yogurt is supposed to help with upset digestive systems, and chicken soup is presumably an aid to getting over colds and sniffles.

Turkey is a producer of alcoholic drinks, which may surprise Americans, since it is also a country of Muslims. Anatolia has been a grape-growing region since ancient times, however, and Turkey continues the tradition of wine production. Good beer is also readily available, as well as an anise-flavored drink, called **rakı**, that is beloved by Turks, and consumed with food in the evening, with friends. Rakı is clear in the bottle and the glass, until a little water or ice is added. Then the water or melting ice turns the drink a milky color.

Meze

One of the glories of Turkish cuisine is the wide variety of hors d'oeuvres that can be a meal in themselves, or that comprise the courses served to guests before the main course in homes and restaurants, or spread out at buffets. The idea of a number of small dishes served to whet the appetite before the main part of the meal goes back more than two thousand years in the Mediterranean, though in classical times, the food eaten could be somewhat different from today. It might include exotic fare from nightingales and edible iris bulbs to sea urchins and crickets, in additional to more familiar foods such as chickpeas and shellfish.

These days, meze dishes can be seafood or meat dishes, or stuffed vegetables, called **dolma**, which means "stuffed" in Turkish. Dolma are often squash, tomatoes, eggplant, grape or cabbage leaves, or tender green peppers filled with meat, rice, pine nuts and spices such as cinnamon, mint, or dill. Mezeler also include bean salads, eggplant salad, cucumber and yogurt dishes, and foods like the green and black olives, pilafs, and chick pea spreads similar to ones that Americans may be familiar with from other Mediterranean and Middle Eastern cuisines. Turks also make many different kinds of börek, a pastry that is filled with cheese, or cheese and meat, and spices, and deep fat fried, or baked.

Seafood

Most Turks love seafood, and are especially fond of taking guests out to restaurants that specialize in cooking it. Such establishments abound in Turkey, and many restaurants specializing in this fare overlook the water. With coasts to the north, west and south, many kinds of fresh fish, as well as shellfish, octopus and calamari, are available, in season, and are finely prepared.

Grilled Meats

Of course, Turkey is the land of **kebap** (kebab), which likely came with the Turks out of Central Asia. Lamb is the most usual meat eaten in Turkey, although beef and chicken are also available. Even if you are not normally a lover of lamb, try it if you go there. It tastes deliciously different from the lamb sold in this country.

The method of butchering is similar to a kosher style, and removes blood from the meat. As in Judaism, pork is proscribed by Islam, so Muslims are not supposed to eat it. Turkish cuisine does not include pork, and it is rare to see it in shops and restaurants, except sometimes those that serve foreigners and the non-Muslim communities.

A typical kind of Turkish "fast food" is the **döner kebab** that can be bought and eaten while strolling along the street. Döner means "to turn", and refers to the way the meat turns on the spit to cook. Many thinly sliced layers of meat are packed onto the spit and grilled. As the outer edge of the meat is finished cooking, it is carved off and served. A host of other kinds of grilled dishes are made, and there are also restaurants that specialize in this type of fare.

Sweets, Desserts and Coffee

Turkish Delight, called **lokum** in Turkish, is probably the most famous sweet from Turkey. There are many varieties and flavors of lokum, including mint, lemon, and pistachio. There is even one that is delicately flavored with rose petals. Baklava is also well known. But there is an extensive and less well-known tradition of desserts, many of which were invented to please the Sultan and the court. Some of the most subtle desserts are milk-based. There is another that sounds strange but is exquisite; it uses chicken breast as one of its ingredients.

Dinner is often concluded with a cup of Turkish coffee. This drink is prepared differently from the drip method typical of American coffee. The beans are ground more finely, to begin with. The ground coffee is then measured, and cold water, and as much sugar as the drinker desires, are added into the small container (a **cevze**) in which the coffee will be prepared. The water and coffee are heated just to boiling, and the coffee poured into small cups. Some of the foam from the top of the cevze should go into each cup, and the diners are careful to drain the cup only down to the grounds, leaving them in the bottom of the cup.

Vocabulary

ayran ("ay" is the diphthong represented by the "i" sound in the English word "glide")

beyaz peynir (literally "white cheese;" this type of cheese is usually known as feta in America)

börek (the "oe" in the French word "oeuvre." English does not have this sound)

cacık (pronounced jah•jik, "c" is always the English "j" sound)

cevze

dolma

döner kebab

lokum (lo·koom)

rakı (rah-ka) (very short final vowel sound, close to "a" in about or short "i" sound of "it;" *not* an "ee" sound)

simit

Recipes

Not only do traditional Turkish foods look and taste wonderful, even their names are often delightful, such as "The Sultan Smiled," "Lady's Navel," "The Imam Fainted," "Lady's Thighs," and "Nightingale's Nest." Here are a few recipes, chosen because they are both tasty and not difficult to make. They are slightly adjusted for available American ingredients and measurements, for you to try.

Meat   Lamb is the most usual meat for meze and entrees in Turkey, though beef and chicken are also easy to find, and seafood is much loved as an alternative.

Köfte
(Meatballs)   *Turks make a variety of köfte. They can be grilled or fried, and made with lamb, beef, a combination of the two, or less commonly, with vegetables.*

> 1 lb. ground lamb or beef
> 1 onion, preferably a red one, grated
> 1 egg
> 3 cloves garlic, minced
> 2 Tbsp. tomato paste (or ketchup, in a pinch)
> ¼ cup bread crumbs
> ½ tsp. paprika
> 2 tsp. cinnamon
> 1 tsp. dill, or small bunch of fresh dill, chopped
> 1 tsp. parsley or small bunch of fresh parsley, chopped
> 3 Tbsp. pine nuts (optional)
> salt and pepper to taste

▶ Mix together the ground meat, grated onion, and minced garlic in a large bowl.

▶ Add the remaining ingredients and mix thoroughly with a spoon or by kneading the ingredients with your hands.

▶ Shape small amounts of the mixture into sausage-like meatballs by rolling between your hands until it is round and as long as a finger.

▶ These can be skewered to place on the grill and cooked, turning every couple of minutes until they are done. Or they can be rolled in flour and browned in hot oil on the stove, turning until they are done on all sides, then drained on paper towels.

▶ Serve with cacik (recipe below on page 233) or plain yogurt.

~

Pilavs (pilafs)
and Börek   There are many different rice and bulgar pilafs made in Anatolian kitchens, and they are quite easy to prepare. Some versions are made with ground meat or small pieces of cooked meat mixed in. Traditionally, they were a course in their own right, but pilaf also makes a great side dish for a meal, and may now be served with meat dishes in Turkish restaurants.

Börek dishes are also many and varied. Even fussy eaters love the ones made with a cheese filling that is folded up in pastry dough triangles or rolled into cigar shapes and fried. The recipe here has a similar flavor, but is made in a pan and baked instead.

Spiced Pilav

2 c. rice
1 medium onion, chopped
6 Tbsp. butter
2 Tbsp. pine nuts (you can substitute slivered almonds if you don't have pine nuts)
1-2 tomatoes, peeled and chopped
1 tsp. pepper
1 tsp. salt, or to taste
1 tsp. cinnamon or cloves
4 c. water or beef broth
1 Tbsp. currents (these are best, but you can substitute raisins or golden raisins, if necessary)
1 bunch dill, save out a few sprigs, and chop the rest finely

► Sauté onion in butter until softened. Add pine nuts and rinsed rice, and continue to cook and stir for about 10 minutes, until pine nuts are slightly browned.

► Add chopped tomatoes, salt and pepper, cinnamon, water or broth, and currents and dill. Bring to a boil, reduce heat, then cover and simmer until liquid is absorbed.

► Fluff rice with a fork to separate kernels. Garnish with a few sprigs of dill.

≈

Spinach Börek

Nigella sativa seeds (çörek otu in Turkish) have been used since Roman times for cooking, and in Asia they have been used for medicinal purposes from antiquity. They are said to cure everything except death, but do not use it in large quantities, since nigella is a member of the buttercup family. Too much can be an irritant, and even toxic. As a spice, it can be difficult to locate in America. You may find it under one of its numerous other names; some of the most common include black cumin, black caraway, black seed, nutmeg flower and Roman coriander. Russians, as well as Turks, use it on bread, and Armenians also cook with it, so it may be called charnushka or Russian caraway sometimes. Indian cooks call it kala zeera, kalonji, munga reala or krishnajiraka, and use it in the making of lobhia and in naan bread, so you may find it in stores that carry Indian supplies.

In America, nigella is known primarily from a closely related plant with similar seeds, nigella damascena. Known as a beautiful annual for the garden, which is easy to grow even in bad soil, as long as you have sun and good drainage. Its seeds can also be used culinarily. Its common name in garden catalogues is Love-in-the-Mist.

2 bunches fresh spinach (about 2+ lbs.) or 1 package frozen spinach
1 medium onion, chopped finely
12-14 oz. beyaz peynir (try to substitute Greek or Bulgarian feta if you

don't have a local or Internet supplier of beyaz peynir; American feta
is not as good)

salt and pepper

about 1¼ stick butter

3 eggs

½ c. milk

1 package filo pastry leaves (Turks use a flaky pastry dough called yufka,
but filo dough will work, and is readily available to Americans in most
cities)

sesame seeds or çörek otu (nigella seeds)

▶ Butter or grease a lasagna dish or other large rectangular pan (a sheet cake pan
or jelly roll pan will work).

▶ Thaw, if frozen, or wash and chop fresh spinach. Chop onion and sauté in 3-4
Tbsp. butter until soft. Add spinach and continue to sauté for another 2 minutes. Crumble the beyaz peynir or feta into the spinach mixture, stir to mix,
and add salt and pepper to taste.

▶ Set mixture aside while you melt ¾ stick butter in a saucepan.

▶ Beat 3 eggs with ½ c. milk in a small bowl.

▶ Spread 2 leaves of filo dough on the bottom of the pan, allowing the edges of
the leaves to lie against or overlap the sides of the pan. Spoon a little of the
melted butter over the leaves and spread it with the back of the spoon, or with
a pastry brush, over the layer. Place 2 more leaves of filo dough down to form
another layer, and brush this layer with a few spoonfuls of the egg and milk
mixture. Alternate the pastry leaves, melted butter, more filo leaves and the
egg/milk mixture until half the filo dough is used.

▶ Spread the spinach and cheese mixture as the middle layer, then continue to
alternate the remaining filo leaves with the butter and the egg/milk mixture,
until all the leaves are used, or your pan is filled up. Fold down the edges of the
filo leaves that went up the sides of the pan so that they lie flat on the top, and
seal them down with the melted butter. Brush the top layer with the butter and
the egg mixture, and sprinkle with sesame seeds, if desired. Çörek otu (nigella
seed) is even better, sprinkled over the top. Some people ascribe various
flavors, from "mild peppery" to "oregano or fennel-like" to the seeds, but they
don't really taste quite like anything else. They are another great Mediterrean/
Asian flavor for you to try.

▶ Bake in a moderate oven, about 325 degrees, for 45 minutes, or until golden
brown on top.

∾

Vegetables

Turks do wonderful things with vegetables, so if you are a vegetarian, or know one,
you will find their recipes a welcome change from the usual. They often use spices
and combinations of ingredients that are deliciously surprising, such as cumin with
spinach, yogurt with savory flavors instead of fruit, or cinnamon in dishes that are

not desserts. If you think you don't like vegetables, you may discover that you just didn't like the boring ways they are often prepared.

Spinach with Pine Nuts

2 big bunches (about 1 lb.) of spinach, washed to remove any grit
2 Tbsp. olive oil
1 medium red onion, chopped
1 tsp. sugar
1 tsp. ground cumin
¼ cup pine nuts
¼ cup currants
1 tsp. paprika
salt and pepper to taste

¼ cup plain yogurt
2 tsp. lemon juice, or to taste
2-3 cloves garlic, crushed

► Cook spinach in a few tablespoons of water until just wilted. Then drain and chop it.

► Put olive oil in a frying pan over medium heat, then add the chopped onion, sugar and cumin. Stir and cook this mixture until the onion softens.

► Add pine nuts, currants, and paprika, salt and pepper. (The amounts are approximate; you can use fewer pine nuts and currants, or substitute almonds for the pine nuts, and chopped raisins for the currents, in a pinch.)

► Cook for 2 minutes before stirring in the chopped spinach. Continue cooking for another 2 minutes, then transfer to a serving dish.

► Squeeze lemon juice into the yogurt, stir in the crushed garlic and spoon onto the top of the spinach mixture. Serve immediately.

Mücver
(Squash fritters)

These vegetable fritters are served as meze at parties and for dinner. The white cheese and dill melted inside will make them a favorite. Some Turks do omit the cheese, so if you have leftover zucchini, but no feta, try it anyway. One Turkish friend told me they add in whatever vegetables they like that they have on hand, such as potatoes (which would also have to be grated before mixing). Potato is not typical, but is a nice variant if you like a flavor more like potato pancakes. Usually, they are made with a small squash that is similar to zucchini, which makes a good substitute. The carrot adds a nice touch of orange, but mücver is often made without it.

1½ lbs. zucchini (about 4, depending on their size)
1-2 onions (to taste)
2 or 3 carrots (optional)
4 oz. beyaz peynir or feta (or about ¾ c. crumbled but not packed in)
2 c. flour (depending on moisture content of mix,
     you may have to add more)
3 eggs

1 bunch of fresh dill, chopped
½ bunch of fresh mint or parsley, chopped (optional)
1 tsp. each of pepper and salt (or to taste)
vegetable oil for frying (about 1 to 1½ c., or enough to be 1-1½ inches
    deep in a frying pan)

▶ Grate zucchini, onions, and carrots.

▶ **This step is important**: scoop the grated vegetables up in your hands and squeeze as much of the extra moisture out of them as you can. Place the squeezed vegetables in another bowl. If too much water remains in them, the mücver will not cook in the center, or you will probably have to add too much flour to compensate.

▶ Mix the grated vegetables together in a large bowl with the eggs, herbs and seasonings. Crumble or grate the cheese into the mixture. Add the flour a quarter cup or so at a time, mixing between additions, until the mixture is no longer runny and will stick together.

▶ Heat the oil to frying temperature in a pan. You can see whether it is hot enough by testing a small, marble-sized portion of the mixture first. It should immediately begin bubbling and frying around the mixture if the oil is properly heated. Drop tablespoon-sized balls of the mixture into the hot oil, or teaspoon-sized ones for smaller fritters. Fry on each side until brown, then remove from the oil and drain on paper towels.

Note: Self-rising flour will work also. Just use it instead of the regular flour, and omit extra salt. It is not as authentic, but you may like the fluffier texture that results — it will be more fritter-like.

≈

Çoban Salatası
(Shepherd's Salad)

This salad makes a colorful alternative to leafy greens. Good by itself, it can also be served on a bed of lettuce.

1-2 cucumbers, peeled, sliced and quartered or diced
2 large or 3 medium tomatoes, peeled and chopped into chunks
½ large red onion, sliced thinly
1 bunch fresh Italian or flat parsley, chopped
2 hot green peppers
1-2 cloves of garlic, pressed
juice of 1 lemon (about 3 Tbsp. lemon juice)
about ¾ cup olive oil
salt and freshly ground pepper, to taste

▶ Place the first five ingredients in the salad bowl.

▶ Squeeze lemon juice into a small bowl. Add the olive oil, garlic, and salt and pepper, if desired. Pour over vegetables and stir to mix everything together.

≈

Cacık
(Cucumber and Yogurt)

A dish that is easy to make and wonderfully cool alongside köfte (Turkish meatballs) or other meat dishes, or it can be diluted with water to serve as a cold soup.

> 2 cups yogurt
> 1 large cucumber, peeled and chopped, sliced finely, or shredded
> 2 cloves garlic, or to taste, minced
> bunch of fresh dill or mint, chopped
> salt to taste
> 1 tsp. olive oil (optional)
> ice cubes or shavings (optional)

▶ Stir salt and minced garlic into the yogurt.

▶ Add cucumber, and the mint or dill.

▶ If you want to chill further, add ice cubes or shavings before serving. You may drizzle oil over the top and garnish with a sprig of mint or parsley, if desired.

Sauce
Tarator (Hazelnut/
Walnut Sauce)

This sauce seems to hail from Eastern Anatolia, where it is found in the cuisine of various ethnic groups. Variations are also known in other countries of the Middle East, from Lebanon to Egypt. It is good as an hors d'oeuvre for entertaining, or just to have around as a snack dip. It can accompany almost any fresh, steamed or boiled vegetable, and Turks also serve it with fish and mussels. It can be made ahead and refrigerated, while the food it dresses is freshly prepared, as needed.

> 4 oz. shelled hazelnuts or walnuts (pine nuts are also a variant)
> 2 or 3 cloves garlic
> ¼ cup olive oil
> 2 lemons
> ¼ cup yogurt
> 1 bunch Italian or flat parsley, washed and chopped
> salt and pepper to taste
> 3 apples
> 3 zucchini or other fresh vegetables, such as green beans

▶ Use a food processor or blender to crush the hazelnuts together with the garlic.

▶ Add olive oil and the juice from the lemons, yogurt, parsley, salt and pepper.

▶ Cut apples into wedges and rub a lemon across the cut edge to prevent browning of the fruit. Slice vegetables horizontally into sticks and place on a serving dish with the apple wedges.

▶ Either spoon the hazelnut mixture over them, or serve in small individual bowls beside each plate.

Alternatively, the vegetables and apples can be steamed for 5 minutes before serving topped with the dressing. The walnut version of this sauce is also good with chicken.

Sweets
Rose Sorbet

In Turkey, rose petals are used as a flavoring, to make a kind of jam, and this special drink. The drink is easy to make and fun for hot weather or anytime. It is very sweet, so you may want to water it down once you have tasted it. Or give it an American twist by pouring it over shaved ice to make an exotically flavored snow cone.

Pick the petals from 2-4 (4 if small flowers) fragrant red roses,
    or 2 Tbsp. rose water
2 ½ cups water
1 cup + 2 Tbsp. sugar
2 Tbsp. lemon juice
2 tsp. rose water

▶ Measure the water into a saucepan. Add the washed rose petals or two tablespoons of the rose water and bring to a boil.

▶ Reduce heat, cover and simmer for 10 minutes.

▶ Strain the liquid into a bowl, and keep the petals.

▶ Put the liquid back into the pan, add the sugar, and bring back to a boil, stirring constantly. Reduce heat and simmer for 7 or 8 minutes.

▶ Stir in lemon juice, the 2 tsp. of rose water, and the rose petals. Remove from heat and allow to cool.

▶ Put in the freezer to chill, but stir, shake, or whisk periodically to prevent crystals from forming. Serve in a glass or a julep cup when chilled.

A Drink

This is a cool drink for yogurt lovers.

Ayran

▶ Stir well equal parts of plain yogurt and water in a glass.

▶ Add a pinch of dried or chopped fresh mint (optional), and a pinch of salt.

▶ Add ice cubes if you like, and water it down more if you want a drink that's not so thick (cafes usually make it with a bit more water).

Language, the Alphabet, and Pronunciation

Some Turkish sounds are difficult for English speakers because they do not exist in our language (and vice versa for Turkish, which does not have the "th" sound of English).

But often English speakers do know the sound and simply do not know how to read the Turkish letters. In the 1920s, Turkey switched to a Western alphabet, based on the Latin letter forms, but modified to fit the Turkish language. So reading is fairly easy, once a few simple rules are grasped.

Unlike English, with its many non-intuitive spellings, Turkish is generally spelled logically and phonetically. Where English has a number of sounds all represented by the letter "a," for example, "a" is "ah" in Turkish, like the "a" in "father." Each sound gets its own letter in Turkish. "C" is a redundant letter in English, since the two sounds it can represent could be written with either an "s" or a "k." Turkish uses the "s" for "s" sounds, the "k" for "k" sounds, and this frees the "c" to stand for the hard "j" sound we use "j" to represent in English. The "j" in Turkish stands for the same soft "j" sound the French use "j" to represent. Most other consonents, such as b, t, m, etc., are the same as in English.

Most fonts currently in use do not reproduce all of the Turkish letters, so Turkish words and names may undergo a metamorphosis in English that contributes to our mangling of their sounds, even when the sound exists in our language also. "Ş" is easy for us to pronounce, since it is our "sh" sound, but it comes into our newspaper articles on Turkey looking like a plain "s," so we tend to pronounce it that way. In addition, some Turkish words have a number of spellings in English because they were transliterated into our language in the old days, from Ottoman, when Turkish was written with Arabic letters, and so didn't have a standard Western spelling. Cami, the Turkish word for mosque, is sometimes also spelled Jami or Djami in English, for this reason.

Here are a few pronunciation guides:

a is the same as the "a" in the word "father;"

ay is the dipthong we usually spell with an "i" as in "glide," and pronounced like the word "eye;"

c is *always* the "j" sound we say in words like "jam." This letter is often mispronounced by English speakers, especially news reporters unfamiliar with Turkish names;

ç is the same "ch" sound heard in "lunch;"

e is usually the short "e" in "egg," but it can be drawn out, especially at the ends of words where the sound is almost like a long "a;"

ey is the dipthong represented by "ay" in "bay;"

g is the hard English "g" of the word "game;"

ğ is a silent letter that draws the syllable out longer. The Turkish word doğru (meaning straight) sounds like our words "dough·rue;"

ı (undotted i) does not have an exact correspondence in English. It is similar to our "i" sound in words like "Justin," or the "a" in "about;"

i is pronounced the same as "i" in Spanish. It makes the sound "ee," like in "free" or like "y" at the ends of words such as "sandy;"

j is the French "j" as in "jamais" or the sound of the second "g" in the English word "garage;"

o is the same as our "o" in "so;"

ö is the same as the "ö" in German or the "oe" in French words such as "oeuvre" and "oeuf," but does not exist in English;

ş is the same as the English "sh," like in "shell;"

ü is the same as the "ü" in German, but does not exist in English;

u is the "oo" sound in "school."

So, Topkapı (the name of the old Ottoman palace of the Sultans) should be said almost like "tope′·kahp·a." It is *not* "top·cappy," although it is often mispronounced that way, even by the actors in the movie of that name.

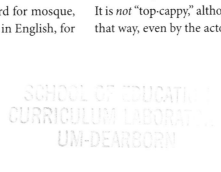

Bibliography

Art, Architecture and Music

Akat, Yücel. et al., *Anatolia: a World Heritage*, Ankara: Ministry of Culture, General Directorate for the Preservation of the Cultural and Natural Heritage, 1991.

Aslanapa, Oktay. *Turkish Art and Architecture*, New York: Praeger Publishers [1971].

Atil, Esin (Ed.). *Turkish Art*, Washington, DC: Smithsonian Institutions, 1980.

Atil, Esin, *The Age of Sultan Süleyman the Magnificent*, New York: Abrams, 1987.

Browning, Robert, *Maqam. Music of the Islamic World and Its Influences*, New York, NY: Alternative Museum, 1984.

Ertuğ, Ahmet, et al., *The Seljuks: a Journey Through Anatolian Architecture*, Istanbul: Ahmet Ertug, 1991.

Goodwin, Godfrey. *A History of Ottoman Architecture*, London: Thames and Hudson, 1971.

Kuran, Aptullah. *Sinan: The Grand Old Master of Ottoman Architecture*. Washington, DC: Institute of Turkish Studies, 1987.

Necipoglu, Gülru, *Architecture, Ceremonial, and Power: The Topkapi Palace in the Fifteenth and Sixteenth Centuries*, MIT Press, Cambridge and London, 1991.

Petsopoulos, Yanni (ed.), *Tulips, Arabesques and Turbans: Decorative Arts from the Ottoman Empire*. London: Alexandria Press, 1982.

Cooking

Başan, Ghillie, *Classic Turkish Cookery*, London and New York, 2002.

Eren, Neşet, *The Art of Turkish Cooking*, New York: Hippocrene Books, 2002.

History: The Ottoman Empire

Babinger, Franz, 1891-1967, *Mehmed the Conqueror and His Time,* translated from the German by Ralph Manheim; edited, with a pref., by William C. Hickman, Princeton, N.J.: Princeton University Press, c. 1978.

Bon, Ottaviano, *The Sultan's Seraglio: An Intimate Portrait of Life at the Ottoman Court,* Saqi Books, 1996.

Braude, Benjamin and Bernard Lewis (eds.), *Christians and Jews in the Ottoman Empire: The Functioning of a Plural Society,* New York, NY: Holmes & Meier. Two volumes, 1982.

Faroqhi, Suraiya, *Subjects of the Sultan: Culture and Daily Life in the Ottoman Empire,* London, New York: I.B. Tauris, 2000.

Goodwin, Godfrey, *The Janissaries,* Saqi Books, London, 1994.

Inalcik, Halil and Quataert, Donald, eds., *An Economic and Social History of the Ottoman Empire 1300-1914*, Cambridge, 1994.

Inalcik, Halil. *The Ottoman Empire: The Classical Age, 1300 - 1600,* New Rochelle, NY: Caratzas, 1990.

Issawi, Charles. *The Economic History of Turkey, 1800-1914*, Chicago: University of Chicago Press, 1981.

Itzkowitz, Norman, *Ottoman Empire and Islamic Tradition,* New York: Alfred A. Knopf, 1972. (reprinted 1986).

Kafadar, Cemal, *Between Two Worlds: The Construction of the Ottoman State*, Berkeley and Los Angeles: University of California, 1995.

Karpat, Kemal H., *The Politicization of Islam: Reconstructing Identity, State, Faith, and Community in the Late Ottoman State,* Oxford, New York: Oxford University Press, 2001.

Kemal Çiçek, et al., eds., *The Great Ottoman-Turkish Civilisation*, 4 vols., Ankara: Yeni Turkiye, 2000.

Köprülü, M. Fuad, (and Leiser, Gary, trans. and ed.), *The Origins of the Ottoman Empire*, SUNY, 1992.

Kunt, Metin, and Woodhead, Christine, eds., *Süleyman the Magnificent and His Age: The Ottoman Empire in the Early Modern Word*, London and Singapore: Longman, 1995.

Landau, Jacob M., ed., *Atatürk and the Modernization of Turkey*, Boulder, Colorado: Westview Press, 1984.

Levy, Aviador, *The Sephardim in the Ottoman Empire*. Princeton: Darwin Press and Washington: Institute of Turkish Studies, 1992.

Lewis, Bernard, *Istanbul and the Civilization of the Ottoman Empire*, Norman, Oklahoma: University of Oklahoma Press, 1963.

Lewis, Bernard, *The Emergence of Modern Turkey*, New York: Oxford University Press, 2002.

Lewis, Raphaela, *Everyday Life in Ottoman Turkey*, New York: Putnam, 1971.

McCarthy, Justin, *The Ottoman Peoples and the End of Empire*, London: Arnold; New York: Oxford, 2001.

McCarthy, Justin, *The Ottoman Turks: An Introductory History to 1923*, London; New York: Longman, 1997.

Nicolle, David, and McBride, Angus, *Armies of the Ottoman Turks*, London: Osprey, 1983.

Ottoman Empire in Drawings, Istanbul: Historical Research Foundation. Istanbul Research Center, 1987.

Peirce, Leslie Penn. *The Imperial Harem: Women and Sovereignty in the Ottoman Empire*, New York: Oxford University Press, 1993.

Pitcher, Donald E, *An Historical Geography of the Ottoman Empire*, Leiden, Netherlands: E.J. Brill, 1972.

Quataert, Donald, *The Ottoman Empire, 1700-1922*, Cambridge; New York: Cambridge University Press, 2000.

Runciman, Steven, *Byzantine Style and Civilization*, Baltimore: Penguin, 1975.

Shaw, Stanford J., *The Jews of the Ottoman Empire and Turkish Empire*, New York: New York University Press, 1991.

Shaw, Stanford J., and Ezel Kural Shaw, *History of the Ottoman Empire and Modern Turkey*. 2 vols., Cambridge: Cambridge University Press, 1976-87 (reprinted 1984).

Wheatcroft, Andrew, *The Ottomans*, London: Viking, 1993.

Literature

Emre, Yunus, *Yunus Emre and His Mystical Poetry*. Indiana: Indiana University Press, 1981.

Evin, Ahmet O., *Origins and Development of the Turkish Novel*, Minneapolis, MN: Biblioteca Islamica, 1983.

Halman, Talat Sait, *Contemporary Turkish Literature: Fiction and Poetry*, Fairleigh Dickinson University Press, 1982.

Menemencioğlu, Nermin (ed.), *The Penguin Book of Turkish Verse*, London, England: Penguin Books, 1978.

Pocketful of Turkish Proverbs, Lubbock, TX: Texas Tech University Libraries.

Uysal, Ahmet & Warren S. Walker, *Tales Alive in Turkey*, Lubbock, TX: Texas Tech University Press, 1990.

Walker, Barbara, (retold by), *A Treasury of Turkish Folktales for Children*, Linnet Books, 1988.

The Republic of Turkey

Abramowitz. Morton, ed., *Turkey's Transformation and American Policy*, New York: Century Foundation Press, 2000.

Ahmad, Feroz, *The Making of Modern Turkey*, New York: Routledge, 1993.

Barchard, David, *Turkey and the West*, London: Royal Institute of International Affairs, 1985.

Economist Intelligence Unit, *Country Profile: Turkey*.

Economist Intelligence Unit, *Quarterly Economic Review of Turkey*.

Gökalp, Ziya. *The Principles of Turkism*, trans., Robert Devereux. Leiden: 1968.

Hale, William M., *Turkish Foreign Policy, 1774-2000*, London, Portland, Oregon: Frank Cass, 2000.

Howard, Douglas A., *The History of Turkey*, Westport, Conn.: Greenwood Press, 2001.

Landau, Jacob, ed., *Atatürk and the Modernization of Turkey*, Boulder, Colorado: Westview Press; Leiden, the Netherlands: E.J. Brill, 1984.

Oz, Yilmas (translated). *Quotations from Mustafa Kemal Atatürk*. Ankara: Ministry of Foreign Affairs, 1982.

Shaw, Stanford J., *From Empire to Republic: The Turkish War of National Liberation*, 5 vols., Ankara, Türk Tarih Kurumu, 2000.

Walker, Barbara, et al., *To Set Them Free: The Early Years of Mustafa Kemal Atatürk,* Grantham, NH: Tompson & Rutter, Inc., 1981.

Zürcher, Erik J, *Turkey: A Modern History,* New York: I. B. Tauris, 1998.

Travel and Tourism

Brosnahan, Tom. *Turkey: A Travel Survival Kit.* Berkeley, CA: Lonely Planet, 1985.

Bean, George. *Aegean Turkey.* (J. Murray, UK) North Pomfret, VT: David & Charles, 1989.

Bean, George *Lycian Turkey.* (J. Murray, UK) North Pomfret, VT: David & Charles, 1989.

Dindi, Hasan et al. *Turkish Culture for Americans.* Boulder, CO: International Concepts, 1989.

Edmonds, Anna G., *Turkey's Religious Sites,* Istanbul, Damko, 1997.

Freely, John *Turkey.* (Companion Guides). London, England: Collins, Second revised edition, 1984.

Halman, Talat. *The Turkish Americans.* (The People of North America Service), New York., NY: Chelsea House, 1990.

Orga, Irfan. *Portrait of a Turkish Family.* (Eland Travel Classics Service), New York, NY: Hippocrene Books, 1989.

Web Sites

Art and Literature

Contemporary Turkish Literature
http://www.turkish-lit.boun.edu.tr

Iznik Tiles and Ceramics
http://www.iznik.com

Les Arts Turcs (in English)
http://www.lesartsturcs.com

Turkish–Islamic Arts
http://www.adnarts.com

Turkish Poetry Homepage
http://www.cs.umd.edu/~sibel/poetry/poetry.html

Business Organizations

Istanbul and Marmara, Aegean, Mediterranean and
Black Sea Chamber of Shipping
http://www.chamber-of-shipping.org.tr

Istanbul Chamber of Commerce
http://www.ito.org.tr

Istanbul Chamber of Industry
http://www.iso.org.tr

Istanbul Commodity Exchange
http://www.istanbulticaretborsasi.org.tr

Turkish Industrialists' and Businessmen's Association
http://www.tusiad.org.tr/english

Further Information

All About Turkey
http://www.allaboutturkey.com/links.htm

Anatolia.Com
http://www.anatolia.com/anatolia

Discover Turkey
http://www.turkishnews.com/DiscoverTurkey

Web-Reyting.Net
web-reyting.net

History

*The Ministry of Foreign Affairs site also contains a
detailed history.*

Atatürk Page
http://www.ataturk.org

Memâlik-i Mahruse
http://www.members.ams.chello.nl/olnon/start.htm

Ottoman Page
http://www.ottoman.home.mindspring.com

Ottoman Studies Resource Index
http://www.ottoman-links.co.uk

Ottoman Web Site
http://www.osmanli700.gen.tr

Newspapers and News in English

Anatolia News Agency
http://www.anadoluajansi.gov.tr

Turkish Daily News
http://www.turkishdailynews.com

TurkishPress.Com Daily News
http://www.turkishpress.com

Turkish Times
http://www.theturkishtimes.com

Research, Scientific, and Research Organizations

Center for Eurasian Strategic Studies
http://www.avsam.org

Center for Strategic Research
http://www.mfa.gov.tr/grupa/sam
Institute of Turkish Studies
http://www.turkishstudies.org

Ottoman Archives
http://www.devletarsivleri.gov.tr

Scientific and Technical Research Council of Turkey
http://www.tubitak.gov.tr/english

Turkish Economic and Social Sciences Foundation
http://www.tesev.org.tr/eng

Turkish Foreign Policy Institute
foreignpolicy.org.tr/index_eng.htm

Turkish Historical Society
ttk.gov.tr/ingilizce/index.htm

Turkish Studies Association
http://www.virgo.bsuvc.bsu.edu/~tsa

Statistical Information, Economics, Demography
Many of the Turkish Government sites also contain statistical information.

CIA World Factbook
http://www.cia.gov/cia/publications/factbook

International Monetary Fund
http://www.imf.org/external/country/TUR/index.htm

Ministry of Foreign Affairs Statistical Indicators
http://www.turkey.org/business/a23.htm

State Institute of Statistics
http://www.die.gov.tr/ENGLISH/index.htm

U.S. Census Bureau. IDB Summary Demographic Data
http://www.census.gov/ipc/www/idbsum.html

World Bank
http://www.worldbank.org/data

World Trade Organization
http://www.wto.org

Tourism

Istanbul City Guide
http://www.istanbulcityguide.com

Istanbul.com
http://.www.Istanbul.com

Ministry of Tourism
http://.www.turizm.gov.tr

Turkish-American Organizations

Assembly of Turkish American Associations
http://www.ataa.org

American Turkish Council
http://www.americanturkishcouncil.org

Atatürk Society of America
http://www.ataturksociety.org

Federation of Turkish American Associations
http://www.ftaa.org

Turkish Governmental Organizations

Armed Forces
http://www.tsk.mil.tr/index_eng.htm

Central Bank
http://www.tcmb.gov.tr/new/englindex.htm

Education Ministry
http://www.meb.gov.tr/indexeng.htm

General Directorate on the Status and Problems
of Women
http://www.kssgm.gov.tr

Ministry of Foreign Affairs
http://www.mfa.gov.tr

Turkish Embassy, Washington, D.C.
includes links to government ministries
http://www.turkishembassy.org

United States Diplomatic Representation in Turkey

United States Consulate General in Istanbul
http://www.usist.org.tr

United States Embassy in Ankara
http://www.usemb-ankara.org.tr